Pitt Series in Policy
and Institutional Studies

Contemporary Community Health Series

The U.S. Experiment in Social Medicine

The Community Health Center Program, 1965–1986

Alice Sardell

UNIVERSITY OF PITTSBURGH PRESS

Published by the University of Pittsburgh Press, Pittsburgh, Pa. 15260
Copyright © 1988, University of Pittsburgh Press
Feffer and Simons, Inc., London
Manufactured in the United States of America

Library of Congress Cataloging in Publications Data

Sardell, Alice.
   The U.S. experiment in social medicine.

   (Contemporary community health series) (Pitt series in policy and
institutional studies)
   Includes bibliographies and index.
   1. Community health services—United States—History—20th century.
2. Medical policy—United States—History—20th century.   3. Social
medicine—United States—History—20th century.   I. Title.   II. Title:
United States experiment in social medicine.   III. Title: US experiment
in social medicine.   IV. Series.   V. Series: Pitt series in policy and
institutional studies.
[DNLM: 1. Community Health Services—history—United States.
2. Health Policy—history—United States.   3. Primary Health Care—history
—United States.   4. Social Medicine—history—United States.   WA 11
AA1 S2u]
RA445.S27   1988   362.1'2'0973   87-35847
ISBN 0-8229-3825-1
ISBN 0-8229-5803-1 (pbk.)

Contents

List of Acronyms

AAAHC	Accreditation Association for Ambulatory Health Care
ABA	American Bar Association
AFDC	Aid to Families with Dependent Children
AFSCME	American Federation of State, County, and Municipal Employees
AHA	American Hospital Association
AHPA	American Health Planning Association
AMA	American Medical Association
ANYNHC	Association of New York Neighborhood Health Centers
APHA	American Public Health Association
BCHS	Bureau of Community Health Services
BHCDA	Bureau of Health Care Delivery and Assistance
CAP	Community Action Program
CCMC	Committee on the Costs of Medical Care
CHAP	Child Health Assessment Program
CHC	Community health center
CHS	Community Health Service
CNI	Community Nutrition Institute
DDHS	Department of Health and Human Services
DHEW	Department of Health, Education, and Welfare
EPSDT	Early and Periodic Screening, Diagnosis, and Treatment Program

FRAC	Food Research and Action Center
GAO	General Accounting Office
HCFA	Health Care Financing Administration
HMO	Health maintenance organization
HRSA	Health Resources and Services Administration
HSMHA	Health Services and Mental Health Administration
HURA	Health Underserved Rural Areas Program
MOA	Memorandum of agreement
MUA	Medically underserved area
NACHC	National Association of Community Health Centers
NANHC	National Association of Neighborhood Health Centers
NENA	North East Neighborhoods Association
NHC	Neighborhood health center
NHSC	National Health Service Corps
NIMH	National Institute of Mental Health
OEO	Office of Economic Opportunity
OMB	Office of Management and Budget
PHS	Public Health Service
RHI	Rural health initiative
UHI	Urban health initiative
VISTA	Volunteers in Service to America
WIC	Women, Infants, and Children (supplemental food program)

Acknowledgments

Many people contributed to the fulfillment of this project and I'd like to acknowledge some of them by name. Peter Beitchman was crucial to the initiation of this study in 1977. He introduced me to the neighborhood health center movement—actors and issues— and shared his valuable insights into both. Joann Lukomnik also shared her extensive knowledge of primary care programs with me, although I did not interview her formally. Jude Thomas May and Peter Kong-ming New were extremely generous in providing transcripts of interviews they had conducted in the mid-1970s. Tom was always interested and encouraging whenever I talked to him about my research. David Blumenthal and Robert Hollister were similarly generous in sharing with me their unpublished studies of the politics of the neighborhood health center program. I thank Sally Guttmacher for suggesting the title of this book.

I deeply appreciate the guidance that Ralph Straetz, Martin Schain, and Louanne Kennedy gave me as I researched and wrote my dissertation on the neighborhood/community health center program. Martin Schain provided absolutely crucial encouragement and advice during the process of additional research and rewriting. Douglas E. Ashford, Peter M. Manicas, and Lawrence D. Brown read the first draft of the book manuscript and made extremely valuable substantive comments on its structure and ideas. Although their comments were central guideposts during the revision process, the responsibility for the final product, is of course, all mine. Their encouragement and support of the work also should be gratefully acknowledged.

Helen Cairns, Dean of the Graduate School of Arts and Sciences, provided Queens College Research Funds to travel to Washington, D.C., to conduct interviews. Thelma Silver graciously and expertly typed many pages of handwritten material. Julia Kwartler and Arlene Diamond worked on the final draft in the same way. Other staff of the Word Processing department at Queens College, including Wendy DeFortuna, Ruth Liss, and Pearl Sigberman, were always very helpful.

Paula Kleinman encouraged me to keep going during years and years of work. Harvey Catchen was a source of love and support throughout.

This book would not have been written without the willingness of those interviewed to be enormously generous with their time and knowledge. These were people with very busy work schedules in Congress, DHEW/DHHS, private law practice, health programs and associations, and at the National Association of Community Health Centers, who spent hours responding to my questions. I thank them all.

I would also like to thank the members of the Health Council of the Sunset Park Family Health Center in Brooklyn, New York, and the administrative, medical, and nursing staff of the Center. I have learned a great deal about the delivery of primary health care and the operation of a community health center from them.

Finally, I'd like to thank Molly Rebecca Sardell Catchen for sharing with me the joys of curiosity, learning, and laughter for the last three and a half years.

I dedicate this book to my parents, Martha and William Sardell, who taught me to be interested in ideas and in social justice.

The U.S. Experiment in
Social Medicine

1

Perspectives on the Policymaking Process in Primary Care

Innovation in Health Care Delivery: The Neighborhood Health Center Program

In the 1960s, federal policymakers set out to "reform" the American health care system. In 1964 Medicare and Medicaid were enacted into law. These programs marked a major expansion of federal responsibility for the provision of health care services. Prior to this time, federal responsibility was limited to the care of only a few specific population groups, such as merchant seamen and veterans.

The Medicare and Medicaid programs were designed to increase access to health care for the elderly and the poor by paying for the services of existing providers (doctors and hospitals). In 1965, the United States Office of Economic Opportunity (OEO) funded an even more radical health services innovation, a new model for health care delivery. In that year, OEO gave grants to medical schools, hospitals, health departments, and community groups to plan and administer "neighborhood health centers" in low-income areas. These health centers embodied ideas that had been espoused by health care reformers since the early twentieth century, including concepts of comprehensive health care, social medicine, and community participation. The advocates of the neighborhood health

3

center program in its formative period believed that these projects would provide high-quality health care to low-income populations lacking access to such care and, at the same time, serve as a model for the reorganization of health care services for the entire U.S. population. The funding of these health projects marked the first time in history that the federal government was directly funding an experiment aimed at the reform of health care delivery.

Federal support for such reform activity was a direct departure from a previous unwillingness to interfere in the organization and delivery of health services by the private sector. Support for other innovations—the establishment of the National Health Service Corps (NHSC), subsidies for the training of primary care practitioners—both physician and nonphysician—and federal grants and loans for the development of health maintenance organizations —were to follow in the 1970s.

The history of the neighborhood health center program, renamed the community health center program in 1975, is the subject of this book. An examination of the program since its genesis in the sixties provides crucial lessons about health care reform that are relevant to health policy and planning in the current period. (Note: discussions of the program before 1975 will refer to *neighborhood* health centers; discussions of the post-1975 period will refer to *community* health centers.)

The American health care system was not restructured on the basis of the neighborhood/community health center model, but the program survived long after the War on Poverty had ended and is a potential model for health care reform efforts in the very different health policy climate of the 1980s and 1990s. In 1980, 876 community health centers, the descendants of the first projects, were providing health services to six million persons (President's Commission, vol. 1, 1983:131). A considerable body of research has documented the ability of these health centers both to improve health status and to reduce the costs of health services (Freeman et al., 1982; Goldman and Grossman, forthcoming; Geiger, 1982).

The fact that the neighborhood health center program did not fulfill its original objective to serve as a model for health care delivery for the whole population was not because the model was inadequate, but rather because of the nature of the American policy process itself. It is this policy process that must be understood. Realistic policy planning cannot go forward without an understanding of the links between the policy process, including the values and structures of relevant institutions, and the outcomes of that process (Jones, 1983; Dye, 1981; Anderson, 1984). Future innovations in health care delivery will also depend on the political environments in which they are formulated and implemented.

Almost all of the existing literature on the neighborhood health center program was written during and about its formative years, when it was funded by the OEO. No substantive examination has been done of this area of federal policy since 1971. This study analyzes the policy processes that made possible the initial funding of the neighborhood health center program and, then, the program's survival and expansion. Changes in the nature of the program itself will be explained in terms of those policy processes. The last chapter of this book will review the health planning lessons of the health center case.

The neighborhood health center case also presents the opportunity to examine closely a phenomenon that has been discussed in the political science literature but infrequently studied. That phenomenon is the nature of policy networks that support programs serving politically and economically disadvantaged groups. With the expanded role of government in social policy since the 1960s, new sets of interests have been articulated at the federal level. Policy networks representing such interests have been identified in the political science literature (Beer, 1976; Heclo, 1978) but little case study material is available to test these formulations. *The U.S. Experiment in Social Medicine* traces the development of such a policy network over two decades and suggests a typology of networks based on this research and on a comparative analysis of this study and another case.

The second chapter of this book is a history of "primary" or "first contact" health care in the United States during the nineteenth century and the first part of the twentieth century. (The definition of the term "primary care" will be discussed at the end of this chapter.) The focus is on the political conflicts that helped to shape the delivery of such care and the resulting "mobilization of bias" in American primary health care policy. This provides the background for understanding how the neighborhood health center model reached the health policy agenda in the 1960s (see chapter 3). The nature of the power relationships in the U.S. health policy system precluded primary care as part of the regular health policy agenda. Support for the establishment of neighborhood health centers did not emerge from health policy networks in Congress and the Department of Health, Education, and Welfare (DHEW), but rather as a result of programmatic social innovation— the War on Poverty—which was a response to the politics of Democratic voting, the "discovery" of poverty in America, and a fear of urban unrest. The concerns of health care reformers were thus linked with a broader concern for the needs of the urban poor, primarily minorities.

Precisely because the neighborhood health center program was funded as part of the War on Poverty and limited to serving a low-income population, its very survival became problematic when a Republican administration, opposed to the continuation of such social programs, took office in 1968. The program did survive the demise of the War on Poverty and was expanded during the Carter administration. An analysis of the policy processes responsible for program survival and expansion provides insight into the nature of policy networks supportive of programs whose constituents are themselves without political resources (see chapters 4–7).

This first chapter will describe the framework used to analyze the policy processes related to the neighborhood/community health center program.

The Subgovernmental Model and
Distributive Policymaking

The dominant perspective from which the American political process was viewed during the 1950s and into the 1960s was that of "interest group pluralism," which emphasized the role of the private voluntary association in representing the interests of citizens in the policy process while assuring the stability of the political system.[1] Public policy was the result of bargaining and accommodation among such groups. Changes in the society would be reflected in politics through the activity of interest groups and the activation of "potential groups" (Truman, 1951). By the mid-1960s, social scientists found that the pluralist assumption that all interests were represented within this group process did not fit the reality of civil rights marches, antiwar demonstrations, and other nonelectoral expressions of discontent during that decade (Smith, 1974:9–10; Bellush and David, 1977:5).

The "neoelitist" critique of pluralism did not dispute the fact that organized interest groups were a central feature of the American political process but, rather, challenged pluralist ideas about the "representativeness" of those groups and about the openness of the system to new groups (Kariel, 1961; McConnell, 1966; Connolly, 1969; Lowi, 1969; Bellush and David, 1977). These critics said that public authority in the United States was not separate from private interests, and that government was often a captive of private groups rather than a mediator among them. Instead of group struggle, there was a system of logrolling in which private groups reinforced each other's dominance in various areas of policy. The consequences of this system were a lack of accountability to the general public, the reinforcement of the power of group leaders over their membership, the exclusion of unorganized groups and broad interests from the policy process, and "the simple conservatism of resistance to change" (Lowi, 1969:90).

By the end of the 1970s, there was widespread acceptance of this characterization of the American political process among political scientists. Randall B. Ripley and Grace A. Franklin, authors of a major textbook on congressional-bureaucratic relations in the United States (first published in 1976), state: "In general, American public policy can be characterized as slow to change, as more responsive to special interests than to general interests, as more responsible to the privileged in society than to the underprivileged, and as tending to be defined and treated as distributive when possible" (1987:209).

One of the reasons for this bias toward privileged social groups, and one of the central characteristics of the American policy process, is the "widespread occurrence of subgovernments" in many functional areas of policymaking (Ripley and Franklin, 1987:6). A "subgovernment" (Cater, 1965) or "subsystem" (Freeman, 1965) is an informal network of individuals involved in a specialized area of policymaking within the decentralized U.S. political system. Subgovernments—"clusters of individuals that effectively make most of the routine decisions in a given substantive area of policy"—usually consist of members and staff of the committees or subcommittees with jurisdiction in that policy area, government officials from the bureau or agency that administers (or would administer) policy in that area, and representatives of interested private organizations (Ripley and Franklin, 1987:8). The tenure of participants in subgovernmental networks is stable over time, since the participants are carrying on the routine functions of government at the bureau and subcommittee level. Typically, the relationships between subgovernment actors are cooperative and disputes are resolved through compromise within a subgovernment, without the involvement of political actors outside this network (1987:8, 90).

The subgovernments most often described in the literature are those supporting the interests of business groups with large financial resources, or groups able to deliver large numbers of votes, such as farmers' or veterans' associations. Attempts to challenge the policies supported by such subgovernments, even by the president, are usually unsuccessful (Ripley and Franklin, 1987:100–10). The ability of such networks to repel challenges successfully is the origin of their characterization as "iron triangles" (Seidman, 1975).

One of the organizing principles of Ripley's and Franklin's work on Congress and the bureaucracy is that the importance of the "subgovernmental phenomenon" varies with policy type and particular environmental conditions. They have classified types of policies in terms of the involvement of specific categories of political actors, the "nature of the interaction among these actors," and the "visibility" of the issues (1987:20).[2] The subgovernmental model of relationships among policy actors is characteristic of distributive policies, those most common in American politics.

Distributive policies are those that provide a subsidy to private groups to do certain things (or not do them) for the general benefit of society. Examples are payments to farmers to grow certain crops, or not to grow them, hospital construction, and mass transit programs. Distributive interactions are of "low visibility" and decisions are "disaggregated," that is, the assumption made is that some will benefit, but no one will be hurt (Ripley and Franklin, 1987:21).

The goal of "redistributive policy," in contrast, is the reallocation of wealth or other values from relatively advantaged to relatively disadvantaged groups. Examples are national health insurance, affirmative action programs, and the progressive income tax. Redistributive policy involves conflict between coalitions of political actors over issues in which there are thought to be "distinct winners and losers." It also involves ideological debate and often includes the president as a primary actor (Ripley and Franklin, 1987:25–26, 145). As Lowi and others have noted, all types of policies can actually be redistributive in their effect on the relative economic position of large numbers of people (Lowi, 1964:690; Hayes 1978:155). It is, however, those issues that are *perceived* by a certain number of actors as capable of producing some redistribution from one sector of society to another that activate large numbers of groups and result in a high level of conflict.

Variation in Subgovernments

While "clientelism" is frequently discussed in the literature on American politics, "perhaps *the* pervasive theme . . . of commentaries on policymaking," few studies have analyzed specific subgovernments in detail or examined how they vary (Davidson, 1977:30–31).[3] In his classic work on the Indian affairs "subsystem," J. Leiper Freeman calls for comparative research and suggests that subsystems differ in terms of two variables: the scope of the policy in which they are involved and the size of the subgovernment. He cites Douglass Cater's discussions of the "large" defense policy network and the "small" sugar subgovernment as an example of the latter variable (Freeman, 1965:68).

Ripley and Franklin describe "four major variations in the situations in which subgovernments function." These are "subgovernmental dominance," "major subgovernment adaptation," "competing subgovernments," and "subgovernmental disintegration" (1987:97). These categories represent variations in the extent to which subgovernments triumph over challenges to a set of mutual policy interests. The discussion of these variations makes clear that subgovernments, though stable, are not "static" (1987:123), but may change in response to changes in external conditions. The authors describe cases in each of these four categories but do not attempt to specify the characteristics of subgovernments or their environments that would make a change to a situation other than "subgovernmental dominance" more likely. They do not, in other words, specify the variables related to the strength or autonomy of a subgovernment. Thus, a major question in the literature is the extent of specific subgovernment autonomy and the conditions for that autonomy (Freeman, 1965, ch. 3); or conversely, the means by which political actors at higher levels can reduce the autonomy of subgovernmental actors (Seidman, 1975; Heclo, 1977).

While Ripley and Franklin, like Freeman, focus on relationships between bureaucratic and congressional actors and do not analyze the relationships between interest groups and other subgovernmental actors, they note their importance: "All actors have a major stake in supporting and pleasing the interests of their clients because it is, in part, client satisfaction that can produce critical political support for both the bureau and the subcommittee as they seek to enhance their positions in their respective institutional settings" (1987:96).

During the Johnson administration, a large number of federal programs were created to serve the needs of low-income, predominantly minority populations. These were populations with few, if any, political resources that could be used to provide support for bureaucratic or congressional actors sympathetic to their interests. How then did these programs survive? Was there a different kind of policy network (or networks) operating to help sustain such programs? This analysis of the neighborhood/community health center program provides data on how such a policy network operated initially and then changed, and how it functioned to support the program once the era of concern with poverty ended. It provides the opportunity to compare a policy network supportive of a social welfare program with a low-income constituency to the traditional subgovernments discussed in the literature.

Alternatives to the Subgovernmental Model

As government has become more involved in social policy, new voices have been heard at the national level. Recent studies have discussed the increase in the number of interest groups and the growth of their activities in Washington (Schlozman and Tierney, 1982; Walker, 1983), the types of groups articulating policy concerns (Salisbury, 1984), the techniques used to influence the policy process (Schlozman and Tierney, 1982), and how new groups are formed (Walker, 1983). The existence of policy networks different from the traditional subgovernments described in the literature have been discussed by both Samuel Beer (1976) and Hugh Heclo (1978). They each relate the emergence of different types of policy networks to the expansion of the scope of government in the United States, particularly since the Johnson years.

Beer describes "a professional-bureaucratic complex," consisting of professionally trained bureaucrats and functionally specialized congressional committee members and staff who initiate policy. Interest groups representing the beneficiaries of the programs that are developed may also be involved, but it is the first two components of the policy network that are more influential (1976:159–60). In the professional-bureaucratic complex, "initial causality is reversed: it is the program that creates the lobby, not the lobby that creates the program" (1976:160). While Beer delineates a distinct process by which the professional-bureaucratic complex acts to create support for social welfare programs, he does not discuss the characteristics of the resulting policy networks. He assumes that they will be the same as any other "triple alliance or . . . iron triangle" (1976:160).

Hugh Heclo describes more diffuse "issue networks" of political actors that have emerged in the last twenty years. "An issue network is a shared-knowledge group having to do with some aspect . . . of public policy" (1978:103). It may contain a large number of participants with various degrees of independence from their institutional (bureaucratic, congressional, or organizational) environment. Participation in such issue networks is transitory rather than stable and it is based on a commitment to the issue rather than a hoped-for economic or institutional gain. Members of an issue network, in contrast to a professional-bureaucratic complex, may not agree on the issue and may not be involved in mutual activity related to it (1978:102–4).

Although the existence of groups advocating social programs has been discussed as a significant phenomenon in recent work on interest group politics (see Cigler and Loomis, 1983), only a few studies have examined the policy networks within which such groups operate. One of these studies, on the "manpower" subgovernment, is limited to a brief two-year period (Davidson, 1972). Pratt's description of the aging subgovernment (1976) covers many years but is not focused on theoretical issues about the nature of policy subsystems generally. In contrast, this study analyzes relationships among political actors over a long period of time so as to draw conclusions about the nature of such networks. It examines how the professional-bureaucratic complex that initiated the health center program changed to include a constituency group of health center directors and patients and a broader congressional membership.

The term *policy network* will be used throughout this book as a general term to include subgovernments (iron triangles), professional-bureaucratic complexes, and the more open issue networks. When one of these specific terms is appropriate, that term will be used.

Doubts About the Subgovernmental Model

Several empirical studies have raised questions about the extent to which the subgovernmental model can be usefully applied to the current period. This work underscores the critical importance of longitudinal and comparative studies of policy networks.

Gais, Peterson, and Walker (1984) describe changes in the American policy process since the 1960s that suggest that the dominance of subgovernments in policymaking is no longer accurate as a description of the policy process. The emergence of public interest groups and other citizens' groups with concerns based on ideology rather than economic interests and the emergence of redistributive issues on the political agenda have meant that a great deal of recent policymaking has involved disputes between coalitions of groups with opposing values and a wider public following the issues through the media (1984:164–66). Gais et al. present data from their 1980 mail survey of national voluntary associations concerned with public policy that reveal unexpected relationships among political actors within a universe of subgovernments. For instance, more than three-quarters of the citizens' groups and about 70 percent of the occupational groups working in the profit-making sectors of the economy reported that groups with positions opposed to theirs were working in the same policy area. A large number number of groups also reported engaging in tactics that would intensify conflict rather than limit it to stable subgovernments. In addition, the groups surveyed experienced changes in the degree of access to government after the election of Jimmy Carter (1984:170–77). A 1981–1982 survey of Washington-based interest groups conducted by John T. Tierney and Kay Lehman Schlozman produced similar findings (Tierney, 1985:9–12). Gais et al. suggest that a "conflictual, permeable, unpredictable system has evolved in the United States. Many iron triangles remain in operation, but their influence is less persuasive than in the 1940s and 1950s, and the system can no longer accurately be characterized as a loose collection of subgovernments" (1984:163). Yet in an 1985 report on a second mail survey of interest groups, Peterson and Walker found that many groups were not affected by Reagan administration efforts to reduce their influence "because of their ties with virtually independent subgovernments or iron triangles" (1985:8). It appears that while some policy networks continue to enjoy a great deal of autonomy, there is at the same time much more conflict within the policy process. This is asserted by Heclo (1978:105) and also by de Haven–Smith and Van Horn (1984), who report on a study of the participation of traditional economic groups in public policymaking. In their study of the HIRE program, a federally sponsored employment program for Vietnam veterans and other disadvantaged groups in the late 1970s, they found conflict between two existing subgovernments, one concerned about employment and training programs and the other concerned with veterans' issues. There was also conflict within the employment and training subgovernment over the nature of the program. This conflict was limited during the formulation phase of the policy process when some major decision areas were left unresolved, but they resurfaced during the implementation process and were a serious obstacle to the program's success (de Haven–Smith and Van Horn, 1984:632–37). De Haven–Smith and Van Horn suggest that policy formulation that looks distributive may become conflictual during implementation and therefore emphasize that "longitudinal policy analysis" is crucial (1984:639).

The policy networks described by de Haven–Smith and Van

Horn are far more unified and structured than the kind of issue network Heclo discusses, yet these authors record a level of conflict that does not fit the classic subgovernmental model. Possibly these subgovernments are in a transitional phase, undergoing the kind of transformation discussed by Ripley and Franklin (1987) and Heclo (1978:105) in response to changes in the larger environment.

David Wilsford (1984) has studied this kind of transformation over time in one policy arena—that of telecommunications. The telecommunications policy network operated for more than thirty years as a quiet, "closed" network of a small number of participants with mutually supportive interests. This began to change during the late 1960s. By 1976, when AT&T was deregulated, telecommunications policy was an "open" arena with many groups that could not agree on policy (Wilsford, 1984:436–37). Wilsford's case suggests that the consequence of subgovernmental "disintegration" may be a configuration like the issue network described by Heclo.

All of this recent literature points to the need for further analysis of the applicability of the concepts of policy subgovernment and issue network and underscores the need to study and compare such policy networks over a long period of time. Longitudinal analysis is crucial because one of the major characteristics of a subgovernment is that it operates autonomously, in spite of changes in the larger policy environment. Thus, such subsystems need to be analyzed before, during, and after major changes in the environment. This study of the community health center program covers more than two decades, examining the relationships among bureaucratic, congressional, and interest group actors during five different presidential administrations.

Only one other published study done to date, *Feeding Hungry People,* by Jeffrey M. Berry, has examined the policy network relating to a social program—food stamps—over time and compares it to the models of such networks found in the literature. Berry finds that the food stamp program was much more like an issue network than a subgovernment or iron triangle. This study comes to a different conclusion. While the policy network supporting the health center program did not have all of the characteristics of a subgovernment, it also differed in important ways from the issue networks described by Heclo.

Chapter 8 compares the food stamp and health center networks and suggests that each represents a different form of social welfare policy network within a typology of such networks. This is a first step in developing generalizations about these phenomena.

The Nature of This Study

This analysis of the community health center program is both a "deviant" and a "hypothesis-generating" case study (Lijphart, 1971: 691–93). It is a deviant case study because it examines a policy network that supports a program serving a poor, largely black and Hispanic population, whereas most subgovernments discussed in the literature support programs whose constituencies have substantial political resources. It is a hypothesis-generating study because one of its goals is to analyze how such a policy network differs from the traditional iron triangle discussed in the literature.

All of the historical discussion presented in chapter 2 and much of the discussion of the OEO period in chapter 3 are based on secondary materials. The analysis of the neighborhood health center policy network during the Nixon, Ford, Carter, and Reagan years (chapters 4–7) is based on primary research, both archival data from government and interest group sources and interviews with individuals involved in the policy process. These individuals included health center administrators, House and Senate Appropriations Committee staff, the congressional staff who worked on each major piece of legislation that authorized funding for the health center program, staff and officials within the Public Health Service (PHS), officials and staff of the National Association of Community Health Centers (NACHC), and staff of the American Hospital Association and the American Medical Association (AMA).[4]

The interviews were designed to elicit information on the actions of and the relationships among political actors involved in the formulation and implementation of health center policy over a fifteen-year period, focusing especially on the 1975, 1978, and 1981 reauthorizations of the program.[5]

The Definition of Primary Care

Primary health care has been defined in various ways over the last twenty years. Underlying this variety of definitions are political differences about which institutions and health care workers should deliver such care (see Rogers, 1975; Parker, 1974; McDermott, 1974; CCHS, 1975; AHA, 1973). The definition of *ambulatory care* is clear; it is "health care service given to a person who is not a bed patient in a health care institution" (Jonas, 1986:125). The definition of primary care, in contrast, involves a description of the scope of services to be provided, and that varies considerably from writer to writer.

The concept of *primary care* is based on a theory of health planning that involves a regional organization of care on three levels of increasing specialization and technical complexity. Primary care is the treatment of simple conditions that are found most often in a given population (colds, arthritis) and is provided in a location easily accessible to the population being served. *Secondary care* is concerned with the treatment of more serious conditions occurring somewhat less frequently (such as bone fractures or appendicitis) and is usually provided in a community hospital serving a population larger than that served by primary care practitioners and institutions. *Tertiary care* involves the most complex treatment for the rarest conditions by the most highly specialized practitioners, usually in teaching hospitals that serve a broader geographical area and a larger population than the first two levels (Batistella and Rundell, 1978:298; Parker, 1974:18–22). This planning model assumes that the health care system will treat populations rather than individuals. This assumption is made explicit in those definitions of primary care that have a community-based, epidemiological approach and include public health services as part of their definition (Parker, 1974; Geiger, 1972, 1982; Abramson and Kark, 1982). This was the concept on which the neighborhood health center program was based.

However, primary health care has also been defined in terms of services provided to individuals. This definition is more appropriate to care provided by solo, fee-for-service practitioners as well as care delivered within institutional settings such as health maintenance organizations (HMOs) and hospitals. One such definition lists the functions of primary care as (1) the provision of "ready access for solutions to ordinary problems," (2) the identification of and provision of treatment for potentially serious medical problems "from innocent-appearing situations," and (3) the provision of "science-based Samaritanism" or "human support and reassurance" based on scientific expertise (McDermott, 1974:293). This definition appears in an article arguing that primary care must be delivered by a highly trained physician based at a hospital.

Primary care has often been characterized as involving "responsibility" and "continuity." A primary care practitioner assumes the responsibility for assessing health needs, planning and coordinating care, and making appropriate referrals to other levels of care. Primary care services are said to include preventive care, health education, treatment and rehabilitation services (Kirkham, 1977:9, Batistella and Rundell, 1978:310–12; CCHS, 1975:xi). This concept of primary health care (also a part of the neighborhood health center model) was the basis for efforts to restructure hospital outpatient clinics in the 1970s so that care provided in clinics would no longer be fragmented and episodic. The U.S. Congress became involved in this effort in 1978 and the legislation developed was viewed by health center supporters as a political challenge to the community health center program. This will be discussed in chapter 6.

The term *primary care* thus resonates with different meanings, depending on the health policy perspective of its user. In this book, outpatient care is discussed in several different historical periods and institutional and social contexts. Therefore, the term primary care will generally be used in its narrowest sense. This is as "basic or general care which emphasizes the point when the *patient* first seeks assistance from the medical care system and the care of the simpler and more common *illnesses*" (House, *A Discursive Dictionary,* 1976:127, emphasis in original). Efforts to deliver more comprehensive or community-based services will be discussed specifically.

2

The Mobilization of Bias
and Primary Care Policy

Neighborhood health centers were to provide comprehensive care, both preventive services and treatment, to all of the residents of a specific community. In 1965, the concept of health services was broadly defined to include activities aimed at changing aspects of the social and physical environment that negatively affected the health status of the population served. In addition, individuals from the community were to work with physicians and nurses as part of a health care team, and consumers were to participate in the governance of each center. Thus health centers were models for health care delivery that challenged the existing health care system. (The term *system,* as it is used here, does not imply rationality, but merely a regularized set of interactions.) It was for this reason that federal funding of the neighborhood health center (NHC) program was not initiated as part of the regular health policy agenda, but rather as part of the War on Poverty, a new policy that was to be implemented outside the existing social welfare, labor, and health bureaucracies.

In order to develop this argument fully, it is necessary to analyze the institutional arrangements for the provision of primary care in the United States and the forces responsible for shaping those arrangements. Underlying this approach are the concepts of "mobilization of bias" and "nondecision-making" developed by

Peter Bachrach and Morton S. Baratz (1970), building on the work of E. E. Schattschneider (1960).

Bachrach and Baratz argue that power is exercised "when A devotes his energies to creating or reinforcing social and political values and institutional practices that limit the scope of the political process to public consideration of only those issues which are comparatively innocuous to A" (1970:7). "Political systems" and "subsystems" develop a "mobilization of bias, . . . a set of predominant values, beliefs, rituals and institutional procedures ('rules of the game') that operate systematically and consistently to the benefit of certain persons and groups at the expense of others. Those who benefit are placed in a preferred position to defend and promote their vested interests" (1970:43). Bachrach and Baratz identify the means by which a certain mobilization of bias is sustained as nondecision-making. Nondecision-making involves the ways in which

> demands for change in the existing allocation of benefits and privi-
> leges in the community can be suffocated before they are even
> voiced; or kept covert; or killed before they gain access to the relevant
> decisionmaking area; or failing all these things, maimed or destroyed
> in the decision-implementing stage of the policy process. (1970:44)

One of the forms of nondecision-making they describe is to label a "challenge" or "demand for change" as illegitimate according to the norms of the system (1970:45).

Thus, Bachrach and Baratz call attention to the fact that poten-tially redistributive issues or policies may be prevented even from becoming part of the policy agenda. Michael T. Hayes has incorpo-rated the concept of nondecision-making in his typology explaining the roles of interest groups under various legislative conditions (1981:25–38). A situation labeled as involving nondecisions is either one in which leaders are able to keep certain issues off the agenda even when there is dissatisfaction with existing arrange-ments, or when the challenging groups have few political resources and cannot overcome institutional barriers and force action on an issue. In either case, no legislation is enacted (1981:35–6).

The concepts of the mobilization of bias and nondecision-making are particularly relevant to U.S. health care policy in the twentieth century. While the issues of inappropriate, inaccessible, and costly health care were raised by health care reformers at various times, for long periods these issues were not part of the political agenda.

I use the concept of the mobilization of bias in health care policy to explain both why an experiment in health care delivery began as part of the War on Poverty, and why some of its innovative characteristics were modified within a very short period. One problem related to the use of this concept, however, needs to be discussed.

In Bachrach's and Baratz's case study of antipoverty policy in Baltimore and its relation to "an ideology of white supremacy" (1970:170), the content of the mobilization of bias is fairly straightforward.[1] In addition, a shift in the mobilization of bias could be measured approximately in terms of outcomes—for example, membership of blacks on antipoverty boards and the actual distribution of income. In areas such as health policy, however, determining the content of the mobilization of bias is a far more complex issue, a central methodological problem in measuring change that Bachrach and Baratz do not discuss. Before determining that a demand or policy challenges the existing order, that order must first be described. The challenge must be viewed in relation to the status quo.

The specific nature or content of the mobilization of bias in primary care policy in the United States developed historically, along with the structural arrangements for delivering such care. This chapter will review the development of these arrangements, the result of a series of political struggles, and then describe the content of the mobilization of bias in primary care policy in the 1960s.

As I retrace this history, I will also examine earlier efforts that challenged these arrangements. Some of these reformist efforts were based on ideas about how health care delivery should be organized, ideas similar to the views of advocates of the neighborhood health center program in the 1960s.

Power Relationships and the Delivery
of Primary Health Care

THE DISPENSARY

The distinctions between inpatient and outpatient or ambulatory care, which are so important in today's health policy debates, are made within the context of a hospital-centered health system. However, the hospital did not assume this position until the early twentieth century. In fact, until the development, at the end of the nineteenth century, of "scientific medicine" and new modes of medical practice that involved the use of antiseptic operating rooms and laboratories, little actual medical treatment was done in hospitals (Jonas, 1977A:165–66). Hospitals were traditionally established "to care for strangers and the poor" (Duffy, 1974:178), and in the United States during most of the nineteenth century they continued to have a protective or custodial function.

For the middle and upper classes during the eighteenth and nineteenth centuries, physicians provided treatment in the patient's home. "Decent, respectable people expected to be treated at home" (Duffy, 1974:178). Workers who lived in large cities could obtain care at a dispensary, a free-standing clinic that offered treatment such as minor surgery, tooth extraction, and the prescription of drugs for common ailments. Most dispensaries also sent young doctors to visit patients who were too sick to leave home (Rosenberg, 1974:32–33). Dispensaries, originally founded for charitable motives, were financed privately in most cities.[2]

During the nineteenth century, dispensaries were the major form of medical care for urban residents who could not afford to pay a physician (see Rosenberg, 1974:32). For instance, in 1871 in New York City, twenty-six dispensaries treated 219,851 patients or approximately one-fifth of the city's population (Duffy, 1974:185). By 1900 there were approximately one hundred dispensaries in the United States (Davis and Warner, 1918:10).

Charles E. Rosenberg cites several important factors in the development of the dispensary as the primary medical institution serving the urban working class. The dispensary was "consistent" with "available therapeutic modalities," with the organization of the medical profession, with the small and "homogeneous" community, and with a tradition of private charitable activity. However, most fundamental in Rosenberg's view, is that the dispensary served the interests of the elite, European-trained segment of the American medical profession. Early in the development of the dispensary, medical training was an integral part of its organization. At the beginning of the nineteenth century, established physicians provided their apprentices with clinical experience at the dispensaries. In fact, the training function of the dispensary was a major argument made in efforts to raise funds for their support. As medical schools began to include clinical training as part of their curriculum, they established their own dispensaries. Dispensary organization followed the development of specialization within the medical profession; dispensaries had separate departments for specific organs of the body and categories of disease.

As the number of American hospitals began to increase during the post–Civil War period, they established their own dispensaries or outpatient departments. In some areas, hospital outpatient departments and the older, free-standing dispensaries competed for patients. Medical schools even advertised the services of their clinics in handbills and newspapers. During the same period, medical schools began to become affiliated with hospitals and to establish internships and residency programs. The hospital-based programs thus provided the clinical training previously provided at the dispensary (Rosenberg, 1974:37–50). By the 1920s, the free-standing dispensary had all but disappeared. By then, it "had become as marginal to the needs of the medical profession as it had been central in the first two-thirds of the nineteenth century" (Rosenberg, 1974:49).

The same elite (or potentially elite) physicians who had worked in the dispensaries were now most likely to be closely linked to a hospital. Hospital outpatient departments were also organized by specialty into separate clinics. This structure reflected their function as sites for the selection of interesting cases to be admitted to hospitals where they would be used for training purposes (Davis, 1927; Freymann, 1974).

While the establishment of dispensaries and outpatient departments was related to the interests of one segment of the medical profession, another part of the profession found these institutions threatening to their interests. During the last part of the nineteenth century, as earlier, the majority of American physicians practiced individual fee-for-service medicine outside of the hospitals. As part of a series of political efforts by newly energized medical societies, a campaign against "dispensary abuse" was conducted, beginning in about 1890.

THE CAMPAIGN AGAINST DISPENSARY ABUSE
The American medical profession at the end of the nineteenth century was fragmented, conflict-ridden, and politically ineffectual (Burrow, 1977:16–20). When Dr. Joseph N. McCormack, the chief political organizer of the AMA during the Progressive Era, began his tenure in 1900, he "found that legislators seldom trusted doctors and that professional endorsement of a measure often was tantamount to defeat" (Burrow, 1977:19).

However, under McCormack's direction, state medical societies and the AMA began to mobilize politically. They became engaged in struggles about the harmfulness of patent medicines, overprescribing by pharmacists, and the threat to maternal and infant health posed by midwifery (Burrow, 1977: 113–17). Underlying these efforts was a sense (a recurrent theme in medical journals of the period) that physicians had low status and an inadequate and dwindling income in an inflationary economic time (Burrow, 1977:14–15; see Markowitz and Rosner, 1973:88). Many in the profession believed that an "oversupply" of medical schools had resulted in an excess of physicians in relation to the number of patients seeking treatment (Burrow, 1977:106; see Markowitz and Rosner, 1973:89–90). Midwives, who in 1900 delivered about half of the babies in the United States, were viewed as a threat to the physician's livelihood as well as to the health of the population (Burrow, 1977:117).

The economic issue was faced most directly when state medical societies set fees,[3] "blacklisted" patients who had not paid their bills,[4] and complained that dispensaries were treating patients who were able to pay for private medical treatment. Dispensary policies were thought to reduce the potential patient population by treating patients who could afford to pay for their care. Concern was voiced by medical societies in many states about the policies of both free-standing and hospital dispensaries (Burrow, 1977:106–13). Organized physicians "publicized accounts of wealthy citizens crowding the indigent away from dispensary doors 'clothed in fine raiment, decked with jewelry.' According to this account, the 'Diamond Dispensary' (apparently in New York City) got its name from its gratuitous service to the rich" (Burrow, 1977:111).

Physicians in New York State helped to enact legislation that dealt with these concerns. An 1899 law mandated that all dispensaries be regulated by the Board of Charities and established that dispensaries would provide "means test" or "charity" medicine to the poor. Patients who misrepresented their income would have to pay fines or go to jail (Burrow, 1977:112–13).

The attacks on the dispensaries were made without solid evidence of the charges. The reality was found to be quite different. A 1911 survey of Manhattan dispensaries concluded that 90 percent of those studied could not afford to pay for care, and that this was true of the average poor family (Burrow, 1977:112). However, as a result of pressure from private practitioners, hospital clinic and dispensary services were to be limited to those who could prove that they were unable to purchase private medical care. A "two-class" system of health services was to be clearly delineated via a means test.

THE OPPOSITION TO CONTRACT MEDICINE

Some poor families, especially working-class immigrants, avoided "the stigma of charity medicine" by consulting contract physicians employed by fraternal societies. This form of medical care was found in the ethnic neighborhoods of small and large cities in all parts of the United States during the first decade of the twentieth century. On the Lower East Side of Manhattan, for example, five hundred physicians had contracts with Jewish lodges and benevolent societies.

Contract practice had been used on plantations in the South before the Civil War but expanded during the Progressive Era in areas outside the South. In addition to the employment of doctors on a capitation or salaried basis by groups of working-class patients in the cities, such arrangements were used by the railroads and mining and logging industries. Large industrial corporations in northern cities also employed contract physicians, and in some places hospitals and hospital associations sponsored contract plans (Burrow, 1977:120–22).

The medical profession claimed that physicians were paid very little by such plans, and Burrow suggests that these claims were valid (1977:122–23). What made such arrangements attractive to the participating physicians was that in a time of great competition for patients, contract practice at least provided a regular income (Duffy, 1974:179).

Physicians in private practice were uncomfortable with contract medicine both because salaries were low and because it challenged the fee-for-service system (Burrow, 1977:119). Local medical societies varied in their position on this issue. Some opposed all contract plans; others approved such arrangements if they were in geographically isolated industries such as lumber or mining or if patients were clearly unable to pay a physician. In 1911, the AMA took a position opposing all contract plans; in 1913 it approved physician participation in fraternal society contract plans in which members were below a certain income level. Clearly, the same concept of means-test medicine was operating here as had been successfully institutionalized in the dispensaries as a result of the campaign against dispensary abuse.

By about 1920, the number of contract physicians had declined to "negligible proportions" (Duffy, 1974:298). It is not clear whether the activities of organized medicine on this issue was the primary reason for its decline (see Burrow, 1977:132). The decline of contract practice could also have been related to the successful reorganization of medical education on the basis of scientific principles. The "reform" of medical education included limits on entrance into the profession. As the number of physicians decreased, so did competition among them. This enabled individual practitioners to raise fees and still maintain a private practice (Duffy, 1974:299–300).

The organized medical profession equated its economic survival with the fee-for-service system and, even in times of economic hardship, resisted forms of medical care organization that would challenge this payment system. Local medical societies and the AMA opposed group practice and prepaid medical care in the 1920s and 1930s as they had opposed contract practice during the first decade of the twentieth century. This opposition to group practice and its consequences will be discussed briefly later in this chapter.

It is clear that the professional and economic interests of American physicians were crucial factors in determining how primary health care services were organized over time. The urban dispensaries of the nineteenth century provided teaching material and clinical experience for one segment of the American medical profession; as hospitals took over this training function, freestanding dispensaries disappeared. Another, larger segment of the American medical profession organized against dispensary abuse and succeeded in establishing a means-test policy so that the line between private and charity medicine would be clearly demarcated and maintained.

While political activity by the medical profession significantly shaped the structure of primary health care delivery in the United States, the profession was also operating within a sympathetic political culture—that of American liberalism (Hartz, 1955). The concern of some physicians with dispensary abuse echoed and reinforced deeply felt American beliefs about individual responsibility, the causes of poverty, and the relationship of the state to society.

AMERICAN IDEOLOGY AND
THE FINANCING OF HEALTH CARE

Since the colonial period, poverty has been viewed as a consequence of an individual's failings, and stigmatization went along with the acceptance of "poor relief." In the mid-seventeenth century, colonial officials required paupers to wear large identifying badges on their clothing. During the nineteenth century, newly founded schools, work houses, and temperance societies were supposed to end poverty by "reforming" the poor. Although many men became disabled and unable to work as a result of the Civil War, and large-scale immigration, urbanization, and a number of economic depressions increased the magnitude of poverty in the United States at the end of the nineteenth century, Social Darwinism reinforced the notion that individual rather than structural factors made people poor (Feagin, 1975:24–37). The major conclusion drawn by Michael B. Katz from his empirical case studies of poverty in the nineteenth and early twentieth centuries (1983) is the great disparity that existed between the economic realities that shaped people's lives and the social perception of that reality. The nature of unskilled work in the nineteenth century was such that "dependence was a structural, almost normal, aspect of working-class life" (1983:183). Yet central to the American belief system was (and is) the idea that hard work will bring success and that failure to achieve is a consequence of a defect of will or character (Feagin, 1975:91–92). Such a set of assumptions about the social world would work against arguments for state actions to ameliorate the conditions related to poverty. This "ideology of individualism" (1975:91) was a factor in the success of the American medical profession in limiting the private and public provision of primary care services.

Charles Rosenberg points out that the concept of dispensary abuse had an important ideological function in directing health policy. If "abuse" did not explain the rapidly expanding population that was seeking treatment at dispensaries, then "large numbers of worthy and hard-working Americans were indeed too poor to pay for even minimally adequate medical care" (1974:52).

The inability of many workers to pay for medical care was recognized by those reformers involved in the unsuccessful movement for compulsory health insurance between 1912 and 1920. These reformers (who rejected the individual defect explanation of poverty) were part of the larger Progressive movement concerned with improving the living and working conditions of urban dwellers.

A campaign to establish state-administered health insurance for workers and their families was initiated by the American Association for Labor Legislation, founded in 1906 by a group of social scientists (Numbers, 1978:16–19). Compulsory health insurance was supported by other organizations of social scientists and social workers, by hospital-based, academic, and public health physicians, by some unions, by the Socialist party, and by some Democratic and Republican politicians, including five governors. Opposition was led by commercial insurance companies (1978:57–61) and joined by many state medical societies. Debate on the issue was interrupted by World War I; after the war this debate was affected by fears of foreign bolshevism and domestic radicalism. Health insurance bills failed in all of the legislatures in which they were considered (1978: chs. 8 and 9).

American social reformers had been influenced by European health insurance plans. But the political conditions under which they were established were quite different from those in the United States. In Germany, where a health insurance program began in 1883, and in Great Britain, where one was enacted in 1911, politicians in power viewed health insurance as an issue that would gain them support among working-class voters who might otherwise support growing socialist parties (Numbers, 1978:10; Heidenheimer, Heclo, and Adams, 1975:9). In the United States, the socialist party was far smaller and trade unions were split on the issue.

During the decade after the defeat of health insurance bills in the United States, large numbers of city workers sought medical care at outpatient departments and other clinics, including dispensaries. These institutions were the major source of care for "as much as a fourth of the urban population" (Stevens, 1971:146).

Unmet need for medical services during the 1920s was documented in a series of reports published by the Committee on the Costs of Medical Care (CCMC) in 1932. The CCMC, a research group established by foundation funds in 1928, did a five-year study of American health services, the most comprehensive study of American health care up to that time. It presented abundant evidence that access to medical care was inequitably distributed by income and that a significant proportion of low-income families were receiving little or no medical or dental care. At the end of its work, the committee issued a majority report recommending the development of hospital-affiliated group practices (including nurses and technicians, as well as physicians) and prepaid financing of health care. The report left open the question of whether such prepaid mechanisms should be administered privately or by the government. A minority group of the committee, which included all of the AMA representatives, dissented from the final report. (Stevens, 1971:183–86; Rayack, 1967:147–50).

The AMA attacked the proposals of the CCMC as it was to respond to any proposals that might alter the solo, fee-for-service, privately financed system of medical practice, including health insurance bills introduced in Congress during the 1930s and 1940s. A 1932 editorial on the CCMC report in the *Journal of the American Medical Association* stated:

> The alignment is clear—on the one side the forces representing the great foundations, public health officialdom, social theory—even socialism and communism—inciting to revolution; on the other side, the organized medical profession of this country urging an orderly evaluation guided by controlled experimentation which will observe the principles that have been found through the centuries to be necessary to the sound practice of medicine. (Quoted in Harris, 1966:68)

Clearly, the AMA response to the majority report of the CCMC was to label it as illegitimate according to the values of American society. This form of nondecision-making was effective; the CCMC proposals were not seriously discussed as part of the health policy agenda. Nondecision-making occurred again when the Roosevelt administration, fearful of potential AMA opposition, removed the issue of health insurance from the Social Security bill it presented to Congress in 1935 (Stevens, 1971:187–88; Starr, 1982:266–69).

Thus, although a substantial part of the working class was apparently unable to purchase medicine from the private sector, efforts to finance such care through the state were unsuccessful in the pre–World War I era and continued to be so until the New Deal. When a limited amount of public money was provided for medical care beginning in the 1930s, the recipients were subject to the stigmatization of means-test provisions and federal money was used to pay for the services of private providers (Stern, 1946:110–13). Beginning in 1935, the federal government did provide grants-in-aid to local governments to provide health care for the poor. The recipients of such care were selected on the basis of a means test (1946:114, 20–36).

THE LIMITATION OF THE SPHERE OF PUBLIC HEALTH
At the same time that the medical profession's campaign against dispensary abuse and contract practice (as well as vast changes in medical theory and practice) were helping to shape primary care services in the private sector, a public health movement had developed, concerned with the role of government in assuring the health of large populations. But the influence of a "science" of medicine oriented to the individual patient, traditional American beliefs about the role of government in society, and the political pressure of organized medicine combined to greatly limit the sphere of public health in America.

Activities related to the health of the public can be traced to efforts during the colonial period to limit the spread of yellow fever in port cities, but the systematic study of the health status of the general population, including environmental factors related to that status, began in the mid-nineteenth century. In 1839, the American Statistical Association was established and during the next several years studies were published on the health conditions of the population of various American cities. These studies related health to the urban environment and problems such as inadequate sewerage, housing and water supply, overcrowding, and poverty. During the same period, voluntary associations were formed to deal with these problems. For instance, the New York Association for Improving the Conditions of the Poor (established in 1843) focused on tenement conditions in that city. Other groups worked on issues such as pure water and food and health education. Many of the physicians, public officials, and others involved in these public health activities viewed themselves as part of the larger social reform movements of the latter part of the nineteenth century (Rosen, 1949:317).

George Rosen suggests that this "first phase" of the public health movement embodied a concept of "social medicine," in that health was viewed as a product of the social and physical environment of the population:

> It is clear that by the middle of the seventies considerable advance had been made in America toward a socially oriented view of health and disease. Physicians, lay sanitarians, and public administrators had come to recognize that health and disease were in considerable measure an expression of collective behavior, that social and economic conditions were inextricably intertwined with morbidity and mortality. (1949:320)

This perspective, however, changed within the next twenty years so that activity aimed at the prevention and treatment of specific diseases replaced a concern with their causes. Beginning in the 1890s, for example, settlement houses and other voluntary agencies began to provide screening for tuberculosis and venereal disease and preventive services for infants and small children as part of public health campaigns. Rosen comments that at this point the public health movement's orientation

> was empirical and pragmatic. It had no well-articulated system of ideas . . . into which such diverse problems as poverty and dependency, infant mortality, sweatshops, prostitution, tuberculosis prevention and tenement house reform could be fitted; . . . their uncoordinated attacks on specific diseases did little to advance a comprehensive

formulation of the environmental and more particularly of the social relations of health and disease. (1949:321)

The broad, environmental perspective on health changed to a narrow, disease-oriented approach because of the influence of the new science of bacteriology that was shaping medicine generally. Bacteriology focused on specific diseases and found its source in specific agents. Just as physicians specialized narrowly in various organs and parts of the body, the public health movement focused on specific diseases. Moreover, the public health movement also limited itself primarily to disease prevention. The public sector provided little treatment because of its responsiveness to the interests and demands of private medical practitioners.

PRIVATE MEDICINE AND PUBLIC HEALTH

During the first two decades of the twentieth century, public health and physician activists became concerned with rationalizing the provision of health services to the poor. As a consequence of such concerns, health centers were established in many cities in the United States. They were based on the district concept of serving the population of a given geographical area and were intended to coordinate the health, welfare, and recreational services provided by several different agencies (both public and private) by placing them in one central location. Their health care focus was on the prevention of disease through education, maternal and child care, food inspection, and immunization. By 1926, there were more than a thousand such centers across the country (Wilinsky, 1927:677–80, Hiscock, 1935:30).[5]

By offering only preventive services, the health centers avoided competition with the treatment services provided by private practitioners. A 1927 paper by the health commissioner of Boston states this explicitly. "In order to promote properly the principles of preventive medicine it is important that only such services as are truly prophylactic shall be part of the health center, leaving the curative field to the practitioner, hospital and existing dispensary" (Wilinsky, 1927:679).

In one case where this division of labor was not scrupulously observed, health centers sponsored by the Los Angeles County Health Department provided emergency care and other treatment services. Private practitioners complained and these services were shifted to the county hospital (Hiscock, 1935:45). "Private practice would not permit competition by centers in care outside of the hospital or to have treatment dominated by public authorities" (Stoeckle and Candib, 1974:31–32).

The limitation of the sphere of public health in response to opposition by the medical profession was also seen in New York, a city in which much innovation in public health services took place. Beginning in about 1910, professionals in the New York City Department of Health attempted to expand the scope of its activities. In 1913, New York City opened its first venereal disease clinic. The next year, the department's Division of Child Hygiene became a bureau and operated fifty-six infant milk stations, six dental clinics, and five clinics for children with tonsil and nasal problems. In 1914, Dr. Sigismund S. Goldwater (then superintendent of Mount Sinai Hospital) became the health commissioner of New York. He began to move the Department of Health toward involvement in the direct provision of health services. A model health district was established on the Lower East Side of Manhattan as part of an attempt to coordinate the fieldwork of the department and bring it closer to citizens. Goldwater also suggested that everyone in the city be given a physical examination by the department (Duffy, 1974:263–67).

Goldwater's suggestions and actions were perceived by the organized medical profession as a threat to its interests. At a meeting of the Society of Medical Jurisprudence, "the Health Department was accused of virtually committing the city 'to a policy of Socialism' and its health programs were described as 'ruinous to the business of the medical practictioners of the City'" (Duffy, 1974:269–70). Goldwater's tenure as commissioner was quite short. In 1915, during a period of budget-tightening under the next health commissioner, the city's nose and throat clinics for children were closed. This was "a step which the Public Health Committee of the New York Academy of Medicine heartily approved" (1974:270).

"As long as the department's medical inspectors merely reported thousands of physical defects among school children, the medical profession had no objection, but the opening of clinics to correct these conditions was another story" (1974:269–70).

Another effort to broaden public responsibility for the delivery of health services was made at the state level by Dr. Herman Biggs, a New York State health commissioner. In 1920, Biggs wrote a plan for the establishment of health centers all over New York State that would provide integrated preventive and therapeutic services to both rural and urban workers. The centers would be run by county governments, but the state would provide funding for their construction and operation (Terris, 1946:390). Biggs's vision was that such centers would provide "for all medicine, preventive as well as diagnostic and curative" (1946:398).

The proposal was introduced into the New York state legislature in 1920 as part of the Sage-Machold Bill. During the previous legislative session, a health insurance bill had been defeated by a coalition made up of the private insurance industry, businessmen, and the state medical society. The chairman of the Assembly Rules Committee had called the bill "bolshevistic" and similar charges were made during the debate over the health center legislation. The bill was defeated.

The activities of organized medicine in New York were central to the limitation of public health activity at both the city and state level. But it is significant that one of the strategies used in both instances was to label proposals for the expansion of public health services as challenging the prevailing societal value system— "socialistic," "bolshevistic." This was the same strategy used against proposals made by the CCMC to reorganize primary care.

The Structure of the Primary Care Sector

Although New Deal programs expanded public health services in areas such as school and child health (Stevens, 1971:178–79), the basic structural arrangements for providing primary care in the 1960s had already taken shape by the 1920s (see Anderson, 1968:15–16). Personal health services were to be provided by the private sector; in the 1920s this was the fee-for-service physician (both the general practitioner and specialist) in solo practice. The hospital outpatient department would also provide primary care, but only to charity patients as determined by a means test (Jonas, 1986:134, 144–45).

Public health providers at the local level had three types of tasks. The first was to provide environmental, health-related services such as inspection of food and water and the maintenance of public health laboratories. The second was to collect vital statistics. Third, local health departments generally provided preventive personal health services (especially those that would help to control communicable disease) such as the innoculation of infants and adult screening for tuberculosis and venereal disease (Jonas, 1986:145). Local government services were clearly supplementary to private medicine and the federal government respected this arrangement.

The first element in the mobilization of bias in primary care was thus the dominance of the private sector in the delivery of medical treatment. Means testing was intended to reinforce this dominance. A second factor is related to, but also distinct from, the first. The dominant mode of primary care was care provided not only within the private as opposed to the public sector, but also care delivered by a physician, a solo practitioner who was paid on a fee-for-service basis. A third characteristic of the structure of the health system was that responsibility for the health of individuals was clearly separated from that of large populations. An earlier concern with health as a product of the physical and social environment had been superseded by the "medical model" in both prevention and treatment—a focus on specific diseases as manifested within individual patients.

There were efforts to challenge these dominant arrangements, both small-scale experiments and proposals for large-scale reform. These efforts provide evidence of discontent with the existing system and, in some cases, opposition to them reveals the exercise of power to prevent the consideration of these as alternative arrangements.

Challenges to the Mobilization of Bias

AN EXPERIMENT IN COMMUNITY ORGANIZATION
Some early experiments in health care delivery viewed health as an arena for community involvement and organization. This notion, of course, challenged the professional dominance enjoyed by organized medicine. One such project was the Cincinnati Social Unit which operated from 1918 to 1920. It was directed by Wilbert and Elsie La Grange Phillips, who were socialists, and was funded by "wealthy progressives" (Betten and Austin, 1977:13–14). It is interesting to review this experience briefly, since in several respects it is a predecessor of the neighborhood health center movement of the 1960s.[6]

The goal of the Social Unit was to deal with the problems of a mixed working-class, middle-income neighborhood of 12,000 in Cincinnati, Ohio, by providing social services and organizing its residents to participate directly in neighborhood governance. Citizen participation was actualized in the form of elected block workers who represented their blocks in a neighborhood policy-making body called the Citizens' Council.

The block workers also served as health educators and outreach workers. They were responsible for visiting all of the families on their block, conducting surveys of health status and health needs, registering births, reporting disease, providing information on health care and on the unit's health programs, and arranging for medical services. Most block workers were housewives who received a small salary for this work (Betten and Austin, 1977:14–15). Similarly, the neighborhood health centers of the 1960s provided for citizen participation in project governance and employed community residents to provide health care and advocacy services to patients in their homes and at the centers.

Another similarity between the two experiments was that those responsible for the programs anticipated the reactions of private physicians and made concessions to their interests. Local physicians' organizations, fearing that the provision of free medical services by the Social Unit would reduce the income of doctors, opposed its establishment. Wilbert Phillips assured the Cincinnati Academy of Medicine that the Social Unit would use the fee-for-service method for paying physicians and argued that the unit's existence would help to "prevent health insurance," a financing system "strongly opposed" by the academy (Betten and Austin, 1977:19). While the Social Unit provided free classes on prenatal and infant care and nutrition, medical and dental exams for both children and adults, and medical care for preschool children, it did not provide medical treatment by physicians for the general population. Instead, patients who were examined at the unit's health station were then referred to family doctors for treatment (1977:16).

In spite of these concessions, the Social Unit lasted only two years. The same kind of political labeling was used against it as was used against the expansion of public health services in New York during this general era of red-baiting. It was first attacked by Cincinnati politicians as socialistic and a move toward the Soviet form of government. Attacks by local social service agencies and the local medical society followed: "Institutions and groups which considered the unit a threat to themselves . . . used the radicalism charge as the vehicle for their own purposes" (Betten and Austin, 1977:19). The outside financiers withdrew their support and the Social Unit experiment ended (1977:20).

EFFORTS AT HEALTH SYSTEM REFORM

Other efforts attempted to change some of the most fundamental aspects of the health services arrangements described above by establishing institutions that would provide comprehensive health care—both preventive services and treatment—and/or by providing services to that part of the working population that might (with difficulty) be able to pay for the services of a private practitioner.

A key figure in such efforts was Michael M. Davis, a medical sociologist, health administrator, and author of many books on health care delivery and financing. Davis's career as a health care reformer spanned almost fifty years, from his establishment of the first "pay clinics" in the United States in 1913 to his advocacy of prepaid health care in *Medical Care for Tomorrow,* published in 1956 (Rosen, 1972:322). Davis received his Ph.D. in sociology from Columbia University in 1906; before and for a few years following his studies he worked in settlement houses and did community organizing on the Lower East Side of Manhattan (Rosen, 1972:321; Pumphrey, 1972:31). In 1910 he became the director of the Boston Dispensary and thus began a twenty-year period of involvement with innovation in the delivery of ambulatory health care.

When Davis began his tenure in Boston, he found the dispensary organized into many separate clinics, all operated as charity institutions (Pumphrey, 1972:32), without regular budgets and staffed by volunteer physicians. Davis instituted an annual budget, increased the number of social workers, and concentrated on improving the quality of care provided at the dispensary. This included emphasizing the continuity of the doctor-patient relationship and instituting a regular system of patient follow-up by the social service staff (Pumphrey, 1975:453–57). (It is interesting to note that the same "reforms" in outpatient clinics were made in hospitals in the 1970s.)

Davis's most radical "break with medical charitable tradition" was the establishment of pay clinics at the Boston Dispensary (Pumphrey, 1975:460). These clinics were held in the evening to meet the needs of a working population. Physicians were salaried and patients paid small fees. The first clinic, an eye clinic, opened in 1913, and between 1914 and 1919 several other evening clinics— for gynecology, venereal disease, and care of the ear, nose, and throat—were established (1975:459–62).

In *Dispensaries: Their Management and Development* (1918), Davis and his co-author, Andrew W. Warner, discuss their vision of the dispensary as the institution that should be responsible for the delivery of primary care in the urban community. "The Dispensary is the medical organization which must cover the major portion of the field in caring for disease, standing between the Hospital on the one hand which provides for the relatively small proportion of acutely incapacitated patients, and the Public Health Department on the other hand which deals usually with preventive work alone" (Davis and Warner, 1918:viii).

Davis and Warner argue that dispensary physicians should be employed on a full-time, salaried basis, and that patients should see the same doctor each time they come for care. Health services should not be limited to narrowly defined medical needs; the dispensary should work with other institutions to change the social and physical environments that threaten the health of patients (1918:355–65). Davis, in fact, argues elsewhere for the efficiency of social medicine. "The community is becoming wearied of a policy which spends two dollars a day for 'curing' a patient in a hospital, and leaves untouched the home conditions which with reasonable certainty will compel the patient or his family to return for the same expensive process" (quoted in Pumphrey, 1975:456).

Davis and Warner are also concerned that the cost of "specialized medicine" is beyond the means of the general public and argue that dispensaries should provide health services to workers as well as to the unemployed poor (1918:329, 364). They also call for group practice ("cooperative" medical practice) as opposed to "the very slightly tempered individualism of private practice" (1918:351–52).

The "philosophy of health care" that Michael Davis worked to implement throughout his long career may be summarized as follows:

> First, he was convinced that curative services divorced from preventive aspirations were unproductive and wasteful. Second, medical services should be accessible to all people, which meant, under the existing system, that ways had to be found to serve a "middle class" which neither qualified for charitable care nor could afford regular medical fees. Third, the provision of good medical care was not the exclusive responsibility and burden of the medical profession, but required the integrated cooperation of persons from many professional and occupational groups. (Pumphrey, 1975:463)

In 1920, the Rockefeller Foundation established a Committee on Dispensary Development and Davis became its director. Its purpose was to "introduce new concepts of ambulatory care in dispensaries and hospital outpatient department units" (Rosen, 1972:322). During Davis's seven-year tenure as director (the life span of the committee) the committee sponsored three demonstration projects: a reorganization of a hospital outpatient department, a health maintenance clinic, and a pay clinic affiliated with New York Hospital and Cornell Medical School (Rosen, 1976:41–43; Pumphrey, 1972:38–39). The first two demonstrations did not achieve their goals, but the third, the Cornell Clinic, was "an outstanding success" (Pumphrey, 1972:39).

The Cornell Clinic employed salaried physicians in a group practice and used a sliding-scale method of payment while providing comprehensive ambulatory care services (Rosen, 1976:41–43). Clinic physicians were paid what they would earn in private practice. The clinic achieved self-sufficiency after eighteen months and "became a standard of the possible in the organization of medical care for the middle classes" (Pumphrey, 1972:39).

In 1928 Davis became the director of medical services for the Julius Rosenwald Fund (Pumphrey, 1972:39). The goal of the fund's work in this area was "to make good medical care more readily available to persons of moderate and low incomes by reducing sickness costs or by making it easier for people to pay for them" (Julius Rosenwald Fund, 1937:3). (Davis was one of the organizers of the CCMC, a group whose work has already been discussed.) In addition to conducting studies of the organization and financing of medical care and working with other organizations on these issues, the fund gave grants to institutions that were innovating in these areas. These included the University of Chicago and the International Ladies Garment Workers Union in New York, both of which had established pay clinics; and hospitals experimenting with "middle-rate payment plans" in which physicians' and surgeons' fees were included in a flat rate for hospitalization (Julius Rosenwald Fund, 1937:4–11). In 1936 the fund abolished its own Department of Medical Services but gave large grants to two other organizations to carry on its work. One grant went to the American Hospital Association for the study of group hospitalization plans and the other to a newly established Committee on Research in Medical Economics which was to do research, training, and consultation in order to make medical care "more widely available to the people at costs within their means" (Julius Rosenwald Fund, 1937:25–26). Davis headed this committee until 1951 (Rosen, 1972:322).

While Davis's work contributed to the development of voluntary insurance plans for hospitalization (such as Blue Cross), his encouragement of pay clinics did not have the same success. In *Medical Care for Tomorrow* (1956) Davis says: "The opposition of practitioners has . . . prevented pay clinics from developing to any extent as adjuncts of nonprofit hospitals" (144). However, he is not specific about the form of this opposition or its consequences in his writings (Pumphrey, 1972:35). A study of the fate of the pay clinics established between 1910 and 1940 has yet to be done.

THE GROUP PRACTICE MOVEMENT

The CCMC had looked toward the creation of group health plans through local initiative (Stevens, 1971:188). The committee estimated that about two hundred such practices existed, mostly in the West and Midwest (Rosenfeld, 1971, vol. 1:12–13). There were two different types of group practice: cooperative group health associations and proprietary group health associations. Cooperative group health associations were prepaid group practices (medical personnel shared equipment and worked together) in which lay members made administrative policy; in proprietary associations a group of physicians provided services to subscribers who did not have a policymaking role. Both the cooperative health associations, which emerged in areas where other cooperative ventures had existed, and the proprietary groups were opposed by the AMA (McDonagh, 1942:9–10, 16, 334–35).

The opposition of organized medicine to group practice was a major obstacle to the formation and survival of such plans (Stevens, 1971:188). Local medical societies took action against physicians who worked in a prepaid health care consumer cooperative in Elk City, Oklahoma, and against the staff of the Roos-Loos Medical Group, a proprietary group serving the employees of the Los Angeles County Department of Water and Power (Rayack, 1967:180–82). In one famous 1943 case, the Supreme Court found the AMA and the District of Columbia Medical Society to be in violation of the Sherman Anti-Trust Act. These organizations had tried to prevent doctors working for the Group Health Association of America, a prepaid consumer-controlled group, from getting hospital-attending privileges or referrals from medical society members (Harris, 1966:17, Rosenfeld, 1971, vol. 1:18).

It is significant to note, as Michael Davis did in 1941, that such activity by organized medicine not only had a negative effect on existing group practices, but also was an inhibiting force in relation to the establishment of other such groups (1941:139). In addition to taking punitive actions against individual physicians, the AMA campaigned against prepaid group practice in the pages of its journal and through other educational channels of its organization. One of the primary arguments against such practices was that they were a move toward socialized medicine. Physicians who read or heard these arguments made them, in turn, to their patients. The labeling of group practice in this way was a significant barrier to its expansion (McDonagh, 1942:335–38).

The Policy Setting for
the Neighborhood Health Center Program

PRIMARY CARE IN THE 1960S
During the 1940s and 1950s, American medical practice became more specialized and the number of general practitioners declined (Stevens, 1971, chs. 14–15). Between 1931 and 1963, general practitioners decreased from 80 percent to 28 percent of all physicians in active practice (Batistella and Rundell, 1978:297). Specialization reduced access to comprehensive primary care for all patients (Richmond, 1969:86). Patients buying their care from the private

sector often chose their own specialists and would go to several different physicians for different problems. In such a situation no one health care professional would coordinate and "manage" their treatment.

In spite of the recommendations of groups like the CCMC, the overwhelming majority of all physicians—specialists and general practitioners—remained solo practitioners. As specialists' fees increased, patients without the means to buy care in the private sector were left to find health care in public health departments (still primarily limited to preventive services and screening) or hospital outpatient departments. Also during this period, low-income populations from rural areas of the United States and the Caribbean emigrated to mainland cities while more affluent populations moved to suburban areas. Many physicians in private practice moved to the suburbs; low-income areas of cities were left with few office-based practitioners, most of them aging (Hudson and Infeld, 1980:31). During the 1950s and 1960s the number of visits to hospital outpatient departments increased greatly, especially in urban areas (Stevens, 1971:421).

Hospital outpatient departments were organized along the specialty divisions of the hospital, and patients had to attend different clinics for different complaints. Care was unlikely to be coordinated. It was difficult for patients with either simple illnesses or multiple health problems to receive appropriate treatment (Jonas, 1986:136). Medical work in the hospital outpatient department, which was less compatible with the research and teaching orientation of specialty medicine than inpatient care, provided little status or other professional recognition (Knowles, 1969:176–77). Physicians working in these clinics were either rotating house staff in training (residents or interns), part-time attending physicians, or outside doctors hired to work by the session. Patients would see a different physician each time they came to the clinic (Jonas, 1986:135–36).

The use of hospital emergency rooms also increased during this period. In addition to treating true emergencies, emergency rooms began to care for patients without private physicians when hospital outpatient clinics were closed or crowded, and to provide backup care for private patients whose doctors were not available or who did not have the equipment needed to treat their condition. Thus, a large proportion of those seeking treatment in hospital emergency rooms did not have emergent conditions (Jonas, 1986:138).

Socially concerned physicians and others interested in health services described these conditions in very critical terms and identified them as a major problem of the American health system in the 1960s:

> In most of our large cities, the hospital out-patient department together with the emergency room is the basic source of care for the poor. Today's out-patient departments still retain some of the attributes of their predecessors, the 18th Century free dispensaries. They are crowded, uncomfortable, lacking in concern for human dignity and to make it worse, *no longer free*. (Yerby, in Richmond, 1969:85, emphasis in original)

> The long, hard bench with the four-hour wait, multiple referrals, incredible discontinuity of care and various other indignities suffered in an anti-social and decadent environment remains the order of the day in most ambulatory clinics in this country. A two-class system of care has prevailed whether it be the contrast between inpatient and outpatient care or private versus clinic patient. (Knowles, 1969:178)

One commentator at a 1964 New York Academy of Medicine Conference on the "Expanding Role of Ambulatory Services in Hospitals and Health Departments" referred to Michael M. Davis's discussions of the need to reform hospital outpatient departments and his own "persistent feeling of *déjà vu*" as the very same issues were being debated (Jonas, 1986:136). The neighborhood health center program was conceived within the context of these policy concerns.

THE FEDERAL ROLE IN HEALTH CARE DELIVERY
One final aspect of the American health care system needs to be described as background to the analysis of the neighborhood health

center program: the relationship of the federal government to health care delivery over time.

Until the end of the Second World War, the federal government's role in the health sector was very limited. During much of that time federal responsibility extended only to the provision of health care to a few isolated groups in the population: merchant seamen, members of the armed forces, veterans, and Native Americans (Stern, 1946:145). In 1921, Congress passed the Maternity and Infant (Sheppard-Towner) Act, a program of grants-in-aid to states to establish demonstration programs for maternal and child health services (Roemer, Kramer, and Frink, 1975:66). This was the first time the federal government had provided money to the states for health services. Sheppard Towner was "enacted over the bitter opposition of the AMA" (Jonas, 1986:355) and lasted only until 1929 (Roemer, Kramer, and Frink, 1975:66). In 1922, the House of Delegates of the AMA passed a resolution against "state medicine," defined as treatment provided or financed by any level of government. Specifically exempt from this prohibition were the detection and treatment of communicable diseases, medical services provided by the armed services and the U.S. Public Health Service, and care of the "indigent sick" (Stevens, 1971:144). From that point until the mid-1960s, when Medicare was passed, organized medicine was successful in its efforts to limit the role of the federal government to those areas it had specified or others it did not oppose.

In the late 1940s, the Veterans Administration expanded the health services that it provided to veterans (Sidel and Sidel, 1977:241), federal monies were channeled into biomedical research, and grants were given to the states to build hospitals under the Hospital Survey and Construction Act of 1946 (the Hill-Burton Act). The AMA supported the Hill-Burton program and did not take a position on biomedical research (Brown, 1978:49). It did, however, strongly oppose President Truman's proposal for national health insurance and spent large sums of money to defeat pro-insurance senators in elections and to mount a national propaganda campaign against "socialized medicine." National health

insurance was not passed by Congress, and the Truman administration shifted its focus to a proposal for hospital insurance for the
elderly (Marmor, 1973:12–15). It was not until fourteen years later
that Medicare was enacted.

THE FEDERAL ROLE AND THE MOBILIZATION OF BIAS
The movement for universal, government-administered health
insurance failed in the 1940s, like earlier movements for health
insurance at the state level, because of the ideological advantages
enjoyed by the AMA. In Paul Starr's words, "Employers shared a
desire to draw the line against socialism" (1982:288). "Between the
two sides in the conflict, there was a gross imbalance in resources—
partly material, partly social, partly symbolic. And these imbal-
ances reinforced one another: the edge the opposition enjoyed in
its social bases of support could be translated into material advantages and means of influence" (1982:287). Although Starr doesn't
use this term, clearly he is describing the operation of "systemic
power" (Stone, 1980), one of whose components is the mobilization of bias.

Comprehensive national health insurance bills were introduced
in Congress every year from 1935 to 1949, but none of these bills
ever came out of committee. The issue of national health insurance
seems to have moved back and forth between Hayes's categories of
"the politics of nondecision" and "the politics of redistribution"
(Hayes, 1981), depending on whether the issue was kept off the
agenda or whether there was major conflict between supporters
and opponents at a particular time.

Richard E. Cairl and Allen W. Imershein (1977) use the concept
of the mobilization of bias to analyze the issue of national health
insurance in the U.S. Congress in the 1970s. They assert that
Medicare changed the nature of federal involvement in the social
service area and therefore "could be considered a successful challenge to the prevailing bias against such federal involvement." But
they also make the very important point that in health policy
there were "at least" two elements of the mobilization of bias, one
relating to federal financing of health care services, the other to

certain "structural" arrangements that were responsible for the way in which health care was delivered. They also state that the passage of Medicare did not challenge this latter aspect of the mobilization of bias in American health policy (1977:170).[7] Although health services for the elderly were to be publicly financed, decisions about the delivery of that care, as well as the price, were to be determined by the private sector. Personal care and public health would continue to be separated, and fee-for-service solo practice was to be maintained—in fact, reinforced—by Medicare reimbursement policy.

Because the neighborhood health center model challenged these elements of the mobilization of bias in primary care policy, nondecision-making characterized the agenda-setting phase of the policy process. This aspect of the policy process—the emergence of the neighborhood health center program on the policy agenda—will be discussed next.

3

The Neighborhood
Health Center Program

Policy Entrepreneurship and Health Care Reform

The first neighborhood health centers were funded as part of the Community Action Program established by the Economic Opportunity Act of 1964. This legislation was at the center of the Johnson administration's War on Poverty, an effort to provide basic education, job training, and other services to low-income individuals by funding new community agencies in which the poor would participate.

The War on Poverty, in James Q. Wilson's terms, was a "new policy" in contrast to the more usual, incremental "amendment of an existing one" (1973:330). Nelson W. Polsby includes the creation of the Community Action Program as one of eight cases in a study of "policy innovation" in America (1984:13). Polsby analyzes "the key to policy innovation" in the Community Action case, as well as in another one of the cases he studied, as "the presence within the government of policy entrepreneurs, persons who knew whatever there was to know about programs in the area, with ideas of their own and opportunities to write these ideas into the law of the land" (1984:144). Analysts of the War on Poverty agree that it was a policy initiated within the executive branch, with Congress having a very limited role, little input from interest groups, and little attention from the general public (Donovan, 1967: ch. 1; Piven and Cloward, 1971:257; Friedman,

1977:26). It was a potentially controversial policy—its legislative enactment was quiet, but conflict and controversy later emerged— and for this reason the 1964 legislation was quite general, leaving decisions about the substance of actual programs to administrators (Hayes, 1981:123). This in turn provided the opportunity for health system reformers themselves, both in and outside of government, to act as policy entrepreneurs in establishing the neighborhood health center program.

The Creation of
the Neighborhood Health Center Program

One of the mandates of the Office of Economic Opportunity (OEO), created by the 1964 legislation, was to work "toward elimination of poverty or a cause or causes of poverty, through developing employment opportunities, improving human performance, motivation and productivity . . . bettering the conditions under which people live, learn and work" (Donovan, 1967:40). Health was not one of the areas in which OEO initially planned to fund projects, although medical care, at least in the form of an initial physical examination, was a part of most OEO programs.

Such examinations revealed that many of the participants in programs like the Job Corps and Head Start had untreated health conditions. Local community action agencies began to submit proposals to purchase medical services from the private sector. OEO officials decided that it would be less costly and ultimately more useful to fund health service projects directly, especially projects that would effect basic changes in the way that health services were delivered to the poor (Levitan, 1974:51; Schorr and English, 1974:45–46; May et al., 1979:7–8).

The first grant for the development of a health care delivery project was awarded in June 1965 to Dr. H. Jack Geiger and Dr. Count Gibson, both of Tufts University Medical School. Geiger and Gibson had come to OEO with a proposal to establish a model health center that would provide comprehensive health care, train and employ community residents, and involve them in community development. This model of combining the delivery of health services with community organization was based Geiger's earlier work with Dr. Sidney L. Kark in South Africa and Gibson's work in Boston. The grant they received was to develop two comprehensive health projects, one in an isolated Boston housing project called Columbia Point, one in a southern rural area. About the same time, other health professionals began to develop similar models of health care delivery and to negotiate with OEO officials for funding (Levitan, 1974:53–54; Geiger, 1972:157–67; Anderson et al., 1976:8–12). Grants were awarded for six additional health center programs for the fiscal year 1966 (Levitan, 1974:54). This first group of health centers were funded as demonstration projects by the Research and Demonstration Office of the Community Action Program (May et al., 1980C:110–11).

Authorization for the program, and thus the number of projects that could be funded, was greatly expanded in 1966 with the passage of an amendment to the 1964 Economic Opportunity Act. This amendment, sponsored by Senator Edward Kennedy, provided monies specifically for the planning and operation of "comprehensive health service programs" in urban and rural low-income areas that lacked adequate health services. The amendment discussed the importance of consumer participation and the need to provide employment opportunities and other social services along with health services (Anderson et al., 1976:13).

In the latter part of 1966 (fiscal year 1967), an Office of Comprehensive Health Services was established within the Community Action Program to administer neighborhood health center grants. At the same time, an Office of Health Affairs was created within the Office of the Director of OEO. The latter was a staff agency responsible for the coordination of all of the OEO medical and health programs, including those in Volunteers in Service to America (VISTA), Head Start, and the Job Corps. Neighborhood health center policy was made by this office in cooperation with the Health Office within the Community Action Program (May et al., 1980C:122–24).[1]

Fifty million dollars was appropriated for the neighborhood

health center (NHC) program under the 1966 amendment. By 1968, more than fifty centers had been funded under this authority; by the end of 1971, the number was up to one hundred (Anderson et al., 1976:15).

The NHC Model as a Challenge to Mainstream Medicine

The neighborhood health center was to be a new model of health services organization that would provide dignified, accessible, comprehensive, and community-based care. The three community-based elements of this model were: (1) community health services, (2) community economic development, and (3) community participation. These will each be described briefly.

THREE ELEMENTS OF COMMUNITY–BASED HEALTH SERVICES

The term *community health services* is used here to refer to those services which are based on a view of health status as a product of the social and physical environment, and treatment as involving intervention in the environment of the population being served (see Geiger, 1982:94). This idea, as discussed in chapter 2, is part of a long tradition of social medicine and was basic to the public health movement of mid-nineteenth-century America.

The first OEO health centers implemented this concept by helping community residents to act together on economic and environmental issues. Children treated at the Tufts-Delta Health Center in a poor rural area of Mississippi suffered from malnutrition and dysentery. Residents worked together to construct wells, repair their homes, and establish a farm cooperative to grow food (Klaw, 1976:198–99; Geiger, 1974:140–41). In other areas of the rural South, center personnel and community members also dealt with problems related to sanitation, sewerage, and housing conditions (Davis and Schoen, 1978:168). The staff of a health center and hospital in Sunset Park, Brooklyn, helped local residents to create an organization to rehabilitate housing in the area and to work on zoning and other community issues (Jacobs, 1981:79–97). The 1968 OEO guidelines included preventive services, transportation to and from the centers, "patient and community health education," and environmental health services, as well as traditional medical care and social services, as services that could be offered at neighborhood health centers (Davis and Schoen, 1978:165).

A second aspect of community health services is the decentralization of health care, bringing it closer to the people. This was also not a new idea but was one of the principles of the health center movement of the second decade of the twentieth century. Neighborhood health centers in the 1960s, like their predecessors, were to serve the population of a defined catchment area, but in contrast to the earlier centers, were to provide integrated treatment as well as preventive care and to involve community residents in the operation of the centers.

Health care would also be brought closer to the people by employing residents of the community to visit patients in their homes and to act as liaisons between patients and the centers' professional staff. Underlying this liaison function was the notion that residents could provide important information about the community and its people that would not otherwise be accessible to professionals from outside that community (Geiger, personal communication, 1983). These workers, often called family health workers, were to function as part of a health care team along with a physician and a public health nurse. They were to provide bedside care, health education, and social advocacy services such as assistance with housing, welfare, and other aspects of the patient's social environment (Wise et al., 1974:283–87).[2]

The employment of family health workers at neighborhood health centers implemented principles of community health services in terms of both outreach and social medicine. The recruitment, training, and employment of these workers was part of another aspect of the original neighborhood health center model — the idea that these projects could be centers for community economic development as well as health care. By providing jobs to individuals from the community, the health centers were also to be "potential tools for the development of human resources and economic well-being in poor communities. Each center's health activities could provide members of the community with employment, training in job skills, the opportunity to develop stable work histories, and experience in managerial positions" (Davis and Schoen, 1968:162). In addition, health center staff provided the expertise needed to help initiate community development in areas other than health care. Programs were funded, for instance, in housing and water conservation (Davis and Schoen, 1968:175–77).

Finally, "maximum feasible participation" of the poor was mandated in the legislation authorizing the War on Poverty, and OEO staff responsible for funding the first neighborhood health center demonstration projects "were strongly committed" to that idea (May et al., 1979:11). However, the operationalization of that concept was an evolutionary process that at some points involved conflict between health center consumers and project administrators. (This will be discussed in chapter 4.)

Thus, the neighborhood health center model was based on the principles of social medicine (or what has been called community health services), on the concept of a health care institution as a vehicle for community development, and on the notion of participation by community residents in decisions about health needs and health services.

COMMUNITY-BASED HEALTH SERVICES AS
A CHALLENGE TO THE EXISTING SYSTEM
The neighborhood health center model challenged the existing health care delivery system in several ways. First, it was to "reintegrate" the traditional separation between public health and personal health services by defining health broadly and providing preventive, environmental, and outreach services as well as medical treatment at one facility. Second, by providing care to all the residents of a geographically defined community rather than to those who passed a means test for poverty or fit certain demographic or disease categories, health centers disregarded the pre-

viously negotiated boundaries between public and private medicine. Third, the neighborhood health center was a form of group practice employing salaried physicians, and thus challenged the fee-for-service, solo-practice model of health care advocated and defended by the AMA. In addition, health services organizations composed of teams of physicians, nurse practitioners, and family health workers challenged the traditional medical hierarchy in which the physician is at the top (see Friedson, 1972, ch. 3). Finally, professional dominance was also challenged by the notion of consumer participation in decisions about health care services.

A model of health care delivery that embodied these challenges to the existing health care system could not be considered as a part of the regular health policy agenda. It was not. Instead, the neighborhood health center model was initially funded as a research and demonstration program (a new policy) of the War on Poverty.

The events that led to the funding of the first group of neighborhood health centers indicate that the NHC model had two sets of "policy parents." It was a product of both the federal commitment to sponsor community development programs in low-income areas and of a health system reform agenda of activist health professionals both in and outside OEO.

Health Reformers as Policy Entrepreneurs

Gibson and Geiger had originally taken their health center plan to officials in the Public Health Service (PHS), the health agency within the Department of Health, Education, and Welfare (DHEW). As I will discuss below, DHEW had a history of accommodation to the medical establishment. These PHS officials sent the Tufts professors to OEO (Levitan, 1974:53).

OEO officials operated within a conceptual framework in which poverty was seen as a consequence of the lack of opportunity in many areas within American society and perpetuated through a "cycle of poverty" that included both poor health and unemployment. A health care program would intervene in this cycle at several points by providing "high quality health care to a population with little access to such care, by employing community residents, and by involving the community in the policymaking process at the centers" (May et al., 1979:3).

Those OEO officials involved in the funding of the first health centers also believed that if high-quality health care was to be provided to the poor, institutional reform was necessary. As I discussed in chapter 2, by the mid-1960s, policymakers recognized that specialization in medicine and the decline of general practice had especially limited the health care available in low-income urban areas. Poor and working-class individuals and families had to rely on health services provided by hospital outpatient departments, emergency rooms, or local health departments. The care at hospital emergency rooms and clinics was fragmented, episodic, and undignified. Public health departments treated only specific diseases or population groups and did not provide comprehensive, family-oriented care. Lee Bamberger Schorr, an official responsible for funding the first NHC demonstration programs, recalls: "We very quickly decided that if OEO was going to spend any substantial amounts of money on health, it would have to be directed to changing the organizational framework through which health services were being delivered to poor people" (quoted in May et al., 1980B:585).

OEO staff working on the health center program were "assisted by highly respected medical consultants—both practitioners and academicians—who were identified with the small but articulate reformist wing of American medicine" (Pritchard, 1974:27). This group of physicians advocated a number of changes in American health care, including prepaid group practice, the reorganization of ambulatory care delivery, and preventive health services. They had been unsuccessful in earlier attempts at reform because both DHEW and Congress were sensitive to the AMA's opposition to government involvement in the organization of health care delivery. The War on Poverty was viewed by individuals who belonged to this network as a new opportunity for health system reform. OEO did not have relationships with traditional health constituencies and it was located in the Office of the President rather than within another established government bureaucracy, like DHEW (Pritchard, 1974:27–29).

Health center advocates differed as to what the major goals of the OEO program should be and what its effects could be. Some believed that the agency's primary goal was to change the relationship of established health institutions to the poor. The community participation component of the program would help low-income citizens to feel politically efficacious and would force institutions to meet the needs of the communities they were to serve (Pritchard, 1974:31–34). In providing high-quality care, the program would enable the poor "to enter the health care system as equal participants" (May et al., 1980B:598). Others stressed the economic development aspect of the neighborhood health center program in terms of both employment of residents at the centers and the greater employability of people with proper health care. Still others believed that the lasting impact of the program would be to introduce specific innovations, such as team practice and the employment of family health workers, into the health care delivery system (Pritchard, 1974:33–34; Hollister et al., 1974:16–17).

Finally, and most significant from the perspective of this work, many of those involved in the creation of the NHC program (both in and out of OEO) viewed it as a catalyst for change throughout the American health system. According to one former OEO official, some of those within the agency hoped to develop models of health care "that could be adapted to the total population" (Interview, 16 June 1975:19, May and New transcripts). Health services in general emphasized high-technology treatment in hospitals, rather than preventive and primary care, and were fragmented and costly. The hope was that the neighborhood health center model would prove to be a success in providing low-cost, high-quality care so that it would stimulate the reorganization of the entire health care system.

Many of those involved in establishing the first health centers viewed their efforts as part of a "neighborhood health center movement," a movement linked to other movements, those for civil rights and welfare rights (Interviews, 6 April 1978, 17 July 1979; Brandon, 1977:82–83; Hollister et al., 1974:13–21). Several of the physicians in the neighborhood health center movement had, in fact, worked in the civil rights movement in the South as members of the Medical Committee for Human Rights, an organization founded in 1964 to support southern voting registration drives by providing health services to volunteers (Anderson et al., 1976:23).

One commentator describes the "ideology" of comprehensive health services, which was central to the neighborhood health center movement, as including "a vision of an alternative health care system that allowed radicals in the medical profession and in community organizing to come together behind a program of systematic revision that was clearly distinguishable from the *ad hoc* reform of existing institutions by such measures as establishing an appointment system to reduce patients' waiting time or adding medical social workers or physicians' associates to hospital staffs" (Brandon, 1977:82).

In a 1968 speech, Dr. H. Jack Geiger presented such a vision: "The hospital as we now know it is an obsolete and ineffective institution for ambulatory care; . . . hospitals for the future should be vastly different—in effect, intensive care units for patients with critical and complex illness. . . . The hub of the medical care universe would be a network of comprehensive community health centers" (Somers, 1971:34).

The neighborhood health center concept—radical in its emphasis on community health as opposed to medical care, and consumer participation rather than professional dominance in health care decisions—was not to be limited to health services for the poor, but would be an alternative to the hospital-based medical care system for the whole population.

The Politics of
the Neighborhood Health Center Program:
Opposition and Co-optation

This vision of reform was not realized in the years immediately after the creation of the program. Neighborhood health centers were funded by the federal government only as a program for the poor and, in fact, a congressional amendment in 1967 reinforced its status as "poor people's medicine" (Marcus, 1981:45). A reorganization of the health care system as envisioned by Dr. Geiger could come about only as part of a major policy innovation such as the establishment of a national health insurance system. Serious efforts to enact such a policy ceased during the Carter administration (see Califano, 1981, ch. 3).

As a program limited to the poor, the health center model was a less threatening experiment. Even so, OEO officials anticipated the interests of powerful provider groups in an effort to prevent conflict over the program. In spite of these efforts, there was opposition to specific centers by providers at the local level and political action on behalf of the use of a means test in health centers—a policy counter to the original neighborhood health center model.

Local opposition to specific health centers funded by OEO was expressed by pharmacists in communities where a new health center would include a pharmacy, by black physicians in northern ghettos, by officials of southern public health departments, and by local (white) medical societies (Feingold, 1974:95; Interviews, 6 April 1978 and 17 July 1979; Interviews, 11 April 1975 and 11 June 1977, May and New transcripts). Physicians and pharmacists felt directly threatened by the health centers in economic terms, while public health officers viewed the centers as competing with their control of health care services to the poor.

At the national level, southern politicians opposed the program, as they did the rest of the War on Poverty, because they did not wish potential political resources, both money and jobs, to be provided to southern blacks by the federal government (Interview, 6 April 1978; Levitan, 1974:61–62). Although southern congressmen (both Democrats and Republicans) expressed their opposition in Congress, the Johnson administration had enough Democratic votes to win congressional majorities for the War on Poverty in the years 1964–1967 (Sundquist, 1968:146–51).

Both the AMA and the American Hospital Association have a history of opposition to modes of health services delivery that can be viewed as competitive with the practices of private physicians or the operation of hospitals, respectively (Feldstein, 1977). OEO officials and Senator Edward Kennedy, their initial congressional ally, acted to prevent or to modify such opposition.

ORGANIZED MEDICINE AND
THE NEIGHBORHOOD HEALTH CENTER PROGRAM
OEO officials sought to allay the fears of representatives of organized medicine at the national level by providing "guarantees" that OEO projects "would not 'compete with' the private sector" (Marcus, 1981:35). Local health center officials were encouraged by OEO to hire at least one physician active in the local medical society and to invite medical society officials to sit on health center boards and to comment on health center performance (Marcus, 1981:35; Interview, 17 July 1979). In spite of these actions at the national level, there was opposition to the funding of specific health centers by organized medicine at the community level. In Denver in 1966, the board of the Public Health and Hospitals Corporation voted against a proposal to have the corporation apply to OEO for funding to establish Denver's second health center. One of the physicians on this board asserted that the neighborhood health centers were "just another step toward socialism." He declared that it was "unbelievable to think that the centers are not going to hurt the private practice of a physician. . . . When we reach center No. 25, there won't be any private practice" (Hollister, 1971:165). Later the decision to apply was reversed. However, the delegates from Denver to the AMA's House of Delegates meeting in 1967 expressed their concern that the County Medical Society had not been appropriately involved in the decision to apply for the grant. As the program was expanded in Denver,

the opposition from organized medicine disappeared. Doctors found that their fears about the loss of patients had not been justified (Hollister, 1971:166–67).

There was also initial opposition to the establishment of health centers from physicians in St. Louis (Hollister, 1971:257), in Mississippi (Interview, 6 April 1978), and in Texas (Interview, 31 March 1978), among other places. In New York City there were "turf arrangements" made with local physicians and hospitals as to where a center would be located and how it would recruit patients so that the new centers would not draw patients away from existing private practices or hospitals (Interviews, 5 and 16 July 1979).

The position of the AMA on the neighborhood health center program was ambiguous. Some statements made by association officials about the program in this early period were very supportive, while others were very negative (see Levitan, 1974:60). One OEO official recalled that the AMA gave "lukewarm support" to the program (Interview, 31 March 1978), while an aide to Senator Edward Kennedy reported that the 1966 OEO amendment, which specifically authorized monies for neighborhood health services programs, was introduced by Senator Kennedy in anticipation of efforts by organized medicine to prevent OEO from funding health centers (Interview, 4 November 1975:3, May and New transcripts).

Neighborhood health centers were not discussed very often in the pages of the *Journal of the American Medical Association* during 1965–1970. They were only two articles describing health center programs during these years (Maloney, 1967:411–14; "Can Community Health Centers Cure . . . ," pp. 1943–55). Both depicted the program in positive terms.

Speeches and other official statements made by association officers about the neighborhood health center program during this period reflect two distinct themes. The first is that organized medicine should be involved in the administration of the program, at both the local and national level. This is the AMA's traditional position that physicians and not "lay persons" should make health policy decisions. The second is that the line between government medicine (welfare medicine), as defined by a means test, and private medicine for the rest of the population should be firmly maintained.

A report of the AMA's Committee on Welfare Services at the 1966 annual convention stated that at meetings with the OEO staff, its members had "expressed concern" that OEO was "developing standards and guidelines with limited professional medical staff and limited consultation with the medical profession" ("Committee on Welfare Services," p. 443). The committee proposed that a formal advisory committee of physicians be established for the NHC program at the national level (this was endorsed by the AMA House of Delegates) and that the local medical profession develop a similar relationship with individual programs (443–44). "These politically popular programs can well result in the development of new ways of providing care for the poor; the local medical society should be ready to assume a leadership role" (444). The idea that organized medicine should control new modes of health care delivery was repeated in the 1969 and 1970 presidential addresses at annual AMA meetings.

In a 1966 address, the AMA's incoming president suggested that the government's role in health care delivery be limited to "the overall stimulation and support of private enterprise, rather than undertaking specific operational or directional capacities." The exception is programs for "its wards or dependants" (Hudson, 1966:99). The next year, the new president of the association gave his reasons for AMA "opposition" to OEO neighborhood health centers: there were already too many federal health programs; the problems of the poor could be dealt with through Medicaid; and the AMA supported the financing of care for the poor but was opposed "to the doling out of tax funds to the wealthy and the well-to-do" (Rouse, 1967:169–70). Here are echoes of the rhetoric of the campaign against "dispensary abuse" in the 1890s. It was on the means-test issue that private practitioners took action in the legislative arena to alter the original neighborhood health center model. This opposition was also reminiscent of the activity of organized medicine in that earlier period.

Initially, according to OEO policy, each health center would provide care to all of the residents within its geographical area, rather than to persons with certain diseases or those who belonged to particular demographic groups. By doing this, OEO was disregarding the established boundaries between public and private medicine. In 1967, however, an amendment to the OEO act was passed which changed the eligibility criterion from residence in a center's catchment area to income below the poverty level. This effectively prevented neighborhood health centers from serving a mixed-income clientele and thus expanding beyond a poverty population. A 1969 interpretation of the amendment restricted "self-pay" patients to one-fifth of the total (Zwick, 1974:85). This amendment was enacted in response to the demands of "private practitioners and other providers of health care in the private sector" (Davis and Schoen, 1978:164; see also Levitan, 1974:57).[3]

The AMA did not testify at congressional hearings held on the 1967 amendments (as it did on subsequent NHC legislation) and the AMA *Journal* did not report an official association position on eligibility criteria for treatment at NHCs. It is not clear whether the Congress members proposing this amendment did so in response to lobbying by the AMA or in response to the concerns of prominent practitioners in their districts or of county or state medical society representatives.

HOSPITALS AND MEDICAL SCHOOLS

The majority of grants awarded during the first four years of the health center program went not to community corporations or other neighborhood-based groups, but to hospitals and medical schools. One reason for this was to prevent opposition to the program from developing (May et al., 1980A:123–24; Interview, 31 March 1978). This was not, however, the only reason why many of the early grants went to hospitals and medical schools. There were several other reasons.

First, the Office of Comprehensive Health Services within OEO needed to produce successful programs quickly. Hospitals and medical schools were more experienced and therefore seen as more dependable in terms of handling large grants. Their sponsorship would also provide professional legitimacy for health services innovation (Marcus, 1981:23–27).

Second, the awarding of grants to medical schools and hospitals was part of a strategy for stimulating health reform by supporting individual health reformers within established institutions. Health reformers within major medical schools and teaching hospitals would develop innovative programs with federal dollars (May et al., 1980A:124–27; May et al., 1980B:586–87; Anderson et al., 1976:22–23; Marcus, 1981:26).[4]

Finally, OEO legislation required that grants made to "limited purpose organizations" such as community corporations had to be approved by the governor of the state in which the organization was located. OEO officials feared that, especially in southern states, governors would veto health center funds going to community corporations in black areas. Educational institutions, including medical schools, were exempt from this provision (Interview, 31 March 1978; see Sundquist, 1968:148).[5]

The program was made attractive to hospitals and medical schools in several ways. Health center development grants included unrestricted overhead monies that could be used to finance programs in other parts of the hospital and medical school (Pritchard, 1974:71–72). Because federal support for medical research was decreasing (Hollister et al. 1974:16), the medical schools that applied for health center grants were those in need of money, those where students were asking the schools to become involved in the provision of health services to low-income community residents, or those with "key medical-care delivery reformers" on their faculty (Marcus, 1981:30).

Hospitals that were perceived as uninterested in meeting the health needs of neighborhood residents could use the health center program as an "opportunity . . . to mollify low-income-community hostility without displaying any real commitment to reform" (Marcus, 1981:31; see Hollister et al., 1974:16). Although one of the core principles of the program was "community participation," OEO was at first not specific about how participation was to be implemented beyond the community advisory role. This did change as the program developed and community residents asked for a larger role in decision making.

Thus, within the bureaucratic arena, a policy with redistributive aims was to contain "distributive elements." In federal housing and community development programs of the 1960s and 1970s, subsidies went to builders and banks as well as to low-income citizens in need of housing (see Ripley and Franklin, 1984:123–26). Similarly, in this case, substantial benefits went to hospitals and medical schools as well as to the medically underserved communities in which health centers were established. And as with national housing policy in the 1930s, private providers were assured that public programs would not compete with them (see Judd, 1984:264).

The Presentation of the Issue in Congress

Shortly after the first group of health centers were funded, Senator Edward Kennedy (D–Mass.) became interested in the health center program. Kennedy was beginning to view health policy as a major field of concern at this time (Interview, 6 April 1978) and he was particularly interested in one of the issues that neighborhood health centers were to address, that of access to care for populations that were underserved (Interview, 4 November 1975:2, May and New transcripts).

After extensive conversations with OEO officials and program staff and visits to centers all over the country, Kennedy became convinced that health centers should be the major health program of OEO. In 1966, he envisioned the funding of at least 800 centers across the country, but by 1968, the general opposition to the OEO program as a whole had resulted in the reduction of its budget (May et al., 1980C:128). The 1966 and 1967 health center amendments to the Economic Opportunity Act of 1964 were both written by Kennedy staff persons in consultation with OEO officials, with whom they had a close working relationship (Interview, 4 November 1975:4, 9, May and New transcripts; Interview, 31 March 1978).

Kennedy lobbied other members of Congress to support the 1966 and 1967 health center amendments. "He personally persuaded the key members of the committees that it was a good program, based on his knowledge of it." Kennedy argued that the program should be considered separately from other War on Poverty programs, that it was "run by professionals," that it was free of corruption, and that it was improving the health care of the poor. Kennedy also had to address the ideological issue raised by publicly supported medical treatment. "It wasn't socialism, it wasn't socialized medicine, it was just the good old American process of trying to give some people who didn't have something, something" (Interview, 4 November 1975: 4, May and New transcripts). Clearly the "mobilization of bias" against the public funding of comprehensive health care was operating in this instance, even when such care was to be provided only to the poor. Kennedy, however, was apparently successful in his efforts to persuade his colleagues in Congress that the neighborhood health center program was not socialized medicine and was different from other antipoverty programs.

During the 1967 congressional debate on the OEO program as a whole, its opponents suggested that it was threatening the stability of American society.[6] There were questions raised about the effectiveness of some programs, such as job training (H. Rep. 90-866:148–63), but also much discussion about the "misconduct" of OEO workers in engaging in political activity (CR —Oct. 3, 1967:27620–21); the promotion of "radicalism" by OEO (CR —Nov. 14, 1967:32342, Nov. 15:32656); the impropriety of the OEO funds for voter registration (CR —Oct. 4, 1967:28021–24; H. Rept. 90-866:174); the generally "disruptive and destructive activities of the Community Action Program" (H. Rept. 90-866:165); and political competition of antipoverty programs with elected officials (CR —Nov. 14, 1967:32364). The neighborhood health center program, in contrast, was not viewed as a politically radical experiment but rather as a legitimate professional and "charitable" enterprise. It was not mentioned very often in the congressional debate. When it was, it was seen as "bringing medical care to people who have not seen a doctor or a dentist in their lives" (CR —Nov. 15, 1967:32707), rather than as an innovative model that might threaten existing providers.

The presentation of the neighborhood health center program in these terms—the "structuring of the issue"—was an important component in its political survival. Congressional support for neighborhood health centers became crucial in the early 1970s when the Nixon administration attempted to dismantle the program. (See chapter 4.)

Policy Entrepreneurs in DHEW

The Office of Economic Opportunity was not the only agency of the federal government that was responding to the social ferment of the 1960s. In 1968, policy entrepreneurs within the Public Health Service (PHS) initiated the funding of a number of neighborhood health centers by that agency, some run entirely by community boards. This departure from previous DHEW policy originated with another group of health care reformers within the federal bureaucracy.

The PHS began as the federal bureau responsible for providing health services to marines in the late eighteenth century and grew as the national government became more involved in the health field (Jonas, 1986:342). In the early 1960s, the involvement of the PHS in primary health care delivery was limited to the funding of state and locally administered programs to diagnose and treat specific types of disease such as rubella, arthritis, and mental illness (Greenberg, 1975:489). Federal support for such categorical disease programs was contingent on fidelity to the agreements made between the public and private sectors at the local level as to their respective spheres of activity.

However, beginning in 1968, the PHS provided grants for the establishment of comprehensive health centers in low-income areas. During fiscal years 1968 and 1969, twenty-four centers were funded (Blumenthal, 1970:3) and by 1972 DHEW had funded fifty-five projects serving 850,000 people. This was the first time in its history that the PHS was directly funding "services to the poor citizens not covered by a special separate beneficiary authority" (Merten and Nothman, 1975:249). This undertaking by DHEW was a result of many of the forces that had shaped the OEO program: an awareness within the government of problems in the health field, a general commitment by the Johnson administration to act on behalf of the poor, and individual reformers committed both to changing the condition of the poor and to reforming the health care system.

The specific mechanism through which these programs were funded was section 314(e) of the Comprehensive Health Planning and Public Health Services Act of 1966 (PL 89-749) which was amended by the Partnership for Health Amendments of 1967 (PL 90-174). The goal of this legislation was the coordination of national health care resources in both the private and public sectors so that "comprehensive health services of high quality" would be provided "for every person" (Merten and Nothman, 1975:248).

Sections 314(a) through 314(d) of the legislation authorized funding for state comprehensive health planning agencies, regional health planning projects, the training of health planners, and formula grants to states for health services (Jonas, 1977A:360). Section 314(e) provided for project grants to develop new types of health services projects. The legislative language of 314(e) was quite broad, allowing the surgeon general to make grants to public or private nonprofit organizations for studies, demonstrations, training, and service programs directed toward innovation in health care delivery (Blumenthal, 1970:12–13). However, traditional PHS politics made the funding of health services innovation unlikely. The PHS "avoided programs in areas in which organized medicine was sensitive: programs that might influence the delivery system of medical care in the United States, and programs that involved the federal government directly in financing continuing integrated care to significant numbers of Americans" (Blumenthal, 1970:3).[7] The system of funding categorical grants for specific diseases was supported by a policy network of high-level civil servants—most of whom were physicians and officers of its Commissioned Corps (Miles, 1974:191–92), members of the Senate Appropriations Committee, and several interest groups: the AMA, voluntary associations concerned with specific diseases, and the Association of State and Territorial Health Officers, an organization representing public health officials at the state and local levels (Blumenthal, 1970:30–31, 49–51, 76, 88, 125–26).

The decision to use 314(e) monies to fund neighborhood health centers was a consequence of the activities of a "coalition" of health care reformers at the middle and top levels of the bureaucracy. DHEW appointees in the Johnson administration believed that the PHS should support comprehensive health service programs rather than categorical programs. These officials included Dr. John Gardner, the secretary of DHEW, Dr. Philip Lee, the assistant secretary for health and scientific affairs, and Dr. George A. Silver, the deputy assistant secretary for health.[8] A 1967 report done for the secretary of DHEW recommended that more than 600 comprehensive health centers be established in low-income areas by 1973 (Blumenthal, 1970:38–39, 45–46, 85, 88). There were other advocates for comprehensive health services within the PHS. During the 1960s, socially concerned young physicians, social scientists, and administrators had joined the PHS to fulfill a two-year commitment to federal government service in lieu of entering the military during the Vietnam War. Many of these people believed in the need for health system reform and in particular emphasized the importance of consumer participation. There were also some career bureaucrats within the PHS who supported these ideas (Interview A, 13 July 1979). There was "a lot of interaction and discussion" between these people and those working on the neighborhood health center program at the OEO" (Interview, 31 March 1978).

A policy of subsidizing community-based projects providing comprehensive health services, however, had to be implemented by the U.S. surgeon general who was chief of the PHS. The surgeon general was also the medical director of the Commissioned Corps and drawn from its ranks (Miles, 1974:191–92). His "constituency" consisted of the agencies and the bureaus within the PHS and the outside interest groups which supported existing programs, as well as the assistant secretary for health (Blumenthal, 1970:149–50).

One of the young physicians doing alternative service at the PHS, Dr. James Block, was particularly concerned about the improvement of primary health care services for the poor (Interview A, 13 July 1979). While a medical student at New York University, Block had worked with Dr. Howard Brown, a pioneer in the development of community-based primary care, at a comprehensive health center in lower Manhattan. Block had also met Dr. George A. Silver, the deputy assistant secretary, through Brown, and Silver had helped Block to come to the PHS. Block arrived at the PHS "committed" to the OEO neighborhood health center concept. He played a central role within the Office of Comprehensive Health Planning, the agency that was to implement the planning legislation, in the decision to use 314(e) money to fund comprehensive health centers.

The vehicle through which this occurred initially was the Neighborhood Service Program of the Johnson administration. The program's purpose was to establish "multiservice centers" in low-income communities. It was to be funded with money from the budgets of existing agencies. When an interagency federal committee asked the Office of Comprehensive Health Planning to fund a health component of the Neighborhood Service Program, the initial response was negative. The 314(e) money was being used to fund the traditional categorical disease programs. However, a short time later, Block was assigned to the Office of Comprehensive Health Planning where he began to argue that 314(e) money should be used to fund neighborhood health projects. Official acceptance of this position within the PHS came with the issuance of the Priority Statement for the Partnership for Health Program issued by the surgeon general in November 1967. It stated that priority in the 314(e) funding process should be given to comprehensive health services for the poor (Blumenthal, 1970:102–07).

The implementation of this policy was facilitated by a reorganization of the PHS in April 1968 by the new DHEW secretary, Wilbur Cohen. First, the Office of the Surgeon General was abolished and the surgeon general became a deputy assistant secretary within DHEW, with a reduced role in policymaking (Greenberg, 1975:497). Second, the Office of Comprehensive Health Planning was moved to one of the three newly created administrative divisions of the PHS, the Health Services and Mental Health Administration (HSMHA). The director of the HSMHA reported to the assistant secretary for health, rather than to the surgeon general.

A few months later, the Office of Comprehensive Health Planning and another agency, the Division of Medical Care Administration, were merged and became the Community Health Service (CHS) (Blumenthal, 1970:146; Shenkin, 1974:119). The CHS had the responsibility of administering 314(e) grants. The director of the new bureau, Dr. John Cashman, supported the funding of comprehensive service programs. Dr. Block, who became the deputy director of a division within the CHS, worked with others to implement the Priority Statement (Blumenthal, 1970:173–74, Interview A, 13 July 1979). In New York, for example, DHEW funded a health clinic sponsored by the North East Neighborhoods Association on the Lower East Side of Manhattan (NENA) and the health component of the Hunts Point Multiservice Center in the Bronx (Interview A, 13 July 1979).

Some of the advocates of neighborhood health centers within the PHS shared with individuals in OEO a desire not just to improve the health care of the poor but also to reform the health care delivery system in general. Health projects funded under 314(e) would be a vehicle for specific innovations such as prepaid practice, the employment of salaried physicians, and the organization of health professions into multidisciplinary teams. During the first few years after the enactment of Medicare, there was a belief within the health policy community that a national health plan would follow. "We had the same dream as OEO, that Medicaid and Medicare would come in and pick up the tab and we were really trying to *develop the delivery structure.*" The DHEW program would be a way to "work it out with the poor and peddle it to the country at large, . . . the means of demonstrating to middle-class Americans that this kind of institutional delivery of care was really the way to go and we were going to make middle-class America so envious that that's what they would begin to follow" (Interview A, 13 July 1979). Section 314(e) of the comprehensive health planning legislation was to serve, after the dismantling of OEO, as the authority under which health centers were funded until 1975.

The Professional-Bureaucratic Complex: An Alternative View

Federal funding of neighborhood health centers was initiated by OEO officials and staff working with socially concerned physicians based at universities and later by reformers within the PHS. Although these individuals can be said to have been part of an "issue network" interested in health care reform (see chapter 1), their involvement went beyond shared expertise (one of the characteristics discussed by Heclo), because they worked together to achieve a common goal. Once Senator Kennedy joined health center advocates in a pattern of mutual activity in support of the OEO program, a set of relationships developed that fit Beer's description of a professional-bureaucratic complex. As Beer notes (1976:160) and as I will discuss in detail in chapter 8, the initiation of policy by such a bureaucratic-professional complex was common to many of the health and other social welfare programs first established in the 1960s and 1970s.

Beer describes the professional-bureaucratic complex as part of a broader discussion of a shift from private sector to public sector politics in the United States. The expansion of government and the increase in scientific and technical expertise as relevant to policy issues has resulted in an increase in "the influence on government that arises autonomously within government itself" (1976:128). Beer contrasts the initiation of policy by professionally trained bureaucratic actors, this "technocratic tendency," with the "older *responsive* models of policy-making" in which interest groups are the initiators (1976:160, emphasis added). The idea that policy coming from within the government is less responsive to societal, group, or individual needs than are policies sponsored by organized interest groups needs to be explored. So does the notion that public sector politics is a relatively new phenomenon.

First, critics of American pluralism have pointed to the lack of responsiveness to the needs and interests of unorganized citizens, as well as to group members, in many oligarchic organizations (McConnell, 1966; Lowi, 1969; Connolly, 1969). Second, in many cases predating the mid-twentieth century, "new interests" did not organize spontaneously into voluntary associations but were often encouraged to do so by government officials and even aided by government monies. This was true in the case of both farmers (McConnell 1966:75–76) and veterans' groups (Harader, 1968:37–38). Thus, the phenomenon of public officials acting to mobilize a set of unorganized interests predates the welfare politics of the 1960s or even the 1930s.

Policy initiation by bureaucratic actors is described in two classic works on policy networks: J. Leiper Freeman on the Indian affairs subgovernment (1965) and Pratt on networks concerned with aging policy (1976). In the case of both the Indian Reorganization Act of 1934 and the 1961 White House Conference on Aging, respectively, the constituencies directly affected were not organized effectively. In these cases, and in the neighborhood health center case, bureaucratic officials were articulating a set of interests that could not otherwise be represented because of structural biases in the political system.

The general obstacles to organizing constituency groups have been described by Olson (1965), and others have discussed the additional barriers to the organization of low-income citizens (Parenti, 1970; Bellush and David, 1977; Piven and Cloward, 1979). Michael Lipsky and Morris Lounds (1976) have described the characteristics of the health services system that make community organization in this specific policy arena especially difficult. Inequalities in access to health services caused by social class differences are less visible than in other areas such as education or housing; health services are used on an episodic rather than a routine basis; those most dependent on health care institutions and services—the chronically ill and the elderly ill—are a difficult population to mobilize for political activity; and finally, the legitimacy and high status accorded to the medical profession by virtue of its expertise make it especially difficult to mobilize citizens on health issues.

The neighborhood health center program was initiated by bureaucratic and professional actors concerned with health services reform and health care for the poor, not directly by the constituency it was to serve. However, enactment of the War on Poverty and other programs of the Great Society was a response by political leaders to the nonelectoral political activities (marches, sit-ins) of large numbers of citizens in the civil rights movement that were undertaken because of the structural barriers to effective political influence of low-income and minority populations via traditional electoral and interest group participation (Piven and Cloward, 1971, ch. 9; Donovan, 1967, ch. 1; Kotz, 1977:48–51).

One could argue that bureaucratic actors were articulating needs that were not being addressed because of the inequalities of political power. This argument follows a tradition of analyzing the democratic functions of the bureaucracy. Long (1952) asserts that the bureaucracy is a more "representative" institution than Congress because those occupying bureaucratic offices are more demographically representative of the U.S. population. Woll (1977) argues that the bureaucracy contributes to American democracy because it can take a national view of policy and is responsive to the concerns of many interest groups, whereas members of Congress who must frequently stand for reelection are responsive to narrow, local constituencies. A. Lee Fritschler (1983) concludes from his study of the tobacco subsystem in the 1960s that the bureaucracy, rather than Congress, has the ability to reject the interests of powerful economic groups in favor of broad interests such as the "health of the public" (1983:146–47).

It is not being argued here that bureaucratic decision making is an ideal form of democracy. Clearly it is not. My argument is more limited: bureaucratic initiatives may serve the interests of unorganized citizens not represented by existing private associations. Public sector actors may, in some instances, be more responsive to such interests than private sector actors.

Beer's discussion of the professional-bureaucratic complex is limited to the initiation of policy. In the neighborhood health center case, a network of bureaucrats and congressional staff members continued to play the central role in shaping the program after its first experimental years.

4

Program Survival
and Institutionalization

The neighborhood health center program was created as part of the War on Poverty mounted by a Democratic administration. The next administration, that of President Richard M. Nixon, planned to reduce or eliminate many Johnson era social programs and to focus health system reform on initiatives within the private sector. In addition, especially during his second term, Nixon and his advisers attempted to reduce the ability of the federal bureaucracy to make social policy through the administrative process.

In spite of this shift in the political environment, the neighborhood health center program survived the Nixon and Ford administrations. It was, in fact, legislatively institutionalized as a separate categorical grant program in 1975 over presidential opposition. This chapter will examine the political processes that produced this outcome.

Nixon Administration Policy and
Neighborhood Health Centers

During the 1968 presidential campaign, Nixon was critical of Great Society programs and promised to reduce the role of the federal government in social policy. His general philosophy was that decision making in domestic policy should be moved to the state level. Nixon's "New Federalism" proposals, made in 1969, were intended to dismantle much of the categorical grant structure that had been erected by previous Democratic administrations.[1] These responsibilities were to be shifted to states and localities, while only transfer payments, demonstration programs, and those programs that involved overlapping jurisdictions would be maintained as federal responsibilities. The devolution of power away from Washington was also to be implemented through decentralizing federal agencies; funding decisions about social programs were to be made at the regional level rather than in Washington (Nathan, 1975).

In health policy, the goal of the Nixon administration was "to radically reduce the federal role in subsidizing health activities" (Iglehart, 1973:645), while stimulating the private sector to restructure health care so that costs would be reduced. The two major health programs proposed by the Nixon administration were a national health insurance plan based on the purchase of private health insurance by employers (*New York Times*, 19 February 1971:1) and federal support of health maintenance organizations (HMOs), or prepaid group health plans. Federal planning grants were to stimulate the development of privately sponsored HMOs which, it was hoped, would decrease the need for hospitalization and therefore reduce health care costs (Bauman, 1976).

These administration policies affected the neighborhood health center program in several ways. First, the administration began to reduce the operational responsibilities of OEO in 1970. All existing health centers were to be transferred to DHEW, and no new freestanding health centers were to be funded by OEO. Consequently, between 1970 and 1973, the Office of Health Affairs supported other types of ambulatory care innovation such as the restructuring of hospital outpatient departments, group practices for minority physicians, "networks" of health care delivery institutions and prepaid capitation projects (Interview, 31 March 1978; see Marcus, 1981:138–39).[2] By fiscal year 1974, all neighborhood health centers were under the jurisdiction of DHEW, a decentralized DHEW.

This meant that decisions about the annual grants for each center, previously made by OEO officials in Washington, were now to be made by DHEW officials at the regional level. Regional DHEW officials had had little experience in working with neighborhood health center projects and "many did not share the philosophy of the OEO centers" (Anderson et al., 1976:19). In contrast, as we have seen, many program officials in both OEO and DHEW in Washington believed strongly in the neighborhood health center concept.

Second, the administration's objective of reducing direct federal funding for social programs, coupled with its cost containment concerns, was reflected in its initial support for the HMO concept and its lack of support for the neighborhood health center model. Before legislation was passed specifically authorizing funds for the development of HMOs, grants for such projects were allocated from general monies authorized under section 314(e), the legislative authority under which health centers were being funded. In the early 1970s, in spite of inflation and increased appropriations for the 314(e) authority in general, funding for neighborhood health centers was not increased. In fact, no new health centers were funded by DHEW between 1971 and 1973 (Anderson et al., 1976:15–19).

Third, in 1972, DHEW announced that it was planning to phase out federal grants for activities such as health centers. Such programs would have to find other sources of funding (GAO Report, 1973:9–10).

When the first health centers were established as OEO demonstration projects, Medicare and Medicaid had just been enacted. Supporters of the program expected that as the NHC program grew, it would be financed largely by Medicare and Medicaid (Zwick, 1974:83). However, state Medicaid plans did not include all of the medically indigent individuals who received treatment at health centers, and Medicare and Medicaid did not reimburse services at health centers to the same extent as they did other health care providers such as hospital outpatient departments. A study issued by the General Accounting Office (GAO) in May 1973 concluded that health centers were not collecting substantial reimbursement from Medicare or Medicaid. "The major existing third-party programs do not reimburse the Centers for all the services they provide and do not cover all the persons served by the NHCs" (GAO Report, 1973:17). Health centers were still being funded primarily by federal grant monies. (See chapter 5 for a detailed discussion of how the reimbursement structures of the Medicare and Medicaid programs have affected health center funding.)

In spite of this situation, DHEW published regulations in the *Federal Register* in May 1973 requiring that health centers recover the maximum amount possible from sources of funding other than federal grants. An accompanying announcement stated that health centers "must be or become self-sustaining, community-based operations with diminishing need for . . . HSMHA support" (quoted in ANYNHC, 1973:1). The Nixon administration's view was that the federal government should directly support health programs only as demonstrations. After that, support had to come from local communities (Interview, 31 March 1978).

In terms of administration support, then, the future of the neighborhood health center program looked very bleak in the early 1970s. This was the conclusion of Isabel Marcus, who studied the program during the OEO period (1981).[3] Marcus was pessimistic about the potential support the program could enjoy at the end of the War on Poverty. She noted that OEO was supported by a fragile congressional coalition and that the NHC program had no other bureaucratic agencies as allies and no influential outside constituencies as potential advocates. OEO officials had not attempted to mobilize either hospital or medical school associations on behalf of the program. The AMA had been assured that health centers would not compete with the practices of its members, and guidelines had been written to encourage local medical society involvement at the centers; but the AMA was an unlikely advocate for the program at the national level. The National Medical Association (the organization of black physicians) supported the program while Dr. John Holloman was its president but reversed its position after he left office. The medical care reformers who were involved with establishing the program were too few to be a major political constituency (Marcus, 1981:35–36, 64–66).

Marcus argues that the only possible constituencies for the program, the centers themselves and their clientele, could not be politically effective. The health centers were dependent on government grants; their clients were poor; both were "preoccupied" with day-to-day survival. "Both . . . were marginal; the centers operated at the periphery of organized medicine; their clientele had been disenfranchised effectively from the mainstream of U.S. life" (1981:66).

Despite these political facts, the neighborhood health center program withstood assaults under the Nixon and Ford administrations and was expanded by the Carter administration. An analysis of how this occurred can contribute to our knowledge of the political processes responsible for the survival of programs serving constituencies with minimal political resources and without powerful interest group allies. That is the task of this chapter.

Bureaucratic Advocacy

While the Nixon administration did not support the neighborhood health center program, there were civil servants within both OEO and DHEW who were personally committed to the NHC concept. These individuals acted to protect specific projects and to preserve the program.

First, regarding the timing of project transfers to DHEW, OEO officials decided to keep projects that needed "nurturance" and to transfer projects "that had achieved a level of stability and were not considered to be politically volatile in their states or communities." Generally, northern projects went first, while projects in the South were more likely to remain at OEO (Interview, 31 March 1978).

Once individual projects were transferred to DHEW, regional

offices decided which health center projects should be supported and at what level of funding. This was one consequence of the decentralization of DHEW. Some Washington-based DHEW officials were afraid that the regional offices "would function in an arbitrary and capricious manner" concerning the continuation of specific grants. During 1973 and 1974, the first and second years in which all health center programs were under the jurisdiction of DHEW, HSMHA officials "negotiated" grant levels with the regional office on a project-by-project basis. "Literally, we would argue with them about how much money was going to X center, how much to the Y center." This process, however, was too time-consuming, and the Washington office developed a series of performance measures and funding criteria that could be used by the regional offices to make funding decisions. The development of such performance measures was also a response to concerns expressed by the White House, the Office of Management and Budget, and sympathetic congressional health subcommittees about the lack of concrete data on health center operations.

Agency officials were themselves concerned about the management capability at some centers. Information from an evaluation study, from site visits made by project officers, and from grant applications indicated that many centers did not have adequate financial management systems and were therefore not "capturing" all the third-party revenues they could. Some programs had "excessive" administrative costs. Program advocates believed that these problems had to be dealt with if the program was to survive (Interview, 31 March 1978). This was the beginning of a policy of monitoring program performance in quantifiable terms by the grant-awarding agency administering the health center program. This policy, which has continued through the 1980s, has been an important source of congressional support.

In addition to careful monitoring of project transfers and the development of measurable performance criteria, bureaucratic advocates of NHCs attempted to organize a constituency for the program. In this activity particularly, civil servants were acting like "guerrillas" inside the Nixon administration (Rourke, 1976:112). While some HSMHA officials hoped that neighborhood health centers would become a model for health care delivery for the whole population (see chapter 3), the centers funded by DHEW were located in underserved areas and served low-income communities. This meant that the program's constituents were from that part of the general population with the fewest political resources and the least ability to influence the policy process. Supporters of the NHC concept within the bureaucracy believed that in order to survive, health centers needed the support of "a large national constituency" and took steps to consolidate their efforts toward that goal (Interview A, 13 July 1979).

During 1970 and 1971, a highly placed HSMHA official organized a series of meetings at which liberal health professionals, representatives of voluntary health agencies, medical academics, and neighborhood health center consumers were brought together. This was done after official hours—in the evenings and and on weekends—and without the knowledge or approval of the Nixon administration. This coalition was to work not only to increase the number of health centers in low-income areas, but also to establish health centers "as a model for health care delivery in the whole country." After six or seven meetings, the organizers concluded that such a coalition was not possible; there was a lack of trust among the diverse groups and individuals involved. Regional efforts were more successful. An association of health centers was organized a short time later in New York and applied to DHEW for a training contract that was awarded (Interview A, 13 July 1979).

New York State had a large number of health centers, and a communication network developed among them regarding common problems. By 1970, it had become clear to some involved in the neighborhood health center movement in New York that if they joined together they could pool technical resources and work more effectively to train board and staff members, to influence the development of relevant DHEW regulations, and to negotiate with state government as to the level of Medicaid reimbursement for health centers. Common purchasing of equipment and supplies had also been discussed. The New York Association of Neighborhood Health Centers was formed; in 1971 it received funding from DHEW to provide information and training to health center board members and staff within Federal Region 2 (Interview, 2 July 1979).

At about the same time, another regional association was formed. The Massachusetts League of Neighborhood Health Centers, located in Boston, received its initial funding from the regional office of the Department of Labor (as part of a grant to the Harvard Community Health Plan) and then in 1973 was funded by the New England regional office of DHEW.[4]

In addition to these local efforts to share expertise and information, a national organization was created in 1970 by health center administrators and consumers to establish training programs for staff and members of health center boards. In 1971, this organization, the National Association of Neighborhood Health Centers (NANHC), received a training contract from OEO and opened an office in Washington, D.C.

One of the purposes of these training programs was to increase the managerial capacity of health centers. This was an important task, for, as I have previously noted, there was concern that many centers were not collecting as much third-party reimbursement as they should. In addition, OEO officials were interested in "creating a viable political constituency to support community health centers." In fact, however, during the years 1971–1973, the regional associations based in Massachusetts and New York were far more active in organizing health center administrators and consumers to present information on the program to members of Congress than was the national association (Interview A, 12 July 1979).

The practice of awarding government contracts to private provider associations for technical assistance is very common; the large provider associations such as the American Hospital Association and the AMA regularly receive such contracts. Don K. Price has used the term "contract federalism" to describe the Medicare and Medicaid programs, in which Blue Cross, commercial insurance companies, and Blue Shield administer payments to hospitals and physicians via federal contract arrangements (see Price,

1978:42). Other examples include an ongoing contract (begun in 1972) between the Public Health Service (PHS) and the AMA to provide replacements for National Health Service Corps physicians on vacation (Thompson, 1981:89) and an eighteen-month, $100,000 contract in 1974 between DHEW and the AMA to coordinate the efforts of national specialty societies to develop guidelines for the review of hospital services financed by Medicare and Medicaid ("Amagrams," p. 1414).

In 1973, when the transfer of all health center programs to DHEW was completed, agency officials decided to consolidate the funding of the technical assistance grants to health centers. An agreement was reached whereby the Association of New York Neighborhood Health Centers and the Massachusetts League would give up their individual grants and become subcontractors of the national association. The national body would then attempt to stimulate the organization of additional regional associations in areas where none existed to create a "national network" of technical assistance groups. After the integration of the regional associations into the national association in this way, factional conflict emerged regarding the nature and goals of the organization (Interview A, 12 July 1979; 17 July 1979). (This will be discussed in chapter 6.)

The concern of bureaucrats with clientele interests is common in the American governmental process. However, in this case bureaucrats could not expect reciprocal support for their agency from an influential client group. Rather, officials were helping to organize a group to represent an emerging interest. A parallel can be found in the formation of the American Farm Bureau Federation in the early twentieth century by county agents, supported in part by federal money. A major difference, however, is that it was the wealthiest farmers, those with the most resources in the local community, who were the targets of the agricultural organizing drive (McConnell, 1966:76). In the health center case, by contrast, government officials were helping to organize consumers and institutions with very limited resources of their own.

The creation of a constituency organization for the health center program meant that the professional-bureaucratic complex might develop into a triangular policy network more like the traditional subgovernment. However, not until the late 1970s did that organization become a central actor in health center policy-making. It was not influential in the authorization process for a separate community health center program in 1975. At that point, the policy network supporting the health center program consisted of Washington-based agency officials, consumers and staff from individual health centers, and members and staff of the health subcommittees in Congress.

Congressional Support

ADVOCACY BY
THE CONGRESSIONAL HEALTH LEADERSHIP
Jurisdiction over the neighborhood health center program was held by the Senate Health Subcommittee of the Committee on Labor and Public Welfare and the House Subcommittee on Public Health and the Environment of the Committee on Interstate and Foreign Commerce. Senator Edward Kennedy (D–Mass.) headed the Senate Health Subcommittee; Congressman Paul Rogers (D–Fla.) chaired the House subcommittee. Both men were very supportive of the neighborhood health center program, as was Senator Jacob K. Javits (R–N.Y.) a senior member of the Senate Health Subcommittee (Interview, 31 March 1978).

The NHC program as it operated in the early 1970s was compatible with the ideological positions of both Kennedy and Rogers. Each advocated greater government involvement in the health system, although Rogers was more supportive of the role of the private sector in health financing and delivery than was Kennedy (Bauman, 1976:137).

Rogers "devoted himself to being a health statesman," and this included earning the respect of that part of the health establishment associated with the Democratic party, "not so much the conservative American Medical Association as the more liberal—

although no less self-interested—Association of American Medical Colleges, American Hospital Association, American Public Health Association, Blue Cross and Blue Shield, and many more" (Shenkin, 1974:153). Rogers was therefore "comfortably in the middle of the generally 'liberal' health establishment" on the issues, while Kennedy usually took a position farther to the left and compromised from that position (1974:152, 154). Kennedy's style was to "articulate large goals and seek solutions to broader problems in health," while Rogers's approach was usually narrow and "very pragmatic" (Bauman, 1976:136–37). Rogers, however, worked with a number of young professional staff members on the subcommittee who had been part of the civil rights and student movements of the 1960s and were clearly sympathetic to the goals of the neighborhood health center program (Interview A, 24 July 1979; Interview, 27 November 1979).

Both Kennedy and Rogers had developed considerable expertise in health policy; each had become chairman of his respective subcommittee in 1971 (Shenkin, 1974:152). Senator Javits was also liberal on health issues and the Kennedy and Javits staffs worked together on most issues during this period (Bauman, 1976:137).

This congressional "health leadership" reacted strongly to the Nixon administration's policy of self-sufficiency for health centers. In response to DHEW's announcement that direct federal support for health service programs would end when centers found other funding sources, Senators Kennedy and Javits asked the GAO to study the implementation of the policy and its impact on neighborhood health centers. In requesting this study, the senators said, "The Subcommittee's concern is that the policy will be implemented in a manner which will result in a curtailment of health services currently being provided by project grant programs" (GAO Report, 1973: Appendix 1:29). In a May 1973 press release, Kennedy noted that the GAO study had found that self-sufficiency was not a realistic goal for the centers and that "if the centers must rely on insurance payments to survive, they will have to eliminate many existing health services." He called for a legislative extension of the NHC program until Congress could write new legislation.

Congressman Rogers held a news conference in June 1973 to protest the effect of the DHEW proposed regulations on NHCs. Rogers said that they would "doom" the programs. "It's just another way of saying they are going to cut out the programs completely." The subcommittee chairman announced that he had asked Caspar Weinberger, the secretary of DHEW, to delay the implementation of the regulations for four months and to provide, within two weeks, evidence that it was the intent of Congress to have these programs become self-sufficient (*New York Times,* 21 June 1973:69). The controversy over these regulations was resolved through a series of meetings attended by Secretary Weinberger, staff members of the Bureau of Community Health Services (BCHS), Congressman Rogers, and staff of both the House and Senate Health Subcommittees. In the end, DHEW guaranteed that it would continue financing the centers, but centers would have to maker greater efforts to increase their efforts to collect third-party funds (Interview, 27 November 1979).

LEGISLATIVE ACTION
In addition to opposing administration policy on health center financing under legislation authorizing health services innovation in general, congressional actors worked to provide a new legislative mandate for the community health center program itself. This was in opposition to the wishes of the Nixon and Ford administrations.

The Nixon administration had proposed that six of the thirteen categorical health programs that were to expire at the end of fiscal year 1973 not be reauthorized and that funding for the other seven be reduced. In June 1973, Congress passed a bill that extended for one year all of the major health programs that the administration had declined to continue. These included the Hill-Burton program for hospital construction, the regional medical program, community mental health centers, migrant health centers, and neighborhood health centers. The bill passed each chamber by such a wide margin that, even though the administration had opposed it, on June 18, 1973, President Nixon signed it into law (*New York Times,* 21 June 1973:69).

The next year, rather than simply reauthorizing the general legislation under which the health centers had been funded, the Senate and House Health Subcommittees wrote new legislation that specifically described "community health centers" and authorized separate funding for them. This legislation was enacted at the end of the Ninety-third Congress, but was pocket-vetoed by the president after Congress had recessed. In 1975 identical legislation was passed again in each house (S. Rept. 94-29:37). The Special Health Revenue Sharing Act of 1975 (PL 94-63) became law on July 29, 1975, after Congress voted to override President Ford's veto of the bill (*NACHC, Legislative Status Report,* 4 September 1975:2).

Title V of the Special Health Revenue Sharing Act authorized $215 million for health center operations in fiscal year 1976, $235 million for fiscal year 1977, and an additional $5 million for planning grants in each of those years. This was considerably above the amounts that had been appropriated for health centers under the general authority of 314(e). Title V also described how health center grants were to be awarded, the services to be provided, and the structure of health center governance.

Congress had thus replaced a very general authority for innovation in health service delivery—314(e)—with specific, detailed legislation that directed the administration to fund community health centers. This legislation is seen as a turning point for the NHC program by some of its advocates, because the program now had its own separate legislative authority (Interview, 30 March 1978). What accounted for this congressional action? Why would there be such large congressional majorities for a program serving a constituency with few if any traditional political resources? To answer this question, we must examine the nature of the NHC issue and the broader political environment in which it was considered.

THE NATURE OF THE ISSUE:
THE AUTHORIZING COMMITTEES

David E. Price applies the notion of issue typologies to the work of congressional committees, arguing that variation "in the level and 'quality'" (1978:549) of committee activity on various issues is related to the characteristics of each policy area. He describes legislators as responding to their perceptions about the environment and making calculations about its consequences for their careers. The environment is "fields of incentives, opportunities and constraints that shape their priorities and strategies" (1978:549).[5] Price discusses three aspects of this environment that affect congressional activity on any specific issue: (1) the salience or importance of the issue to the public, (2) the level of group conflict, and (3) the degree and nature of executive agency involvement in that issue area.

Legislators will act on behalf of the interests of well-organized dominant economic groups when an issue does not appear to be salient or potentially salient to the public. Conversely, they are more likely to take positions different from the preferences of organized groups on issues which they perceive to be salient.

The behavior of legislators, even in "clientele-centered" policy areas, those in which interest groups have a major role in shaping policy, is also influenced by the level of conflict within the policy area. When there is disagreement among groups of relatively equal strength, and therefore conflict, members of Congress are reluctant to become involved. If they take a position, one set of interests may be antagonized (1978:569–70). The third "environmental" variable discussed by Price is executive involvement. Members of Congress are less likely, for instance, to actively support clientele interests when an executive agency is already taking this role (1978:552). However, when the executive discourages interests favored by legislators, they have an incentive to act on behalf of these interests (1978:572). This was the case with the NHC program in the early 1970s.

Price describes health as a policy area of generally high public salience, but one involving many interest groups. There is there-

fore much variation in the level of conflict generated on particular
health policy issues (1978:566).

The neighborhood health center program was an issue of low
public salience that generated little conflict. In this case, the low
level of public salience was beneficial to the program. The political environment in which the 1975 health center legislation was
enacted was one of intense conflict, but it was not conflict generated by interest groups opposed to the health center program. It
was, rather, ideological and institutional conflict between the
Nixon and Ford administrations and a liberal Democratic Congress,
and it involved far more than the issue of neighborhood health
centers.

Issue Salience   During the drafting of P.L. 94-63, the NHC program was perceived as having low salience for the general public
and thus generated little interest among most Senate and House
subcommittee members. The Health Subcommittee of the Senate
Committee on Labor and Public Welfare held only two days of
hearings on neighborhood and migrant health centers during
1974. There was, according to a Senate subcommittee staff member,
"an incredible absence of interest in these programs in the Senate,
a real triumph of uninvolvement." Neighborhood health centers
were seen as "small inexpensive programs that did some good for
some people." They were viewed as "business to be taken care of,"
but "*not* a big issue," not "an issue with mileage," and therefore of
little interest to most senators (Interview, 11 July 1979).

For Senator Kennedy, NHCs had been part of a larger plan for
restructuring the health care system. During 1972–1973, Kennedy
and the subcommittee staff had viewed the health center program
as part of the issue of national health insurance, an issue of major
concern to the senator and one of great potential interest to the
public. Subcommittee staff began to draft legislation that would
create "comprehensive health centers" to replace both community
mental health centers and NHCs. These comprehensive centers
were to become part of a national health program when national
health insurance was enacted. After 1973, however, the program

was regarded differently by the senator and subcommittee staff. The political atmosphere had changed; there was a mood of budgetary conservatism in Congress. Neighborhood health centers were no longer discussed in the committee in terms of further innovations in health care delivery. Instead, the question was how to assure the survival of the existing program. Under these conditions, the program seemed to offer few electoral or ideological rewards and aroused little interest. The only senator other than Kennedy and Javits who showed any interest in the health center program was Senator Alan Cranston (D–Calif.), who wanted to make sure that the program would provide health services to Spanish-speaking populations (Interview, 11 July 1979).

The attitudes of House Health Subcommittee members toward this legislation was similar to the attitudes of those on the Senate subcommittee. The committee staff member who drafted the House legislation used almost the same words as his Senate counterpart in describing members' responses to this issue. "Not a lot of people were interested; . . . nobody was passionately committed either way" (Interview, 27 November 1979).

Group Conflict   Redistributive policy differs significantly from distributive policy in the degree of conflict among organized interests (Lowi, 1964; Wilson, 1973; Hayes, 1981; Ripley and Franklin, 1987). As I have noted, Price finds the likelihood of congressional action on an issue to be related to this variable as well. Congress members are more likely to take a position on an issue when group conflict is low. According to this formulation, members of Congress would have been less likely to support NHCs had organized interest groups expressed opposition to the program. In the health center case, the most likely reason for such opposition would be the belief of provider groups (such as those representing physicians or hospitals) that these programs would compete with their constituents (see Feldstein, 1977). In the mid-1960s, OEO officials had defined the NHC program as an attempt at health care reform, but they had also reassured the AMA that health centers would not be in competition with their membership. In addition, a large proportion of the initial project grants had been awarded to hospitals and medical schools. In 1973–1974, the program was defined by its congressional advocates as a limited program for the medically underserved that should be continued. The AMA did take a position opposing legislation authorizing the health center program, but did not pursue this opposition actively.

Representatives of individual health centers, officials of the NANHC, and representatives of the American Hospital Association (AHA) presented testimony on the NHC program at both Senate and House subcommittee hearings. The AMA presented testimony to the House subcommittee but not at the Senate hearings on the program in 1974 and 1975. While the AHA supported a three-year authorization for a separate health center program, the AMA suggested instead that neighborhood health center projects be funded as part of general revenue sharing to the states. This was actually a proposal to eliminate the program. The AMA spokesman raised the issue of competition between health centers and private physicians, stating that such physicians in areas contiguous to health center catchment areas suffered economically and were then forced to leave their own "marginal" areas (House Hearings, 1974:544). The association's representative also questioned the cost-effectiveness of the centers and urged the collection of more data on this issue before the federal government committed itself to the program (House Hearings, 1975:538).

Although the AMA opposed the health center legislation at House subcommittee hearings, it did not take any other action on the issue. No Senate or House staff member recalls hearing from or about the AMA during this period. Staffers do recall hearing from representatives of individual health centers, the NANHC, and the AHA, all of whom supported the legislation but had concerns about its specific provisions. What is the explanation for the behavior of the AMA on this issue?

As I noted in chapter 3, the two themes that appeared continuously in discussions of the NHC program in the AMA *Journal* during the 1960s were the importance of preserving medical care as a private sector activity and the need to maintain physician control of the health care delivery system. These two themes came together in a 1970 speech by the AMA president to the association's House of Delegates on the future of health care. Dr. Walter C. Bornemeier stated explicitly that the neighborhood health center program was threatening, not as a limited program for the poor, but as a model for health care for the general population. It was a threat within the context of discussions of the need for a general restructuring of the health care system:

> Pressures are now mounting for the use of the neighborhood clinic as the focal point for the delivery of most medical services. As the government takes on an increasing role in health care, as costs continue to rise, as local and state governments are confronted with increasing demands on limited public funds, and as groups such as organized labor continue to push for nationalized health services, we can expect federal legislation to zero in on neighborhood medical clinics. It is important for the A.M.A. to take a leadership role so that we may insure that medical clinics remain a part of the free system. (1970:2181–82)

Dr. Bornemeier then proposed that the association sponsor surveys of personnel distribution in various specialties, support medical training in primary care, and establish a Medical Facilities Advisory Association to aid in the establishment of private practices in ghettos. These actions "will keep the delivery of medical care in the control of the physician, rather than abdicting to the hospital, the government, or to the private agencies" (1970:2182).

By 1973, as I have noted, Senator Kennedy no longer viewed the NHC program as a central part of a restructured health system financed through a national insurance plan. As a health program clearly limited to the poor, NHCs were not perceived as directly threatening to the interests of the profession as they were in the earlier period (when no relevant legislation was being considered). A congressional staff member made this point in another way by attributing the association's failure to lobby against the program in 1973–1975 to the program's small size. "Real opposition to the program," he said, will come "when the program gets bigger" (Interview, 27 November 1979).[6]

In addition, other issues more directly related to the structure of the American health care system were being considered in Congress during this period. AMA officers and staff focused their attention on these issues. Medicare, Medicaid, medical school funding, and health planning legislation were discussed in the AMA *Journal* (or *JAMA*) with far greater frequency in the 1970–1975 period than were neighborhood health centers. AMA representatives made the organization's opposition to the 1974 Health Planning and Resources Development Act known to committee members dealing with the legislation (Lander, 1976:2). An AMA spokesperson confirmed that health centers generally have been a low priority issue for the association—"it's never been the kind of priority issue that took personal lobbying" (Interview, 14 July 1982).

The health center program was thus a low-salience issue for interest groups concerned about health policy as well as for the general public from 1973 to 1975. The number of interest groups, like the number of Congress members concerned with the NHC program, was small. The committee staffer who drafted the Senate legislation said: "What surprised me was that no one got more excited about it during that time. There wasn't a lot of knocking at the door saying we want to look at it" (Interview, 11 July 1979).

The salience of an issue and the level of conflict it generates are, of course, related. Groups can widen a conflict by attempting to make it salient to the public (Schattschneider, 1960). If the AMA had found the NHC program an important issue in 1974–1975, it might have used such a strategy, as it did during the long debate over national health insurance and Medicare (Harris, 1966; Marmor, 1973). There was concern in Congress, even among advocates, about managerial efficiency and the levels of "productivity" at individual health centers. Had the AMA dramatized this issue and tied it to the poverty program stereotype of "waste" and "fraud," the reauthorization of the NHC program might have become controversial and problematic. Instead, the 1975 legislation received little publicity.

Low visibility is usually attributed to the distributive policy networks that benefit powerful economic groups. In this case, paradoxically, a program that served a low-income, largely minority constituency benefited from a similar absence of public attention. At the same time, the program profited from intense and open conflict within the larger political environment. This conflict, and its impact on the neighborhood health center legislation, will be discussed below.

Executive Involvement and the Organization of Conflict   While the Nixon and Ford administrations and congressional health leadership disagreed on the issue of federal support for community health centers, this dispute took place within a wider conflict. All of the congressional actors interviewed for this study stressed the importance of this larger context to an understanding of the congressional mandate for the NHC program.

One aspect of this executive-legislative conflict was ideological disagreement between the Nixon administration and a liberal Democratic Congress on the future of Democratic social programs. Congress members and the House Health Subcommittee staff viewed themselves as in a defensive posture. The Nixon administration wanted to "destroy" these programs while Congress was trying to "protect and preserve" them (Interview A, 24 July 1979). Congress was attempting to "save some of the Great Society programs by writing them into law" (Interview, 26 June 1979).

This policy difference was compounded by the congressional staffers' general distrust of the executive branch. This was a consequence of the Nixon administration's attempt to disrupt the political relationships that had provided support for the categorical social programs the administration was trying to end.

During the first two years of the Nixon presidency, the White House focused on the legislative process in domestic policy, and paid little attention to program administration. After encountering opposition to its legislative program in Congress, the Nixon administration initiated what Richard P. Nathan calls "the Administrative Presidency." Individuals who were personally loyal to the president were placed in charge of functional areas of the bureaucracy in order to take control of program administration away from civil servants involved in policy subgovernments (Nathan, 1975:9–10, 62, 74). The president and his closest advisers felt that the bureaucracy "was not loyal" (Nathan, 1975:82; see also Reichley, 1981, ch. 11). According to one DHEW official, "Nixon felt that HEW was a hostile environment" (quoted in Bauman, 1976:133). The HSMHA was seen as especially "tainted because of its longstanding liberal Democratic tradition and orientation" (1976:130).

In addition to "firing agency heads and midlevel political appointees who shared the values and culture of HEW" (Bauman, 1976:138), the presidential loyalists tried to alter the day-to-day working relationships between lower-level executive agency staff and congressional committees within specific policy areas. Several former staffers of congressional health committees initiated discussions of such administration actions. One recalled that DHEW staff were not allowed to meet with the staff of congressional committees without the presence of an individual from the legislative office of DHEW, a "political operative" (Interview, 11 July 1979; see also Bauman, 1976:137, and Iglehart, 1975A). DHEW staff were also required to write memoranda on the content of every phone conversation held with a congressional staff person. DHEW personnel told colleagues who moved to Congress from that agency, "not to call them at work any more" (Interview, 11 July 1979). The result was to enlarge the perceived distance between the administration and Congress. By 1971, said a former House staffer, "[we felt] unable to work with the Administration" (Interview A, 24 July 1979). "We distrusted everything that came out of the Secretary's office," said a former staff member of the Senate Committee on Labor and Public Welfare (Interview, 11 July 1979). It is one of the ironies of the neighborhood health center policy process during the Nixon years that the administration's efforts to control the bureaucracy were among the factors that contributed to congressional support of social programs that the Nixon administration did not want to continue.

Another basis for congressional distrust of the Nixon administration was the view that it was taking action outside of its institutional domain, "abusing" the general authority of 314(e) and therefore going beyond its constitutional role (Interview, 26 June 1979; see also Iglehart, 1975B:1742). The response of Kennedy and Rogers to the Nixon administration's policy of "self-sufficiency" for neighborhood health centers in 1973 reflected the general distrust between congressional liberals and the White House. When Rogers asked for a delay in the DHEW regulation that would implement this policy, he emphasized that such a policy was not the intent of Congress, and most significantly that the administration had not consulted with Congress on these regulations. The administration's actions, in his view, were part of "an assault" on national health programs, which included the impoundment of funds and the failure to fund health programs in the 1974 fiscal year budget (*New York Times*, 21 June 1973:69).

Congressional action to establish a separate legislative authority for the NHC program was part of a larger effort to maintain social programs threatened by an administration perceived as acting unconstitutionally. The reports accompanying both the House and the Senate bills reflect this view. The House committee report says that while the 314(e) authority "has been used well . . . to develop a program of comprehensive health services for underserved populations" that should be continued, the 314(e) provision has also been used "inappropriately" in ways that makes the authority difficult to oversee and guarantees no accountability. For this reason, the committee says, 314(e) should be repealed and replaced with more "specific" legislation (H. Rept. 94-192:81).

The Senate committee makes its discontent with the administration more emphatic:

> The Committee is concerned that the 314(e) authority often has been inappropriately used by the Department of Health, Education, and Welfare to substantially support heavily a wide variety of special initiatives beyond the scope of the legislative intent of this provision. The Committee notes as particularly applicable here the funding of demonstration projects for health maintenance organizations while legislation for funding "HMO's" was actually pending before Congress. Moreover, while the Family Health Center program appears an effec-

tive variation on the Neighborhood Health Center Model, it amounts to a major new Federal program, with 39 funded centers, begun *without legislative review* of its high standardized service package and prepaid approach to health centers. The relationships of this innovative program created by regulation under an overly broad legislative authority to other congressionally authorized programs— such as the HMO program—remains poorly defined. For this reason, the Committee has concluded that it is appropriate at this time to repeal the existing 314(e) authority and to replace it with a new and specific authority which clarifies congressional intent with respect to support for community health centers. (S. Rept. 94-29:118)

Congress members wanted to make sure that DHEW would no longer be "creating" its own programs; they wanted "to regain the legislative initiative" and to tell the administration "what we wanted them to do" (Interview, 11 July 1979; see also Shenkin, 1974:215–16). Because of congressional distrust of the administration, P.L. 94-63, which authorized the community health center program, was very specific in describing how health centers should function. In addition, there was to be continuity between P.L. 94-63 and the existing health center program. The legislation attempted "to describe what was going on at the better centers," not to innovate or create new programs but to "preserve" and "protect" an existing one (Interview A, 24 July 1979).

SPECIFIC LEGISLATIVE PROVISIONS AND
THE HEALTH POLICY NETWORK
As discussed above, few House members, senators, or interest group representatives viewed the community health center legislation as politically significant, and thus did not become involved in drafting the legislation. Professional staff members working with the Senate Health Subcommittee consulted with a panel of advisers, which included health and community mental health center administrators and academics who had advised Senator Kennedy on national health insurance issues. The staff of the House Health Subcommittee talked informally with representatives of NANHC and with bureaucrats in DHEW whom they had

known before entering government service. The background and perspective of these staff members appears to have shaped specific provisions of the legislation.

The two staff members who drafted the CHC legislation for the Health Subcommittee of the House Energy and Commerce Committee were both physicians who had been in the civil rights movement in college and the antiwar movement in medical school. They felt themselves to be a part of a movement for change within the medical profession as well as the larger society. They both understood and supported the NHC concept. One of them, in fact, had worked with a neighborhood health center just before coming to Washington to work in Congress.

These congressional staff members were concerned with writing legislation that would both protect the NHC program and enable health centers to be responsive to the community (Interview A, 24 July 1979; 27 November 1979). As they drafted the legislation, they consulted with two officials of the Bureau of Community Health Services (BCHS) on technical details. One of these officials had gone to medical school with one of the congressional staff members, all four of these young physicians had known each other since they had all belonged to the Student Medical Association (Interview A, 24 July 1979). This interaction occurred in spite of the Nixon administration's attempt to prevent such activity.[7]

P.L. 93-64 divided the services to be offered at community health centers into "primary" (or required) services and "supplemental" services, which could, but did not have to be, provided. Primary services included the more traditional medical services such as physician care, X-rays and laboratory work, as well as transportation and preventive health and dental services. Nutrition education, health education, social services, and outreach were placed in the supplemental category. (P.L. 94-63, Title V, sec. 330). According to the congressional staff members who drafted it, the law defined a set of "primary" required services so that the Nixon (or Ford) administration would not be able to fund less comprehensive models of care (Interview, 11 July; Interview A, 24 July 1979). At the same time, advocates of the neighborhood health center program within the bureaucracy felt that the original NHC model (which would include nutrition and health education and outreach services) was not politically viable in a time of increasing congressional concern about the cost of health care. (The national association's position, in contrast, was that all of these services should be required as primary services [Interview, 16 August 1982].) The consequence of this separation of primary and supplementary services was that DHEW grants to health centers reinforced the tendency of Medicare and Medicaid policy toward financing traditional medical services rather than "community health services." (See chapter 5.)

A second significant provision of the 1975 legislation mandated that each community health center would have a consumer-dominated governing board as the recipient of all federal funds to the center. This board would establish general policies for the operation of the center, approve its budget, and appoint its executive director. A majority of board members were to be consumers who used the center and "who, as a group, represent the individuals being served by the center" (P.L. 94-63). This governing board provision, along with similar requirements in the Community Mental Health Centers Act, was the most advanced form of consumer participation in any health service program up to this time (Lavery, 1978, ch. 2).

As we have seen, many of the first grants to establish OEO-funded neighborhood health centers were given to medical schools, hospitals, or health departments. Consumer input in policymaking was to be provided by an advisory board with a consumer majority.[8] The 1975 legislative provision for consumer control was an affirmation of the increase in consumer-community authority on health center boards. This authority had grown during the life of the program in response to the demands of consumer representatives on these boards. It also reflected support for the concept of consumer participation—even control—among liberal health policy advisers working with the Senate Health Subcommittee and congressional staffers who drafted the legislation for both subcommittees.

The responsibilities of consumers who were members of the first health center advisory boards was unclear (May et al., 1979:15). One reason for this was the lack of existing models for consumer participation in health care delivery. At many health centers during this time, the roles of community representatives on these boards and the relationship of the health center board to the medical school or hospital receiving a grant were being defined. Representatives of the grant-receiving institutions, health center administrators, and community representatives often had different perspectives on the purposes the health center should serve (May et al., 1980B:595–99).

In 1969 the Watts Health Center grant was transferred from the University of Southern California Medical School to the community board at the board's request. Soon afterward, consumer members of boards at other OEO centers asked for such arrangements, and many were negotiated (May et al., 1979:26–33; Anderson et al., 1976:30). Center board members also participated in the first national consumers' health conference in 1969 (May et al., 1979:33) and in the formation of the New York Association of Neighborhood Health Centers, the Massachusetts League of Neighborhood Health Centers, and NANHC (Interviews, 31 March 1978 and 2 July 1979; Interview A, 12 July 1979; Interview A, 13 July 1979).

Consumer board members also raised the issue of board composition, specifically, the validity of health professionals as members of advisory boards. OEO officials responded by issuing regulations that one-third of the members of the boards established by new projects had to be consumers; by 1973 this had been increased to 50 percent (May et al., 1979:35–36).

In both the Senate and the House, the general concept of consumer participation—even consumer control—was widely accepted among the professional staff of the health subcommittees at this time (Interview, 11 July 1979; Interview A, 24 July 1979). On the Senate side, the idea that an advisory board should be replaced by a governing board came from the panel convened by the staff of the Senate Health Subcommittee. It reflected the perspective of national unions that health in the United States "ought to be consumer-run" (Interview, 11 July 1979). The two physician staff members working with the House Health Subcommittee had visited health center projects sponsored by community organizations. They believed that this model was a successful form of "community control" and that advisory boards were "unworkable" (Interview, 27 November 1979). While legislation itself could not guarantee that consumers would function effectively on such boards, it could at least "prevent paternalism" at health centers (Interview A, 24 July 1979).

Since the Nixon administration was opposed to the authorization of the program as a separate entity, it did not take an official position on the governing board issue (Interview, 11 July 1979). Individuals working in the BCHS expressed their support of the governing board provision, as did board members of individual health centers (Interview, 27 November 1979). Some hospital officials opposed the governing board provision, but they did not press their opposition vigorously in 1975 (Interview, 11 July 1979; Interview A, 24 July 1979; Interview, 27 November 1979). However, when P.L. 94-63 was up for reauthorization in 1978, the idea that a consumer-dominated governing board was central to the definition of a community health center was challenged by some hospitals. This challenge will be described in chapter 6.

Writers on Congress have suggested that the large increase in the number of professional staff working with congressional committees, and the fact that new staff are more likely to have professional or technical rather than political experience before coming to Congress, has had a major impact on the legislative process. Congressional staff are said to be increasingly able to influence legislation and may, in fact, be replacing interest group representatives in doing so (Arieff, 1979; Iglehart, 1975A). As I have noted, professional staff had an important role in fashioning the details of neighborhood health center legislation. The NHC case suggests that the influence of congressional staff is probably greater on issues of low public interest and little conflict than on matters that are publicly salient and/or on which powerful interest groups disagree.

THE APPROPRIATIONS COMMITTEES:
THE PERCEPTION OF THE ISSUE

During the years 1969–1974, Congress appropriated money for neighborhood health centers under the provisions of section 314(e) of the Public Health Service Act. In each of these years congressional appropriations for NHCs were higher than those proposed in the presidential budget (Interview, 31 March 1978).

Individuals who staffed the Senate and House Appropriations Subcommittees on Health, Education, and Labor during the Nixon and Ford administrations indicated that the NHC program was seen as a noncontroversial, distributive issue by members of both subcommittees.[9] This was true even though health care providers expressed opposition to program funding to some senators.

The NHC program was seen as one of several categorical grant programs whose goal was to serve disadvantaged populations. According to a congressional staff member working on health for the House Appropriations Committee, "I think that the basic concept that they saw was that these centers brought health care to areas that were in need of health care and they also saw that it allowed the community a voice in how these services were to be provided." It was viewed as a medical care program; many committee members were not even aware of its "social service aspects" (Interview C, 10 July 1979).

A staff member of the Senate Appropriations Committee who was responsible for health programs during the Nixon and Ford years described Senate perceptions of the NHC program in very similar terms. It was seen as a way to provide health care to "unserved" or "underserved" populations that had been neglected in the past. The strongest supporters of the CHC program on the Senate Appropriations Health Subcommittee were senators from rural states and states that contained urban ghettos. "They saw this as an opportunity to provide something to their constituents that they didn't have a sufficient amount of." This was true across "ideological lines." According to this staff member, even some conservative senators from rural states supported the neighborhood health center program.

Physicians' groups and hospitals complained to some members of the Senate Appropriations Committee about competition from neighborhood health centers. Physicians' organizations were particularly disturbed about the use of nonphysician practitioners at NHCs. However, most of the active opposition came from individual doctors and hospital administrators rather than from national organizations. Such opposition, in the form of letters and telegrams, usually came in response to a DHEW announcement of the funding of a particular health center in a specific community. Doctors and hospitals in that community "raised hell" about the opening of the center. After a while, however, when it became clear that these centers "weren't going to put doctors and hospitals out of business," that they were "adjuncts" to other services in the community, the opposition diminished (Interview B, 12 July 1979).

Conclusion

A 1974 study of the politics of the NHC program during the OEO years concluded that the program would probably not survive the opposition of the Nixon administration. This assessment was based on the fact that NHCs served a clientele with minimal political resources and did not have any other influential interest group as sponsor. (See Marcus, 1981.)

This assessment proved to be incorrect. The program survived because of its advocacy by individual bureaucrats acting independently of the Nixon administration and because of the support of congressional health leaders who were allied with them. Its institutionalization as a separate categorical program occurred within the context of conflict between a Republican administration and a Democratic Congress over the funding of social programs.

The bureaucratic advocates of the program were personally committed to health services reorganization and to increasing access to health care. Such individuals are variously described as "zealots," "advocates" (Downs, 1967:88), "missionaries" (Wilensky, 1967:86), or "policy activists" (Heclo, 1978:105). They are said to be "quite rare" but "may have considerable short-run impact" (Ripley and Franklin, 1986:53). However, in this case advocates were more than isolated individual "missionaries"; their political values were those of a specific political generation. Many of the bureaucratic advocates of the NHC program, as well as the congressional staff members who worked with them, shared the experience of political activism in the civil rights and student movements of the 1960s and early 1970s. Their concern with the NHC program was part of their broader consciousness about issues of social justice.

This network of people committed to equal access, comprehensive health care, and community participation was smaller and more activist than the broad issue networks described by Heclo. Yet lacking was the influential interest group that is central to the traditional subgovernment.

The success of their efforts was due to two factors. One was that the NHC program was presented as a distributive issue, as an effort to provide health services to a limited number of low-income people, rather than part of a larger program for general health system reform. (See Nelson, 1985, for a discussion of similar dynamics in the construction and presentation of the issue of child abuse.) The AMA, which opposed the program, did not mobilize its resources on this issue and the health center legislation was perceived by Congress as a low-salience issue involving little conflict. Second, it was considered within the larger conflict between a Republican administration opposed to federal sponsorship of social programs and a liberal Democratic Congress that supported them. It was viewed by Congress members and staff on the health subcommittees as a valuable program that should be protected from an administration acting unconstitutionally and determined to destroy the legacy of the Great Society. This larger political environment was an important factor in the legislative institutionalization of the health center program.

The autonomy of the traditional subgovernment is based on the political resources of the interest group involved (see Ripley and Franklin, 1987:96; Nachmias and Rosenbloom, 1980:216). The neighborhood health center case suggests that when a client group does not have the resources to produce this support, the institutional environment of the bureaucratic and congressional components of the policy network become critical to the outcome of the policy process. This was true of Congress during the Nixon-Ford years, and, as we shall see, of the bureaucratic environment of the Carter years as well.

5

A Bureaucratic Strategy
of Policy Change

Chapters 5 and 6 analyze the policy network supporting the community health center (CHC) program during the Ford and Carter administrations. One major theme to be developed is the central role of bureaucratic actors in building congressional support for the program. The second major theme is how Medicare and Medicaid eligibility and reimbursement policies affected the CHC program. These policies have constrained program expansion over time and are an indication of the limited influence of the CHC policy network within the larger health policy process.

The Rural Health Initiative:
A Bureaucratic Strategy for Program Survival

The crucial importance of bureaucratic actors to the survival of the community health center program went beyond attempts to help create an organized constituency for the program. Beginning shortly after P.L. 94-63 was enacted, the Bureau of Community Health Services (BCHS), which was to administer the program, undertook a series of actions that broadened the population actually served by the program, encouraged direct relationships between CHCs and other BCHS programs, and solidified congressional support for the health centers. Bureau officials were thus continuing to build a policy network supportive of the health center program.

The Bureau of Community Health Services was created by the 1972 reorganization of the Public Health Service (PHS). The first director of the BCHS was Dr. Paul Bataledan. In November 1975, he was succeeded by Dr. Edward Martin, then director of the National Health Services Corps, one of the programs within the bureau. Between 1971 and 1973, Martin had been the deputy director of the Martin Luther King Health Center in the Bronx, New York. Martin assumed the leadership of the bureau at a time when those in policymaking positions within the Ford administration wanted to phase out the CHC program and when there was concern in Congress about the level of productivity and managerial efficiency at individual health centers (Interview A, 25 July 1979).

Bureau leaders responded by strengthening the bureau's capacity to monitor program productivity. In addition, beginning in 1975, there was a major shift in the type of new programs that were funded. Federal resources were to be used in the most "rational" and efficient way. This shift began with the funding of forty-seven rural health projects and the formal declaration of a "rural health initiative" (RHI). These bureaucratic actions were in large part a response to the administrative and political environment of the Ford administration.

THE FORD ADMINISTRATION AND
COMMUNITY HEALTH CENTERS

Gerald Ford assumed the presidency on August 5, 1974, after the resignation of Richard Nixon. Somewhat less than a year later, Ford vetoed the Special Health Revenue Sharing Act of 1975 (P.L. 94-63), which for the first time would have established the community health center program as a separate categorical grant program. Congress overrode his veto and the legislation was enacted.

Although P.L. 94-63 authorized $220 million for the CHC program for fiscal year 1976 and $240 million for fiscal year 1977

(NACHC, *Legislative Status Report,* January 1976:6), the Ford administration requested only $155.2 million for CHC programs in fiscal year 1976. Not only was this less than the $220 million authorized by Congress, it was about 20 percent less than the $196.7 million that had been appropriated for the program in fiscal year 1975. In doing so, the administration suggested that the same number of persons could be served in fiscal year 1976 as had been served in fiscal year 1975 if state and local governments supplied the difference in funding (NACHC, *Legislative Status Report,* 28 November 1975:1).

Congress enacted a supplemental appropriations bill for fiscal year 1976 in December 1975. The CHC program was to be funded at $196.6 million—approximately the same level as the program budget in 1975, and $41 million more than the administration had requested. In its report, the Senate Appropriations Committee rejected the notion that if health center program funds were cut below the 1975 level, the difference could be supplied by local government or other sources (NACHC, *Legislative Status Report,* January 1976:2–4).

One month later, in January 1976, President Ford submitted a rescission request to Congress asking for authority not to spend all of the funds that had been appropriated for the health center program. The amount of the rescission was to be $41.5 million, the amount by which the Fiscal Year 1976 appropriation had been increased over the 1975 budget (NACHC, *Legislative Status Report,* February 1976:1). The request was denied by the House and Senate Appropriations Committees (NACHC, *Legislative Status Report,* April 1976:1), and, as established under the Budget and Impoundment Control Act (P.L. 93-344), the money became available forty-five days after the presidential request had been made (NACHC, *Legislative Status Report,* January 1976:2).

A similar scenario was played out in relation to funding for fiscal year 1977. The Ford budget submitted to Congress in January 1976 proposed a reduction of $100 million for all categorical health programs from the level of the previous year. The request for the CHC program was $155.2 million, the same amount as the administration had requested for fiscal year 1976 (NACHC, *Legislative Status Report,* February 1976:2). In September 1976, Congress appropriated $215.1 million for community health centers, an increase of $18.4 million over the amount appropriated for the previous year. This Department of Labor/DHEW appropriations bill was enacted over a presidential veto (NACHC, *Legislative Status Report,* October 1976:1–2).

The reduction in the budget levels for categorical health programs proposed by the Ford administration for fiscal years 1976 and 1977 was part of an administration plan to replace categorical health programs, Medicaid, and the health planning program with a revenue sharing plan. Under the plan, states would receive block grants for all health programs on the basis of population and income formulas (Iglehart, 1975B:1741; and NACHC, *Legislative Status Report,* February 1976:2–5). The plan would have ended maternal and child health programs, migrant workers' health programs, community mental health center programs, and CHC programs, among others. The block grant proposal, developed by the Office of Management and Budget, was opposed by DHEW.

Ford was continuing Nixon's policies. He hoped to control federal spending and to return power to state and local governments. If the categorical grant system in health was ended, policy networks that dealt with these programs would also cease to operate (Iglehart, 1975B:1741–42). A bill incorporating the Ford administration's block grant proposal (H.R. 12233) was introduced into the House of Representatives in the early spring of 1976, but the proposal did not become law (NACHC, *Legislative Status Report,* April 1976:7, October 1976:2, 4).

THE RURAL HEALTH INITIATIVE:
"CAPACITY-BUILDING"

The rural health initiative (RHI) was undertaken within this context of Ford administration efforts to reduce funds for health centers and to end categorical health programs. It was an administrative policy of allocating more of the health center program's resources to rural areas, establishing small primary care projects that were integrated with other federal programs, and concentrating available resources in areas of "greatest need" (Interview A, 25 July 1979). BCHS officials presented a paper on the need for such a strategy to the Public Health Service Policy Board in July 1975. The initiative was approved as official PHS policy (Interview B, 13 July 1979). There were reasons of both equity and efficiency for such a policy shift.

As early as 1973, it was recognized within the bureau that while most of the resources of the NHC program had gone to urban areas, there was a great need for resources in rural areas. More than half of the medically underserved people in the United States lived in rural areas, but approximately 85 percent of NHC grant funds went to cities (Interview A, 25 July 1979). While rural areas had higher accident rates, more occupational injuries, and an older and poorer population than urban areas, their health services were far more limited. There were fewer physicians and dentists, less accessible emergency and primary care, and fewer public health services than in urban areas. In some rural areas, a very low population density made it very difficult to establish services and retain health professionals (Martin, 1975:292). Between 1968 and 1973, rural areas lost 2.6 percent of their physicians per year, while urban areas did not experience an overall loss (Samuels, 1978:163).

The decision of the PHS to fund more programs in rural areas was coupled with a shift in the type of program that would be funded. First, the RHI programs would be smaller than the first neighborhood health centers. Because rural areas, especially isolated ones, had a "paucity of critical resources" and limited technical expertise and management capacity, bureau officials believed it necessary to establish programs on a much smaller scale than in the past. In their view, the large scale of the earlier NHC programs had resulted in the waste of federal dollars. Under the Ford administration, dollars would apparently be very limited. The RHI projects would begin slowly and grow gradually so that inefficiency and low productivity could be minimized (Interview A, 25 July 1979).

In addition, the RHI involved the attempt to coordinate separate federal grant programs. The first ideas about this came out of experience with the National Health Service Corps (NHSC), authorized by the Emergency Health Personnel Act (P.L. 91-623) in 1970. The act provided for the recruitment and placement of physicians and other health professionals in areas that lacked primary care providers. It was hoped that corps personnel would serve for two years in the program and then remain in these communities as private practitioners (Samuels, 1978:163). However, the program had difficulty in retaining corps personnel once their initial service period ended. This, it was believed, was because corps sites were isolated from other providers and systems of care. Officials decided to work on the coordination of the CHC and NHSC programs as a logical response to the problem of long-term development of health resources in medically underserved rural areas (Interview A, 25 July 1979).

Community health center program sites would provide the NHSC with "a professional atmosphere conducive to the retention of quality medical professionals." NHSC personnel would be operating within a clinic setting with at least two primary care physicians, physician extenders, and other staff, offering "a full range of comprehensive primary care services." This would make the professional experience "more rewarding" (Samuels, 1978:164). For the future, the problem of limited health resources in rural areas would be solved by "the development of a health care delivery system in rural America that links providers to secondary care referral and hospital systems, that decreases professional isolation, and that utilizes extender personnel more effectively in isolated areas" (Martin, 1975:294). The development of such a system became one of the BCHS goals.

A central concern for the bureau in the mid-1970s was the need to help programs deliver services efficiently. Because resources were limited, it was important to integrate programs for underserved populations to the greatest extent possible. The coordination of programs, such as the NHSC and CHCs was seen as more cost-efficient and managerially sound than continuing separate categorical grant programs delivering services to the same population.

A final innovation associated with the RHI was that project grants were to be awarded using a concept called "positive programming." This was a form of outreach by the federal government. Rather than funding those organizations that wrote the best grant proposals, areas with the greatest need were to be selected on the basis of demographic and health status data. The bureau would then provide technical assistance in planning project services and writing proposals to groups in those areas (Interview A, 25 July 1979; Samuels, 1978:165).

In summary, the <u>rural health initiative</u> was

> basically an administrative declaration that first, the rural poor of America were no longer to be second priority, but equal priority based on need. Second, administratively, we were going to find ways to tie together our resources which collectively were still too scarce, so as to maximize them. Third, we were not going to start any huge projects and put two million dollars in one place. Rather, one hundred and fifty thousand dollars in twenty-five places. . . . Lastly, we were going to target projects in the areas of greatest need. (Interview A, 25 July 1979)

After the initial funding of forty-seven RHI projects in fiscal year 1975, the number of grants made to such projects increased rapidly. In fiscal year 1976, 138 RHIs received funding. This number almost doubled the next year to 262 in fiscal year 1977. In fiscal year 1978, 356 RHI projects were funded (S. Rept. 95-860, 1978:10). Thus, the number of funded RHI projects increased more than sevenfold between fiscal years 1975 and 1978.

BUREAU INITIATIVES AND POLITICAL SUPPORT

While the bureau's <u>rural health initiative</u> can be explained as the most rational and equitable way of using scarce resources in a period when the administration did not support funding for health centers, a more direct political consequence was that it increased support for the health center program among important political actors. Its success depended upon a number of factors.

During the early and mid-1970s, members of Congress were interested in the problems of rural poverty and supported the CHC program when it began to address rural needs. According to one source, the health center program would not have survived if it had "continued to be perceived as an urban ghetto program" (Interview B, 17 August 1982).

The National Health Service Corps was initially conceived (in 1970) as a response to the problem of lack of rural health services, and most of the early placements were in rural areas (Redman, 1973; Mullan, 1979:5). Congress also enacted the Rural Health Development Act (P.L. 92-419) in 1972. This legislation required that the secretary of agriculture set goals for rural development in several program areas, including community services, and make an annual report to Congress on progress toward these goals (Martin, 1975:294).

In September 1974, the Senate Appropriations Committee mandated that a five-year rural health service research and demonstration project, the Health [for] Underserved Rural Areas Program (HURA), be established by the Medical Services Administration of the Social and Rehabilitation Service under the Social Security Act (S. Rept. 93-1146, 1974:9). The impetus for this action came from three senators: Warren Magnuson (D–Wash.), Mike Mansfield (D–Mont.), and Norris Cotton (R–N.H.), all from largely rural states. The BCHS worked closely with the Medical Services Administration in implementing the HURA program during its first year. In February 1976 the HURA program was moved into BCHS to be administered along with the RHI by the Office of Rural Health (Interview B, 13 July 1979).

Members of the Senate Appropriations Committee responded enthusiastically to the rural health initiative. The report that accompanied a supplemental appropriations bill for fiscal year 1976 stated that the committee was "pleased to note that 47 rural health projects were initiated in 1975 with CHC funding." The report emphasized the "critical need for centers in medically underserved rural areas" (quoted in *Legislative Status Report,* January 1976:4). In its report on the Department of Labor/DHEW bill for fiscal year 1977, the Senate Appropriations Committee again expressed its pleasure at "the innovative approach the Bureau of Community Health Services is taking in addressing rural health problems" (quoted in NACHC, *Legislative Status Report,* August 1976:4).

The coordination of federal health programs was an additional concern of the Senate Appropriations Committee. In establishing the HURA program, the committee had directed that "programmatic linkages be developed" between HURA projects and several other federal programs—the National Cancer Institute's cancer screening program, the Maternal and Child Health Program, and the Early and Periodic Screening, Diagnosis, and Treatment Program (EPSDT) under Medicaid (Samuels, 1978:165). Coordination was also a central feature of the rural health initiative.

The creation of the RHI program contributed to the view in Congress that the CHC program was a well-managed and productive effort; this belief was crucial to continued congressional support (Interview A, 12 July 1979; Interview A, 25 July 1979). In the early 1970s, program analysts had developed measures of productivity and efficiency (see chapter 4). By the mid-1970s, program monitoring was a central aspect of the operation of the BCHS, and efficiency became a central theme in the discussion of the program by bureau officials in Congress. In 1978, the Senate Committee on Human Resources stated, "One of the successful aspects of the community health center program has been the development of these activities as effective and efficient entities competitive with private providers." The Senate committee also noted that the number of persons served by the program had "significantly increased" by the mid-1970s (S. Rept. 95-860:10–11).

The rural health initiative also made the CHC program "more distributive" (Thompson, 1981:261). The RHI policy involved the establishment of health projects in many areas previously without such projects, thus increasing the number of Congress members with health centers in their districts and improving the potential political effectiveness of the program's constituency (see Arnold, 1979:208–10). In addition, some RHI programs would provide services to low-income white populations in rural areas, whereas the program had been viewed earlier as a program primarily for urban minorities, "a black program" (Interview A, 12 July 1979). This was another way in which the program's constituency was broadened and enlarged.

The rural health initiative was a major change in the nature of the CHC program. It is important to note that this policy shift was developed within the BCHS and "sold" to officials higher up in DHEW (Interview B, 17 August 1982).[1] Bureaucratic actors had initiated a policy that would increase congressional support while operating within an administration that was not supportive of community health centers.

BCHS officials also formulated bureau policies in response to the Ford administration's proposal that block grants to the states replace categorical grant programs in health and to proposals for national health insurance being discussed during the mid-1970s. A 1976 bureau paper discusses the bureau's emphasis on program integration in terms of a strategy called "capacity-building," or the development of service delivery systems in medically underserved areas. It involves integrating primary care resources, maximizing the productivity and efficiency of existing BCHS programs, and establishing new projects in areas where "an independent private sector response, . . . is unlikely. The paper argues that capacity-building would end the duplication of categorical grant programs by establishing an integrated health care delivery system and would provide the institutional structure necessary to implement a national health insurance plan (Rhee, 1976:3–8).

THE URBAN HEALTH INITIATIVE

During fiscal years 1975 and 1976, no new urban health center projects were funded; however, in fiscal year 1977 the BCHS awarded grants for thirty-five "urban health initiatives" (UHIs). The following year the number was increased to sixty (S. Rept. 95-860:10). The basic principles of the rural health initiative were to be applied to urban programs. A large number of projects would be funded, each at a relatively low budget level, "positive programming" would be used, and new primary care efforts would be integrated with both existing federally funded primary care programs and with the provision of secondary care (Interview A, 25 July 1979).

The funding of new urban programs was, in part, a response to pressure from several urban congressmen on the House Appropriations Committee, including Congressmen Rangel (D–N.Y.), Stokes (D–Ohio), and Flood (D–Pa.). Bureau officials believed that it was necessary to "shift the balance" away from an exclusively rural emphasis (Interview B, 17 August 1982). In 1977, there was increased attention to the needs of urban areas by the incoming administration and new UHIs continued to be funded. However, the issue of the allocation of CHC program resources between rural and urban areas was a source of conflict in 1978 when the program came up for reauthorization. (This will be discussed in the next chapter.)

The inauguration of President Jimmy Carter in January 1977 and his appointment of Joseph A. Califano as secretary of DHEW greatly changed the administrative environment of the BCHS. It was far more supportive of health programs for the poor. Yet the larger health policy environment in the late 1970s was very different from that of the mid-1960s, and the BCHS policy initiatives remained central to the health center program during the Carter administration.

The Carter Administration and Community Health Centers

In direct contrast to the Nixon and Ford administrations' attempts to eliminate categorical grant programs and reduce funding for social programs, the Carter administration returned to "the principles of Democratic social programming," including funding categorical grant programs to meet the needs of special populations and centralizing decision making in Washington rather than in the states (Iglehart, 1978:58–59). In addition, President Carter, unlike his Republican predecessors, had political debts to pay to large cities and this had an impact on the kind of health programs initiated by his administration.

The administration's health policies also reflected the experiences, values, and influence within the administration of the secretary of DHEW for its first two and a half years, Joseph Califano. As an official within the Johnson administration, Califano had helped to create the Great Society programs and was sympathetic to programs aimed at low-income populations (Iglehart, 1978:59). Califano's DHEW appointees viewed the provision of services to populations not served by the private sector as a federal responsibility. In contrast to the situation during the Nixon era, many of those in policymaking positions in DHEW during the Carter administration were very supportive of the CHC concept. In fact, the assistant secretary for health, Dr. Julius Richmond, his deputies, Ms. Ruth Hanft and Dr. Joyce Lashof, and the deputy assistant secretary for health planning and evaluation, Dr. Karen Davis, had all been previously involved with the NHC program.

Richmond had served in the Johnson administration and was one of the architects of Head Start (Iglehart, 1978:62). He had also helped to get the first NHC research and demonstration proposal through a screening panel within the Office of Economic Opportunity (Interview, 6 April 1978). Hanft, as an OEO official, was instrumental in developing the first neighborhood health center projects (May et al., 1980A:588). Lashof had been the first project director of a large neighborhood health center in Chicago (Interview, 31 March 1978). Davis was an economist and a senior fellow at the Brookings Institution and had done research on health centers in rural areas of the South (Califano, 1981:93; Davis and Schoen, 1978). "Hanft, Lashof, and Davis [believed] that poor individuals [would] be denied access to quality medical care unless government [created] federal posts to serve them" (Iglehart, 1978:62). In *Health and the War on Poverty* (1978), Davis and her coauthor view neighborhood health centers very positively. They present data showing that health centers are cost-effective models of care and have improved health status.

During Davis's tenure as director of the Office for Planning and Evaluation within the Office of the Secretary of DHEW/DHHS, that office played an advocacy role for the CHC program within the department and the administration.[2] Staff of the Office for Planning, in fact, argued that the BCHS was not expanding the program quickly enough (Interview B, 17 August 1982). This was in direct contrast to the role of the Office for Planning and Evaluation during the Nixon and Ford years (Interview, 18 August 1982). According to one congressional staff person, Davis's focus on the community and migrant health center programs meant that there was "a lot of interest in what the BCHS was doing from the Secretary's Office" (Interview, 18 February 1980). The Carter administration consistently proposed increases in authorizations for these two programs.

The first budget submitted by the Carter administration was a revision of the Ford administration's fiscal year 1978 budget. Funding for almost all of the "discretionary" programs, those other than statutory benefit programs such as Social Security, Medicare, and Medicaid, were increased. While the original budget request for the CHC program for fiscal year 1978 was $215 million, the revised budget request was $229 million. This additional $14 million was part of a special project called Alternatives to Abortion developed by the Carter administration and enacted by Congress in 1978. Thirty-five million dollars would be used to initiate and expand programs that provided sex education, family planning services, pre- and postnatal care, research on attitudes toward contraception, and services to facilitate the adoption of children (NACHC, Legislative Status Report, March/April 1977:1). This program was to deal with an issue important to both Carter and Califano; each had declared their opposition to abortion (Califano, 1981, ch. 2).

The implementation of the Alternatives to Abortion program was designed to emphasize the integration of service delivery in federally funded programs. Neighborhood health centers, maternal and infant centers, and family planning clinics were all to be the sites for these services (NACHC, *Legislative Status Report,* October 1978:6). In 1978, the Carter administration also proposed using community health centers to implement another new proposal, the Child Health Assessment Program (CHAP). This program was to replace the Early Periodic Screening, Diagnosis, and Treatment Program (EPSDT), which provided funding for health screening and treatment of children eligible for Medicaid. The CHAP program would raise the federal matching rate to participating states from 55 to 75 percent, if both screening and treatment were provided for children at "comprehensive health care centers." About a quarter of the total funds authorized for the CHAP program would go to community health centers (NACHC *Legislative Status Report,* 6 November 1980:12).[3] Under the existing EPSDT program, children were often screened but not treated for the conditions that were found (NACHC, *Legislative Status Report,* March/April 1977:2–3).

The first budget developed entirely by the Carter administration was the budget for fiscal year 1979. The health portion of the budget included increases over the fiscal year 1978 budget for community health and mental health centers and other programs providing preventive and primary care services to low-income populations. At the same time it included reductions in the amounts allocated to other PHS programs, such as biomedical research, grants for the education of health professionals, and the repair and maintenance of PHS hospitals. Within the health resources area, financing for physician residency programs in family medicine was increased, as were monies allocated to the National Health Service Corps.

The proposed budget for community health centers in fiscal year 1979 was $39 million more than for the previous year. The centers would be able to serve an additional one million persons; 131 new centers would be funded. During the spring of 1978, the Carter administration requested an additional $50 million for the program. This money was to fund a special "inner city health initiative" as part of a larger program of aid to financially troubled cities. The initiative was to consist of three parts: funds for the conversion of eleven hospital outpatient departments into primary care group practices (a proposal similar to one sponsored by Senator Javits and discussed in chapter 6); grants for four demonstration projects of prepaid capitation plans in public hospitals; and funding for twelve new free-standing UHI projects (NACHC, *Legislative Status Report*, May/June 1978:14–15).

The administration's fiscal year 1979 budget was based on the assumption that its hospital cost containment program would be passed by Congress and implemented, and that the resulting savings of $2 billion would be used to finance the increases for other health programs in the budget (Iglehart, 1978:70). Thus, indirectly, these budget proposals established a competitive relationship between hospitals and health centers, each vying with the other for federal dollars (Schoen, 1978). More direct competition emerged with the introduction of the "Javits amendment" to the legislation reauthorizing the CHC program in 1978. (See chapter 6).

An Analysis of the Urban and Rural Health Initiatives

The community health center program that was expanded by the Carter administration was not, however, the same program that had been funded by OEO and DHEW in the 1960s. Significant policy changes initiated during the Ford administration were continued during the Carter administration.

The BCHS capacity-building strategy involves the integration of not only all federal grant programs in a given community, but also the integration of the private and the public sectors and primary care projects and hospital services. The bureau's *Program Guidance Material* for project grant applications lists seven goals for the RHI. Two of these are the "maximum use of existing health care resources . . . through establishment of linkages between primary, secondary, and tertiary care," and the integration of "primary care delivery that is financially viable, professionally attractive, and able to become self-sustaining." Those receiving RHI grants may be existing providers who will expand their service area, utilize additional manpower, and/or provide a mechanism for the coordination of their services with those of other providers in the area. Applicants for RHI grants must establish projects within a medically underserved area,[4] and create "linkages" with *all* other state and federal health service programs in their community (*BCHS Programs*, 1978:4; BCHS, *Program Guidance Material*, 1978:2–3, 11–13, 16–17).

Both management efficiency and the ultimate self-sufficiency of rural health projects are emphasized. Implementation of the goals of sound management and productivity will be monitored by the bureau's program indicators such as ratios of supporting staff to physicians and proportion of operating expenses that are administrative costs. Projects are expected to "move toward becoming independent" of RHI grant funds. Support for operations of a project will not be provided for more than two years (BCHS, *Program Guidance Material*, 1978:7, 9).

The same themes of coordinating federal resources and developing a health care system linking existing providers are discussed in relation to the UHI. The UHI will also attempt to integrate BCHS program resources; priority in funding will be given to applicants who will use National Health Services Corps personnel to staff their programs. The UHI will help to "develop primary care group practices of health professionals within underserved areas to form the link for patients to an urban health system." The discussion of the UHI, like the RHI, also emphasizes efficiency and economic viability (BCHS, *Program Guidance Material*, 1978:23–24, 28).

It is instructive to compare the UHI concept discussed in bureau publications of the late 1970s to that of the original neighborhood health center model. The majority of OEO-funded NHCs were urban programs. The UHI is different in two important ways.

First, the NHC was to serve as the focus of community development. It was part of the larger War on Poverty and was to be a major *new* community resource, providing jobs and job training, and helping the community to organize itself in new ways. The era in which the UHI was developed was quite different from the

Johnson years. The UHI, conceived in a time of concern about cost containment and the "rational" use of resources, was an effort to coordinate existing resources and/or to have existing providers reach populations that had not previously been served. Thus, one of the examples of a health care system that could be developed with a UHI grant is a satellite clinic of a hospital, using NHSC personnel. Similarly, it is suggested that a group of solo-practice physicians who establish cooperative arrangements and agree to provide primary health care "to the community as a whole" might be eligible for UHI monies. The following is a discussion of a hospital-based UHI project:

> What is envisioned is a community approach to organize a health delivery system in partnership with a hospital, to establish the linkages with ambulatory care and private providers. In this way, the Federal government supports the principal health resources in the community, *rather than imposing an independent provider on the community.* (BCHS, *Program Guidance Material,* 1978:33, emphasis added)

This policy is in clear contrast to the OEO policy of the 1960s in which the neighborhood health center was to be a model for change in the existing health care delivery system.

Second, the thrust of the UHI is to deliver basic "medical" care rather than comprehensive and innovative "health" services. The primary care team members specified in the guidance manual for grant applicants are "family practitioners, pediatricians, internists, nurse practitioners, physician extenders, and dental resources" (BCHS, *Program Guidance Material,* 1978:24). The "essential service" that must be part of an urban health care system are physicians' services, emergency medical services, diagnostic laboratory and radiologic services, available emergency transportation, arrangements for inpatient care, preventive services including prenatal and postpartum care, well-child periodic screening, immunization, family planning services, and preventive dental, eye, and ear care for children. Information and "formal referral arrangements" must be available for "supplemental services," which include transportation, other dental services, mental health services, drug and alcohol abuse programs, nutrition education, social services, health education services, and vision care services (BCHS, *Program Guidance Material*, 1978:31–32). The BCHS refers to "other types of professionals and health advocacy activities" that help patients to establish a system of individual "health maintenance." However, such activities as outreach and health education are clearly not central to the UHI described here:

> The addition of such resources to the urban health system is encouraged; but such additions must be consistent with the responsibility for careful and planned growth based on sound management and financial practices. The core of the system is the group of primary care providers needed to manage the process of patient care. (BCHS, *Program Guidance Material*, 1978:24)

This conceptualization of primary health care reflects the sense of limited resources that characterized health policy in the 1970s. It is in direct contrast to the expansionist 1960s which produced the NHC model.

Those involved in the health center policy network held very different views of the shift away from the original neighborhood health center model. Senator Edward Kennedy and the NACHC were the most concerned that comprehensive services were being limited.

The committee report that accompanied the Senate bill reauthorizing the community health center program in 1978 (S. 2474) expressed satisfaction with the increased efficiency which had been demonstrated by community health centers since 1975 but also cautioned that the program reached less than 10 percent of the medically underserved population, and that only the older centers "are delivering truly comprehensive services" (S. Rept. 95-860:27). In a question submitted to DHEW during the Senate subcommittee hearings on the program reauthorization, Senator Kennedy expressed concern that the new bureau programs were not providing comprehensive services:

> Since 1975 the cost per patient served by Community Health Centers has dropped by 50 percent. This is truly remarkable at a time when

double-digit inflation has characterized the cost of health care services in other sectors. What part of this reduction in cost can be attributed to increased administrative efficiency, and what part results from the fact that of the 574 centers established, only 158 are providing comprehensive services—with the remaining 416 providing little more than the presence of a physician or physician's extender and a very limited range of services.

The response from DHEW was that the 50 percent reduction in cost was a result of both increased efficiency at the older centers (a reduction in administrative costs and an increase in "provider productivity")[5] and "a funding strategy that encouraged an incremental approach to the development of new centers." The incremental approach was that new centers would first provide only "primary" services and later would add "more comprehensive health services" (Senate Hearings, 1978:56).

In testimony before the Senate subcommittee, Dr. Danny K. Davis, the president of the NACHC, stated that reductions in grant levels and the failure to adjust grants for inflation meant that some ongoing programs had had to reduce services, while "supplementary services" were "seldom funded for RHIs or UHIs." He urged that the list of mandated primary care services be expanded to include health education and preventive and outreach services among others, so that the health center model could be maintained (Senate Hearings, 1978:111–12).

Financing Policy: The Limitations of the Community Health Center Policy Network

Davis's reference to the difficulties that the older neighborhood health centers were having in providing comprehensive health services is related to the financing system under which they have had to operate. From the beginning of the program, the assumption was made that health centers would eventually function without grant funds. As discussed in chapter 4, DHEW initiated a policy of self-sufficiency in 1973 that required that health centers recover the maximum amount possible from Medicare, Medicaid, and other sources of funding. This general policy has had the support of the congressional health subcommittees. Members of Congress believed that it was important that NHCs "learn to live in the same third party world as everyone else" (Interview, 11 July 1979). BCHS documents stated that the health systems created by the bureau's capacity-building strategy were also to be self-sustaining. The government's role was to create an independent (private, albeit nonprofit) system which would then be "weaned" from grant dollars. To understand why self-sufficiency was unlikely and the delivery of comprehensive health care services difficult at even the older neighborhood health centers, it is necessary to examine the specific financing mechanisms of the Medicare and Medicaid programs and the underlying politics of financing.

MEDICAID/MEDICARE AND
THE FINANCING OF COMMUNITY HEALTH CENTERS

Medicaid is a federal and state program in which the federal government establishes certain standards and provides a portion of the program funds, while states make decisions about eligibility levels and benefits. Federal regulations require that individuals receiving benefits under the Aid to Families with Dependent Children (AFDC) program must be covered by state Medicaid programs. However, each state decides on the extent to which other groups in the population are covered, including recipients of public assistance programs other than AFDC and the "medically indigent" not receiving public assistance. As a result of both initial state decisions on eligibility requirements and cutbacks imposed in response to program costs, 1978 estimates were that only one-third to one-half of the population with incomes below the poverty level were covered by the Medicaid program at any one time. In addition, many individuals served by community health centers had incomes above the poverty level but could not afford health care (Davis and Schoen, 1978:51–54, 193).

Although eligibility requirements are simpler and benefits are uniform across states, there are problems with the federal Medicare program as well. Medicare regulations provide that individuals receiving outpatient services under Medicare Part B must pay a monthly premium. If these payments lapse, patients must reenroll in the program only during certain specified periods. This procedure acts as a barrier to the continuous enrollment of elderly persons in Medicare and therefore to the recovery of Medicare payments by a community health center or other provider of ambulatory care (Anderson et al., 1976:65). These barriers to the reimbursement for health care affect hospitals as well as CHCs. However, in very significant ways Medicare and Medicaid are biased against health centers as providers of care and against the delivery of community health services.

Medicare did not recognize neighborhood health centers as reimbursable providers until 1973 and has only granted recognition to centers with very sophisticated accounting procedures. In the case of Medicaid, outpatient care provided in hospital clinics is one of the mandatory services that the federal government requires states to provide to Medicaid patients, while care at CHCs is considered to be in an optional service category ("clinic services"). States are not required to provide it under the Medicaid program. A 1977 study of Medicaid reimbursement found that only twenty-two states and the District of Columbia recognized CHCs as "clinics" and reimbursed them for services provided (Kalmans, 1977:2–3). A 1981 update of this study (the last such study done as of 1986), found only a slight increase in the number of states that reimbursed health centers as clinics (NACHC Medicaid Study, 1981:9).

Even when community health centers are reimbursed as clinics under a state Medicaid plan, they are not likely to be reimbursed for all of the services that they provide to their patients. The 1977 study found that "the 'clinic services' category has been used primarily to reimburse traditional medical and dental services (including lab and X-ray), and some non-traditional services, such as family planning and EPSDT, that are mandatory Medicaid services." For example, only five of the twenty-two states that recognize CHCs as clinics reimbursed them for outreach services. Six states reimbursed for counseling services and seven provided reimbursement for health education. Only the District of Columbia reimbursed centers for environmental services (Kalmans, 1977:12). The 1981 *NACHC Medicaid Study* found this situation essentially unchanged (12, 21).

In spite of these facts, there has been pressure on health centers from both Congress and DHEW since the early 1970s to increase the proportion of their revenues from third-party funds. As health centers responded to this pressure, they were forced to cut back on nonreimbursable services, those very services that, some health center advocates argue, are responsible for centers having "a positive impact on health status of the poor and their health resources utilization" (Woodward, 1981:5), and that made them unique as health care providers.[6] In New York City, for instance, health centers attempted to reduce cost by decreasing staff "in 'the fringe areas' such as transportation, personnel, supportive services and outreach. At the same time attempts were made to maintain staffing levels in the areas of direct services by health care providers" (Clark, 1979:227). Direct medical services are those most likely to be reimbursed by Medicaid and Medicare.

A parallel phenomenon occurs with the reimbursement of nontraditional health care providers—nurse practitioners, physician's assistants, and family health workers. As we saw in chapter 3, NHCs pioneered in the integration of such workers in the delivery of health services. Medicare and Medicaid do not reimburse for the services of family health workers. In the case of Medicare, nurse practitioners, nurse/midwives, and physician's assistants were not reimbursed for their services at all until the passage of the Rural Health Clinic Services Act in 1977. However, that legislation applies only to rural health centers (Rosenbaum, 1979:142). Sixteen state Medicaid plans reimbursed health services provided by nurse practitioners, midwives, or physician's assistants in 1977. This was slightly less than a third of all states with Medicaid programs. However, only five of these states allowed separate reimbursement for the services of such nonphysician primary care providers if a physician was not present at the health facility at all times (Kalmans, 1977:15). The 1981 study found that while the total number of states that reimbursed for the services of non-physician primary care practitioners had increased to twenty-six, the number of states that reimbursed for the independent services of such practitioners, other than in a rural health clinic, remained the same—five (NACHC Medicaid Study, 1981:13).

In New York City, the consequences of nonreimbursement of the family health worker by Medicare and Medicaid, combined with the external pressure to reduce overall center costs, resulted in a total decrease of thirty-nine family health workers in seven centers between 1974 and 1977. Five New York City health centers reduced their expenditures for this category of health workers by 50 percent in those years. The reduction in the number of such workers meant a reduction in preventive services such as health education and outreach (Clark, 1979:233–34). A similar phenomenon occurred in the 1980s when Reagan administration policies resulted in large reductions in health center funding.

In addition to their impact on the quality of care provided at health centers, these policies are illogical from a cost-containment perspective. In terms of actual cost (not the proportion of cost reimbursed by third-party payments), nonphysician primary care practitioners are far less expensive than are physicians. Similarly, preventive and primary care services will in the long term reduce overall costs by reducing the number of hospitalizations. In spite of this, cost containment efforts have generally taken the form of decreases in primary care services for low-income populations rather than in overall reductions of more costly inpatient services in hospitals.[7]

THE POLITICS OF HEALTH FINANCING
The health center case makes clear that innovation in health care delivery cannot be maintained without corresponding alterations in financing structures.[8] Health institutions that provide preventive and comprehensive primary care are difficult to maintain within a reimbursement system that operates to support estab-

lished modes of high-technology, hospital-based medical treatment. However, decisions about health financing are produced by a process in which advocates of community-based care have far less influence than do traditional providers such as hospitals. Disparities in political resources are magnified by the fragmentation of the health policy process.

Because many of the policy decisions about Medicaid eligibility and benefits are made at the state level, health center advocates must divide their time and political resources between the state and federal levels. Although this is also true of nursing homes and hospitals, such institutions are more likely to have greater total political resources than are health centers. Federal financing policy is made by a different set of political actors than those involved in authorizing and appropriating grant funds for categorical health programs. The Medicaid and Medicare programs are within the jurisdiction of the House Ways and Means Committee and the Senate Finance Committees. These programs are administered by the Health Care Financing Administration (HCFA) within the Department of Health and Human Services (DHHS). Again, this means that political resources must be stretched. A long-time advocate for the health center program noted that in the early 1980s the members and staffs of the House Ways and Means Committee and the Senate Finance Committee were generally less informed about the CHC program than were members and staff of the health authorizing and appropriations committees. This is a case in which the fragmentation of the American political system operates as a barrier to effective influence by newly emergent interests because such interests must act in several policy arenas at the same time.

During the Carter administration this barrier was breached when the administration itself initiated a change in financing policy that would have reversed some of the bias of the Medicaid program against CHCs. As part of the budget recommendations for fiscal year 1981, the administration proposed that clinic services become mandatory services under Medicaid and that states be required to recognize "organized primary care providers," including community health centers and migrant health centers as "clinics" under this category (NACHC, *Legislative Status Report,* August 1979:11; Communication, NACHC, 22 November 1983).

The provision to mandate state recognition of health centers for Medicaid reimbursement passed both the House and Senate, but a conference committee was unable to resolve the differences between the Senate and House on total budget expenditures for the Medicaid and Medicare programs (NACHC, *Legislative Status Report,* 6 November 1980:13). The mandating of specific providers under Medicaid would commit additional expenditures to the Medicaid programs and there was opposition within the conference committee to this precedent (Communication, NACHC, 8 November 1983). Congress, facing a worsening economy and a large budget deficit, was attempting to meet budget ceilings for all existing programs in order to limit spending. The final legislation agreed to by the conference committee reduced spending for Medicare and Medicaid by $975 million (*National Journal,* 13 September 1980: 1531, 29 November 1980:2047). It is ironic that just when the health center policy network had reached a level of strength that made such a health financing policy initiative possible, the larger political environment of budgetary constraint precluded its enactment.

6

The Health Center
Policy Network

Resource Allocation and Conflict

While Bureau of Community Health Services officials were initiating actions to assure support for community health centers from key congressional authorizing and appropriations committees, the National Association of Community Health Centers, Inc. an organization established in 1971 as the National Association of Neighborhood Health Centers, was developing as a national voice for the centers. Beginning in 1975, the national association focused resources on the policy process and its effect on health centers. In addition, the broadening of the constituency of health center programs was paralleled by the broadening of the membership of the national association.

The national association was not a central participant in the process that resulted in the enactment of legislation authorizing the CHC program in 1975, but it was a highly visible actor in the reauthorization process three years later. By 1978, a policy network supporting the program, consisting of bureaucrats, subcommittee members and staff, and an interest group, was clearly functioning. This chapter describes the political development of the national association during the 1970s and then examines the functioning of the health center policy network in the policy formulation process in 1978.

The Expansion of the Health Center Policy Network: The Political Development of the National Association

As described in chapter 4, DHEW decided to consolidate funding for technical assistance to health centers in 1973 and to have it coordinated at the national level. The New York Association of Neighborhood Health Centers and the Massachusetts League of Neighborhood Health Centers had agreed to become subcontractors of the National Association of Neighborhood Health Centers, which had initially been funded by OEO rather than DHEW. The Massachusetts League was to provide technical assistance to health centers in the New England region; the New York Association was to assume this role for New York State, New Jersey, Puerto Rico, and the Virgin Islands, and later for the other Middle Atlantic states. Southern, western, and midwestern associations were to be established as technical assistance units for those areas of the country. The national association was to continue to run national conferences and institutes for training and disseminating information, but "hands-on" assistance with specific health center management problems would be handled at the regional level (Interview A, 17 August 1982). Grants to the regional associations for training and other service functions continued until June 1980 when the officials of the BCHS decided that these regional technical assistance units were less effective than were outside consulting firms (Interview B, 17 August 1982).

In recent years, new groups without wealthy members, such as consumer groups, have been financed by grants and contracts from government and foundations (Loomis and Cigler, 1983:15, 22; Walker, 1983). During the 1970s, the National Association of Neighborhood (Community) Health Centers received grants from the BCHS to carry out a number of specific projects. The services provided through these grants were available to all federally funded health centers, whether or not they were members of the national association. At the same time, the national association has always had a dues system and has financed a separate set of activities, including conferences, from this source of funds. Up until 1977, dues were $500 per organizational member per year. In 1977, this flat rate was replaced with a sliding scale dues structure ranging from $100 to $1,500 per organizational member, depending on the size of the program's budget (Communication, NACHC, 8 November 1983).[1] The large differences in the size of health center projects in the late 1970s was, of course, the result of the RHI policy begun in 1975.

Once the New York and Massachusetts organizations merged with the national association, conflict over the functions and goals of the new organization developed between two factions of its leadership: those from New York and Massachusetts, and others primarily from the West and Midwest. The eastern groups had worked actively with their congressional delegations in Washington. Both areas had relatively large numbers of centers and sympathetic congressmen and senators—Edward Kennedy and Edward Brooke in Massachusetts, Jacob Javits in New York. In 1973, for example, the staff of the New York Association of Neighborhood Health Centers responded to the DHEW policy requiring health center "self-sufficiency" by contacting centers all over the country and urging them to organize and work with their local congressional delegation against the threat of program defunding (Interview, 2 July 1979). The eastern group believed that a primary function of the national association should be to inform members of Congress about health center programs. The western leaders saw the function of the association as one of "community development" and "education," providing skills and training to staff and board members of individual centers.

This conflict over the direction of the national association was fought out in contests for official positions in the organization in 1974 and 1975. In the 1974 annual election, the candidate from the West won the presidency. The next year, however, the candidate from the eastern faction became the president-elect. The latter election was won as a result of an internal coalition-building strategy. Most of the representatives of migrant health centers, which had recently joined the organization, voted for the candidate of the eastern faction of the association. In that same year, it was determined that a seat on the association's executive board would go to a representative from a migrant health center each year.

These events have had two significant consequences for the association's direction since 1975. First, those leaders of the association concerned with the importance of educating Congress and the public about the value of CHCs have held a majority of seats on the executive board and the organization has developed its capacity to perform that function. Second, the inclusion of migrant health centers as members of the national association has been followed by a continuous expansion of the association's constituency and by a process of coalition-building with other organizations. This has paralleled the expansion of the CHC program.

In 1975 the position of "policy analyst" was created and was assumed by a former staff member of a congressional committee. In that same year the association began publishing a monthly *Legislative Status Report.* This newsletter informed the association's membership of legislative developments and administrative actions related to CHC programs in particular and health policy issues in general. In 1982, the *Legislative Status Report* was replaced by a biweekly information newsletter, *Washington Update.*

Beginning in 1975, the association has held an annual "Policy and Issues Forum" in Washington, D.C., for the purpose of educating health center representatives about current legislative issues affecting their programs and encouraging discussion with members of Congress on these issues (Interview A, 12 July 1979). In 1976 the Department of Policy Analysis was created. By 1981 there were three associate policy analysts working with the director of the department, the individual who had been the association's first policy analyst. By 1983 this group had increased to four (Communication, NACHC, 7 November 1983).

Until 1975, the majority of health center grants went to urban programs. The membership of the national association consisted primarily of urban health centers in predominantly black areas. The national association's first reaction to the bureau's implementation of the rural health initiative policy was negative. Centers were concerned that existing programs could not be funded adequately if limited resources were allocated to large numbers of new programs. The association's position was that a larger number of rural centers should be funded, but that this should be done slowly (Interview, 16 August 1982). Beginning with the incorporation of migrant health centers into the association, however, the organization's constituency has been broadened to include both rural and urban centers and centers whose patients are primarily Hispanic, native American, Oriental, or white, as well as black.

In 1979, rural health organizations participated in the association's Policy and Issues Forum in Washington, D.C. At the opening session of the Fifth Annual Forum in 1980, representatives from two organizations concerned with the health of native Americans discussed the mutual concerns of their membership and the national association. The 1980 forum was sponsored in cooperation with the National Rural Primary Care Association and the American Indian Health Care Association, and sessions were held on rural health services, Indian health services and black lung clinics. In 1980, the national association established the position of director of rural affairs (NACHC *News,* January–February, 1980:4). The Department of Rural Affairs provided education, technical assistance, and other services to people and programs in medically underserved areas and worked with other organizations concerned with health issues in rural areas (NACHC pamphlet, 1980:10). In 1982, when it was decided that rural concerns could be effectively addressed by the functional departments of the association, the Department of Rural Affairs was abolished.

In a 1980 pamphlet, the national association described itself as "a broad-based coalition," and the "national advocate for the many ambulatory health care delivery programs across the country providing health services to the medically underserved." These included "community health centers, neighborhood health centers, family health centers, migrant health programs, rural health programs, Indian health programs, and maternal and infant care programs." A document on the reorganization of the national association, written about 1981, stated that one aspect of the mission of the organization is "to become recognized as ('the') national organization representing ambulatory care." Included as potential group members of the association were "Family Planning Programs," "Mental Health Centers," and "Prepayment Programs," in addition to the BCHS programs listed earlier (NACHC, "Restructuring," n.d.:1, 2). The association was thus claiming a wide variety of ambulatory care programs as its constituency. It continued to have this inclusive orientation through the 1980s. In an April 1986 information sheet, the NACHC is described as an advocate for "community-based health care programs" and "a strong national voice for primary health care" (NACHC, "Organizational Membership Benefits").

Loomis and Cigler (1983) distinguish between two types of groups that have developed as a result of the greater involvement of government in social and welfare policy since the 1960s: "recipients" and "service deliverers." Recipient groups are mass-based organizations such as the American Association of Retired Persons, while service deliverers are trade and professional associations working in specific service areas, such as geriatrics. They suggest that there may be conflict between the interests of service deliverers and recipients in a particular policy area. The NACHC is primarily an organization of service deliverers, yet the mandate for consumer involvement in local health center decisions is incorporated into the policy process of the national association.

The primary category of association membership is organizational membership, consisting of health programs that deliver services. There is, however, also a category of individual membership in the organization, open to all those who support its goals. All officers and committee members must be individual members. As a "trade" association, the NACHC offers various material benefits to its member organizations. The association sponsors a Primary Care Malpractice Insurance Program with special rates, arranges technical assistance for member organizations, and provides a wide range of educational and training programs for health center administrators, clinical staff, and consumers at institutes, conferences, and workshops. In 1979, the association joined with five other organizations (the American Group Practice Association, the Free Standing Ambulatory Surgical Association, the Group Health Association of America, Inc., the Medical Group Management Association, and the American College Health Association) to form the Accreditation Association for Ambulatory Health Care, a nonprofit corporation. This group replaced the ambulatory care section of the Joint Commission on the Accreditation of Hospitals (AAAHC, pamphlet, n.d.).

Although health centers are clearly health care providers, they are an alternative form of ambulatory health care delivery to the solo-practice physician and the hospital outpatient clinic. As political actors, they generally have far fewer resources than do organized physicians or hospitals. In addition, many of the project directors and other staff at health centers are members of minority ethnic groups and/or women, categories of individuals who were traditionally barred from administrative and managerial positions in the health care system. While the national association is a service delivery group representing new interests within the health care system, it also has a decision-making structure that includes service recipients.

The ultimate decision-making body of the organization is the House of Delegates, which holds annual meetings to establish policy and programs, review budgets, and elect the officers of the association. Between meetings, the House of Delegates assigns responsibility for specific policy decisions to a board of directors and an executive committee consisting of the eight elected officers of the association. Each organizational (health center) member of the association has four votes in the House of Delegates. Two of the four are those of consumer representatives from the health center. Thus, 50 percent of the votes in the House of Delegates are cast by consumers. In addition, one of the eight elected officers of the association is a consumer representative.

The Functioning of the Health Center Policy Network

The events related to the reauthorization of the CHC program in 1978 illustrate three important characteristics of the health center policy network. First, they indicate that the national association was far more central to the policy formulation process in 1978 than it had been in 1975. Second, in 1978, in contrast to 1975, the NHC program was an established categorical grant program with support from both Congress and the administration. At this point in the program's development, issues related to the allocation of resources surfaced. Interests represented were rural and urban constituencies, regional interests (the Northeast versus other areas) and hospitals versus free-standing health centers. Interest groups that had not previously participated in the formulation of community health center policy became involved. One of the characteristics of distributive policy is that disputes are resolved through negotiations between members of a subgovernment and political actors outside the subgovernment; "higher authorities" are not involved. Such was the case here.

Finally, the resolution of the conflict over the Javits amendment, a proposal to fund hospital-based primary care centers, makes it clear that groups representing new interests in the policy process (and relatively disadvantaged sectors of the society) have limited political influence when they must battle directly with more established groups over the allocation of resources.

PROGRAM REAUTHORIZATION:
THE NATURE OF THE ISSUE
P.L. 94-63, enacted in 1975, carefully described the services to be provided by CHCs, the relationship of the centers to DHEW, and the governing structure within the centers. The program had been authorized through fiscal year 1977 and was extended for an additional year by the Health Services Extension Act of 1977 (P.L. 95-83). Thus, CHC legislation was again on the congressional agenda in 1978.

As in 1975, the reauthorization of the health center program in

1978 was not a controversial issue. In fact, congressional staff who worked on the bill in 1978 reported the same lack of interest that was reported earlier. One of the professional staff members who drafted the Senate bill said that in 1978, community health centers "were not a hotly contested item" (Interview A, 10 July 1979). In response to a probe asking whether groups other than the NACHC had contacted the Senate subcommittee about the 1978 legislation, another Senate staffer said, "I don't think anybody else cares" (Interview B, 10 July 1979). On the House side, a staff member who had worked on the legislation called it "the kind of issue it was hard to get members to come to because it wasn't controversial; . . . it was difficult to get people in the room for the hearing and for the markup" (Interview, 18 February 1980).[2] The reauthorization of CHC legislation was routine congressional business.

The health center program had the support of all of the members of the Subcommittee on Health and Scientific Research of the Senate Committee on Human Resources (Interviews A and B, 10 July 1979). The committee expressed its satisfaction with the "achievements" of the program and the "improvement in management and efficiency." It viewed the community health center program as "an outstanding model for the delivery of comprehensive health care" and "has reaffirmed its commitment to the health care delivery concepts which are embodied in this program" (S. Rept. 95-860: 27–28).

Subcommittee members disagreed on two issues. These were the primary care proposal, which would have waived the governing board requirement for hospitals receiving CHC funds, and the level of authorization for the program. One Republican senator, also a member of the Senate Appropriations Committee, played the role of "fiscal conservative," and argued that there should be a closer relationship between authorization and appropriation levels for all programs. Other Republicans and a Democrat who also sat on the appropriations committee supported him, and the subcommittee lowered the original amount of funding proposed (Interviews A and B, 10 July 1979).

The Senate committee recommended that the CHC program be reauthorized for five years at the following funding levels: $330 million for fiscal year 1979, $362 million for fiscal year 1980, $397.2 million for fiscal year 1981, $435.5 million for fiscal year 1982, and $478.5 million for fiscal year 1983 (NACHC, *Legislative Status Report,* May–June 1978:1–2; July 1978:12). In opening the Senate subcommittee hearings in February 1978, Senator Edward Kennedy stated that the subcommittee's recommendation that community health centers be reauthorized for a five-year period was an expression of the belief that the program had proven itself and should no longer be regarded as having probationary status (Senate Hearings, 1978:2).

On the House side, the program was supported by the Democratic majority on the Subcommittee on Health and the Environment of the Interstate and Foreign Commerce Committee and by some of the subcommittee's Republican members. Two of the Republican subcommittee members, along with three other members of the full House Committee on Interstate and Foreign Commerce, wrote a separate statement of views on the Health Center Amendments of 1978 in which they attacked the authorization levels contained in the bill (H.R. 12460) as "an exercise in economic fantasy" (H. Rept. 95-1186:106). They were also critical of the fact that the original House bill, introduced in January 1978 as H.R. 10553, was reported from the health subcommittee as two separate bills, the Health Services Amendments of 1978 (H.R. 12370) and the Health Centers Amendments of 1978 (H.R. 12460) in order, they said, to reduce the psychological impact of the total authorization (H. Rept. 1186:107). Within the subcommittee, this group never had "much of a voice," because Congressman Rogers "always had enough votes to outnumber them" (Interview, 18 February 1980).

The House committee proposed a three-year reauthorization at $366 million for fiscal year 1979, $436 million for fiscal year 1980, and $527 million for fiscal year 1981. (NACHC, *Legislative Status Report,* May–June 1978:1–2; July 1978:1–2). These amounts were well above those authorized by the Senate, in part because the

House included funding in its authorization for the Inner City Health Initiative proposed by the president and for new programs in rural areas (H. Rept. 1186:15).

P.L. 95-626 passed both houses of Congress and was signed by President Carter in October 1978. It authorized the community health center program for three years, at $348 million for fiscal year 1979, $405 million for fiscal year 1980, and $472 million for fiscal year 1981 (NACHC, *Legislative Status Report*, October 1978:2). (These amounts did *not* include monies authorized for the planning and operation of "hospital-affiliated primary care centers," which will be discussed below.) This legislation increased the authorization for the program substantially, since only $261.8 million had been authorized for fiscal year 1978 (NACHC, *Legislative Status Report*, July–August 1977:2) and only $247 million had actually been appropriated for the program in that year (House Rept. 95-1186:8). According to one of the House staff members who worked on the legislation, CHCs were given "a very strong congressional mandate in '78." Aside from the authorization of the hospital-affiliated centers, P.L. 95-626 did not make any major changes in the program. "I consider what we did to be basically tinkering with the statute—trying to adjust some problems that we saw" (Interview, 18 February 1980).

CONFLICT WITHIN THE POLICY NETWORK:
URBAN/RURAL EQUITY

One of the two major controversial issues within the health center policy network during the 1978 reauthorization process was that of the relative allocation of resources to urban and rural programs. This issue was discussed at several points in the hearings held on the health center program by both the Senate and House health subcommittees.

In a report on the RHI and HURA projects submitted to the Senate subcommittee, Rural America, an organization established "to assure rural people equity in the formulation and implementation of public policies and programs" (Senate Hearings, 1978:183), asked that the RHI program be "protected" through the passage of specific legislation authorizing RHIs. "In an uncertain political environment, where efforts to meet urban needs have frequently taken precedence over rural needs, the RHI could easily come to an abrupt end" (Senate Hearings, 1978:198–99). In testimony before the Senate subcommittee, Dr. Lorin Kerr, director of the Department of Occupational Health for the United Mine Workers and a member of the Steering Committee of the Rural Health Council of Rural America, cited the rural-urban "imbalance" in health center programs (see chapter 5) and urged that the secretary of DHEW be required to assure that 40 percent of all monies appropriated for the planning and operation of CHCs be used for rural programs (Senate Hearings, 1978:158).

Senator Richard Schweicker (R–Pa.) was concerned about the needs of medically underserved rural areas and of migrant workers throughout the period of the consideration of the health center legislation (Interviews A and B, 10 July 1979). He had introduced a separate bill that addressed the issue of "the imbalance of resources between urban and rural areas" and the "special needs of rural areas." During the Senate floor debate, Schweicker noted that his state, Pennsylvania, had more rural citizens than any other state in the country (*CR*, 29 September 1978:516558). Democratic Senator William Hathaway of Maine, another rural state, asked several questions of DHEW officials about the "urban bias" in the administration of the CHC program (Senate Hearings, 1978:24, 92, 94).

During the House subcommittee hearings, representatives of a rural clinic in West Virginia testified on the need for more money for rural programs, and Dr. Edward Martin, the director of the BCHS, Congressmen Richard Ottinger of Westchester (D–N.Y.) and Dr. Tim Lee Carter (R–Tenn.) discussed funding priorities. The issue was how program allocations should be made when both isolated rural areas and "pockets" within rich metropolitan counties such as Westchester were in great need of health services (House Hearings, 1978A:156–57, 302).

P.L. 95-626 contains a provision that directs the secretary of DHEW to approve grants for CHC in such a way that "the ratio of the medically underserved populations in rural areas which may be expected to use the services provided by such centers is not less than two to three or greater than three to two." This provision that new grant monies should be allocated so that not more than 60 percent or less than 40 percent of the population served should be rural, and vice versa, was originally part of the House, but not the Senate, bill (NACHC, *Legislative Status Report,* May–June 1978:3–4). However, the Senate report (95-860) accompanying S. 2474 stated that "the committee expects that over the next five years equivalent services will be provided to equal numbers of urban and rural medically underserved populations through the programs in this act" (S. Rept. 95-860:18).

The House provision on the rural-urban allocation formula was drafted by two of the subcommittee's staff members. During the period when the CHC reauthorizing legislation was being considered, the Carter administration had proposed that additional funds be appropriated to start new projects in urban areas. House subcommittee staff "were concerned" that the administration intended to reverse its policy of funding new programs in rural areas. They also knew that Dr. Carter of Tennessee, the ranking Republican on the subcommittee, would be disturbed by this prospect. The staff drafted the provision with 60/40 urban/rural ratios and it was accepted by Rogers and Carter and then the rest of the committee. This provision was, in a sense, the House subcommittee's affirmative response to the bureau's rural health initiative (Interview, 18 February 1980).

The allocation of resources to urban areas, especially northeastern cities, was also one aspect of the major controversy related to the CHC legislation: the proposal to provide health center funds to reorganize hospital outpatient departments. Before turning to this proposal, I will outline several of the noncontroversial new provisions of the 1978 legislation and the role of the national association in their formulation.

NEW PROPOSALS:
THE ROLE OF THE NATIONAL ASSOCIATION
Several of the modifications in the health center legislation were suggested by representatives of individual health centers or of the NACHC. These provisions attempted to redress the inequities faced by CHCs as compared to other providers, such as hospitals or HMOs, and to expand the type of services that could be provided by the centers.

Under P.L. 95-626, health centers would be allowed to retain income generated by increased efficiency. If patient fees and reimbursement collected from third parties exceeded reasonable projections for the year, the center could use at least 50 percent of such income to increase the number of persons served or the number of services offered by the center, to improve managerial capacity, to construct new facilities, to modernize existing sites, or to establish a fund to be used for conversion to a prepayment system (NACHC, *Legislative Status Report,* October 1978:3). In testimony presented to the Senate and House subcommittees, representatives of the NACHC argued that health centers should be allowed to use revenues generated by efficient management for improvements and expansion as did other health institutions. "The present system," according to the testimony before the Senate subcommittee, "reinforces a 'spend it or lose it' mentality, dependence on DHEW and a feeling of transience" (Senate Hearings, 1978:13). Both the Senate and House bills included this incentive provision; both committee reports discussed it as a means of encouraging managerial efficiency and the recovery of third party payments by the centers (H. Rept. 95-1186:13; S. Rept. 95-860:29–30).

The national association had also proposed that at least 5 percent of the funds appropriated to migrant and community health centers be available for renovation and/or construction of physical plants. It was argued that health centers must not appear to be second-class institutions, and that "adequate facilities imply a permanence and a commitment to community health centers as important parts of the total health care system. Lack of permanent facilities has led providers, patients, and the general public to regard community health centers as temporary." It was also noted that other types of institutions, hospitals in particular, had received most of the construction money allocated by the federal government under the Hill-Burton program (Senate Hearings, 1978:113). This recommendation did not become a separate part of the legislation, but the monies retained through the incentive provision can be used for construction and renovation of facilities.

Another provision of P.L. 95-636 modified the categories of services mandated by the 1975 legislation. It will be recalled that P.L. 94-63 created two types of services to be provided by CHCs: primary and supplementary services. The Carter administration did not propose any changes in these categories (House Hearings, 1978A:187), but the NACHC urged that some of the supplementary services be designated "primary" services and therefore mandatory, in order to preserve the "community and migrant health center model"; in addition, according to the association, all centers should be funded at levels high enough to provide all of these services (Senate Hearings, 1978:111–12).

This was not done. Instead, P.L. 95-636 created yet another category of services called "priority supplementary services" and required that each applicant assess the need for these services and for environmental services in its catchment area as part of its grant application. If funding for a specific service was not approved, the secretary of DHEW was required to state the reasons for this decision in writing. Priority supplementary services included home health services, dental services, health education, and other social services that would facilitate the use of primary health services. An example of such a service would be the employment of bilingual staff in an area where a large proportion of residents spoke little English (NACHC, *Legislative Status Report,* October 1978:3).

Both the Senate and House bills contained this type of provision and both committees discussed the need to recognize unique local conditions in the determination of services offered. The Senate committee found that "more attention should be given to defining the specific mix of services needed in individual communities." While "public health and preventive services are the most important means of protecting and improving health," certain of these services may not be "appropriate" to an individual health center for various reasons (S. Rept. 95-860:28). The House committee also wished to provide for "greater local flexibility" in the determination of services available at each center (H. Rept. 95-1186:9). This new legislative provision was written in response to the complaints of individual health centers. It was intended to create a "better balance" in the relationship of the health centers to DHEW, to provide communities "a little additional leverage in identifying their problems and not having some regional office person say, 'our policy guidelines say that we're not funding pharmacies this year so you can't have a pharmacy.' There might not be a pharmacy for fifty miles" (Interview, 18 February 1980).

This same concern with enabling local communities to make independent determinations about their own health services needs was reflected in another legislative provision that authorized special funds for technical assistance to local community groups to be provided by private nonprofit or state organizations. This was of special interest to one of the House subcommittee staff members who had worked with a community group in the rural South. That group had planned and operated four health centers, but in this staff person's view, had not received adequate "preoperational technical assistance" from the DHEW regional office.

Clearly, by 1978 the Senate and House health subcommittees were responding to needs articulated by the health centers themselves. A network of relationships similar in many ways to the traditional subgovernment had been created. However, even within this policy network, CHCs did not enjoy the kind of influence typical of interest groups with abundant political resources. This is seen most clearly in the case of the Javits proposal, an attempt to use health center monies to support innovation in hospital outpatient departments.

The Javits Provision:
Hospital Affiliated Primary Care Centers

THE ORIGIN OF THE PRIMARY CARE CENTER BILL
During the winter of 1978, the staff of Senator Jacob Javits, the ranking Republican on the Senate Health Subcommittee, drafted a brief amendment to the health center legislation that would allow hospitals to be eligible for CHC funding. The impetus for this amendment came from hospital officials in New York State who had long complained to Senator Javits that although they wanted to apply for funding under the health center legislation, the governing board requirement made it impossible for them to do so. As legal corporations, they argued, they could not also have independent governing boards. The "Javits amendment" would have exempted hospitals from this provision (Interview B, 10 July 1979).

The New York State hospitals were concerned about two problems: the fragmentation of ambulatory care services and the deficits incurred in their outpatient departments. The state of New York's "ghetto medicine" program was aimed at these problems and it seemed logical to attempt to get the federal government involved in a similar way (Interview C, 25 July 1979). The "ghetto medicine" program (officially called the New York City Ambulatory Care Program in that city) began operating in 1969. It provided state and city funding to subsidize the operation of outpatient departments and emergency rooms in certain voluntary hospitals. The "ghetto medicine" program was the "political model" for the Javits amendment.

The original purpose of the legislation authorizing the "ghetto medicine" program was to enable local health departments to establish clinics providing general medical care in rural and inner-city areas that lacked adequate health services. To minimize opposition, the New York State Health Department officials underplayed the plan to establish publicly funded "neighborhood health facilities," because the provision of direct care by health departments challenged the existing turf arrangements between the public and private sectors. This conscious political strategy appears to have worked, since the two short 1968 amendments to the Public Health Laws of New York State that authorized the program were passed without debate. It was hoped that these health centers would be financed primarily from Medicaid monies so that the state and local government subsidies to the program would be small.

Although "ghetto medicine" programs were established in six other counties, the largest part of the funding went to the New York City program. Originally, the New York City Department of Health planned to contract with voluntary hospitals to provide medical services in Department of Health district health centers. However, in both 1968 and 1969 the New York state legislature made major reductions in the funding of the Medicaid program. Reimbursement rates to hospitals were frozen. Voluntary hospitals in the state attempted to persuade Governor Rockefeller to increase funding to them (Jonas, 1977B:193–95). Some hospitals threatened to close their outpatient departments (Parker, 1973:11). Rockefeller interpreted the "ghetto medicine" legislation broadly and provided $6 million in 1969 for contracts between the New York City Health Department and the voluntary hospitals for the provision of outpatient services in these hospitals. Institutions participating in the program were required to meet certain standards aimed at providing "comprehensive," "family-oriented" health care, and an advisory board with a consumer majority was to be established at each hospital receiving these funds (Jonas, 1977B:196–207).

Neither New York City Health Department clinics nor municipal hospitals participated in the program during most of its existence (NYS–HSM, 1979B:1–20). It was not until its tenth year, when the program had contracted to less than half of its highest annual budget, that grants went to five municipal hospitals, five ambulatory care providers not based in hospitals, and three community health centers, in addition to thirteen voluntary hospitals (NYS–HSM, 1980:42). A 1979 evaluation of the program done by a management consulting firm concluded that the program's impact could not be measured and recommended that the program continue only until alternative policies to provide care for the medically indigent could be developed. The program's goals, the evaluation report said, are "highly diverse," with some participants viewing it as "a deficit funding mechanism," others as "a model hospital ambulatory care program," still others as "a mechanism for supporting fiscally troubled institutions" (NYS–HSM, 1979A:2, 6–7).

The political history of the "ghetto medicine" program illustrates two important themes in the politics of primary care. First, it indicates historical continuity with the earlier efforts (discussed in chapter 2) to provide publically funded comprehensive ambulatory care. It demonstrates the extreme caution which advocates of public health services still used in 1969 in placing such issues on the governmental agenda. The legislation was brief and somewhat ambiguous, came up at the end of the legislative session, and was called "ghetto medicine" to emphasize that low-cost or free health services would be provided only in areas with few private practitioners (Jonas, 1977B:194, 205).

An examination of this case also illustrates the power of voluntary hospitals at the state level, in this case, in New York. A program originally conceived as a "health centers" program was quickly converted into a program that funded voluntary hospitals. One observer comments, "Here is a case of a law having a vast potential for change slipping onto the statutes, but which remained unused in its ambiguity until bent expeditiously to aid the status quo" (Parker, 1973:17–18).

THE DRAFTING OF THE PRIMARY CARE CENTER BILL
The NACHC reacted very negatively to Senator Javits's proposal to allow hospitals to receive health center funding without establishing a consumer-dominated governing board (Interview B, 10 July 1979). The health centers feared that if hospital-based primary care centers were authorized as part of the CHC legislation, health centers would be competing with the "tremendous power of hospitals" during the appropriations process (Interview B, 24 July 1979). Senator Javits responded by introducing a bill that would provide

a separate authorization for hospital-based ambulatory care. This was "a concession to the community health centers" (Interview B, 10 July 1979). Later this bill became a provision of the Senate bill, S. 2474, which reauthorized the CHC program.

Once the hospitals had raised the issue of primary care, Senator Javits and his staff examined it and "realized that there was also an opportunity to encourage positive hospital reforms" (Interview B, 10 July 1979). Hospital outpatient care was subject to the same criticisms in 1978 as in 1965 when the first NHCs were funded. It was fragmented and impersonal. It did not meet the needs of patients for comprehensive, coordinated care of ordinary illnesses and health maintenance services, nor was it organized to meet the needs of patients with multiple health problems. It encouraged individuals to use more than one source of care (including hospital emergency rooms) and it was inefficient and costly. Hospital administrators contended that treatment provided to the medically indigent in outpatient clinics and emergency rooms was a major source of hospital deficits.

While the "ghetto medicine" program was the "political model" for the New York hospitals that attempted to involve the federal government in the direct funding of hospital-based primary care, the actual model of health care delivery described in the Javits bill was based on a program sponsored by the Robert Wood Johnson Foundation. The foundation had given grants to fifty community hospitals throughout the United States between 1974 and 1978 to establish "primary care group practices" (House Hearings 1978B:73). The director of the Robert Wood Johnson Foundation program, Dr. James A. Block, was a consultant to the Senate subcommittee staff writing the primary care bill (Interview B, 10 July 1979). As we saw in chapter 3, Block was a central figure in the effort to have the Public Health Service fund comprehensive health centers in the late 1960s.

In addition to heading the Robert Wood Johnson Foundation program, Block was also director of the Ambulatory Services Department of Genesee Hospital in Rochester, New York, which had converted its outpatient department into a group practice. The group practice had not only expanded service hours and was treating a larger number of Medicaid recipients than previously, but also reduced costs and established a heterogeneous patient population in terms of race and social class (Senate Hearings, 1978:151–2, House Hearings, 1978B:71–75).

The bill introduced by Senator Javits (S. 2879) provided funds for grants to plan, develop, and operate primary care centers in public or nonprofit community hospitals that "primarily service a medically underserved population." A primary care center was to be "a distinct administrative unit of a community hospital." It was to provide primary care services, referrals to emergency and supplemental services, and information about the availability of such services through a primary care group practice of at least three full-time primary care physicians. These physicians were either to be salaried by the hospital or incorporated into group practice. Each patient receiving care was to be assigned to one member of the practice who would be responsible for the management of his or her treatment on a continuous basis.

The bill further specified that "to the extent practicable" primary care services at the hospital should be provided only at the primary care center, and that it should be a "separate and distinct cost and revenue center for accounting purposes." This was to assure that the cost of education, training, or inpatient care could not be "loaded" onto the cost of operating the primary care center. Thus, the reform of hospital outpatient departments, which had been a goal of some OEO officials in establishing the first neighborhood health center, was to be attempted again, more directly.

Finally, the bill mandated that the primary care center meet all of the requirements met by community health centers except for the establishment of a governing board with a majority of consumers. Instead, hospitals would establish an advisory board with a consumer majority drawn from the institution's catchment area. The hospital's grant application would have to be approved by the advisory board, which would meet at least six times a year to develop recommendations on the center's operation. These recommendations would go to the hospital's governing board (S. 2879:11–16).

As the primary care proposal was drafted by Senator Javits and his staff, several different kinds of groups expressed specific concerns about how it would affect their constituencies. The proposal was modified in order to respond to these issues. Senator Javits's staff "worked closely with" the American Hospital Association and the National Council of Community Hospitals in drafting the primary care bill. Since the bill was to cover public as well as private hospitals, representatives of the New York City Health and Hospitals Corporation, the National Association of Counties, and the National Conference of Mayors were consulted as the bill was drafted. Representatives of the American Federation of State, County and Municipal Employees (AFSCME) were afraid that the establishment of primary care centers might displace workers in public hospitals and the bill was rewritten to assure that this would not happen (Interview B, 10 July 1979).

The primary care center bill had originally been viewed as assisting urban hospitals; some hospital officials saw the HURA program as a rural hospital program and felt that the needs of urban hospitals had not been addressed by Congress (Interview B, 10 July 1979; Interview C, 25 July 1979). In fact, in testimony by the AHA, the primary care center provision was referred to as an "urban initiative" (Senate Hearings, 1978:384). Senators and citizens' groups representing rural areas came to the Javits staff and argued that the primary care concept could be just as effective in rural as in urban areas. "So we expanded it to make hospitals in rural areas eligible." Provisions in the bill that would permit the employment of nurse practitioners and physician assistants in primary care group practices "came at the request of some of the rural lobbyists and rural Senators" (Interview B, 10 July 1979).

OPPOSITION TO THE PRIMARY CARE CENTER BILL

Although unions and rural groups had specific concerns about the Javits proposal, the NACHC was the only group that was openly opposed to or critical of Javits's proposal as it was being drafted (Interview B, 10 July 1979; Interview B, 24 July 1979). Because relations between Senator Javits and community health centers had always been good, and Javits had been an early and consistent supporter of the CHC program, the NACHC was able to make substantial changes in the Javits amendment. As discussions of the primary care bill went on, according to the director of policy analysis at the national association, "the Javits staff was amenable to changes."

One of the major issues for the health centers was that in the first draft of the bill, there was "a lot of money" for construction and renovation of hospital outpatient departments. "It looked like money was going into bricks and mortar in established institutions while community health centers were going to be sacrificed." The Javits bill was initially seen by many in the NACHC as "the hospital giveaway program. It simply put in lots of additional money with no strings attached" (Interview B, 24 July 1979). The subcommittee responded to these concerns. In a report accompanying the final version of the bill, the committee stated that development of primary care centers "is used to mean modernization and renovation of space; it is not intended that grant funds be used to cover the costs of new construction" (S. Rept. 95-860:41).

Another change sought by the NACHC was a provision that primary care centers would not be funded in catchment areas already served by CHCs and that priority in grant approvals for service projects in areas contiguous to existing centers should be given to those centers (Interview B, 24 July 1979). The report accompanying S. 2474 stated that in approving grants for hospital affiliated primary care centers, "the Secretary is required to avoid duplication of efforts in areas where existing community health centers, migrant health centers, and other facilities are adequate to meet the needs of the medically underserved population" (S. Rept. 95-860:45).

The NACHC was thus successful in modifying some of the aspects of the proposed bill that were viewed as threatening to its membership. Yet the key issue for the association was the provision that hospital-affiliated programs have an advisory board rather than a governing board. This was, of course, the reason for the bill's development. The NACHC argued that if hospital-based ambulatory care was truly to be "reformed," it had to be made "responsive to the community" and therefore had to have a governing board of consumers.[3] "If that legislation had advocated community boards initially, we probably wouldn't have paid much attention to the Javits bill, wouldn't have been as concerned" (Interview B, 24 July 1979).

Senator Edward Kennedy and the Carter administration also opposed the elimination of the governing board requirement for the hospital programs. Senator Kennedy felt very strongly about the issue; hospitals "ought to go an extra mile" and meet the governing board requirements if they wanted to participate in the community health program (Interview A, 10 July 1979). The Carter administration was opposed to the primary care center provision in the Senate bill because the president's urban health initiative would address the same problems within the framework of the existing program (Senate Hearings, 1978:42–43).

The director of the BCHS argued that the governing board provision was central to the CHC concept because it had been "demonstrated" that consumer acceptance and use of a program was increased by having "broad-based community and user participation" in program governance. The CHC program was, in his words, "not simply an OPD [outpatient department] expansion program. It's a way of giving communities resources and developing independent systems which are dedicated to *ambulatory care* and not simply filling hospital beds" (Interview A, 25 July 1979). Senator Javits maintained that he was firmly committed to community participation, but that it was illogical to prevent hospitals from becoming involved in the improved delivery of primary care to medically underserved populations by requiring a governing board.

After much debate, a compromise was reached between the Kennedy and Javits staff on the governing board issue. Senate bill S. 2474 provided that hospitals establishing primary care centers could have advisory boards rather than governing boards, but that hospitals with governing boards would be given priority in the process of awarding grants. "It was purely a political compromise to keep the legislation going" (Interview B, 10 July 1979; S. Rept. 95-860:44–45).

THE PRIMARY CARE CENTER BILL IN THE HOUSE

The House and Senate bills were both reported out of their respective committees on May 15, 1978 (*U.S. Code,* 1978:9134), but were not passed by both houses until mid-October (NACHC, *Legislative Status Report,* October 1978:1). Unlike the Senate bill, the bill reported from the House Committee on Interstate and Foreign Commerce did not contain a provision authorizing hospital-affiliated primary care centers. The House committee, in fact, was generally doubtful about the ability of hospitals to provide comprehensive primary health care to medically underserved populations. These doubts were outlined in the committee's commentary on the Carter administration's Inner City Health Initiative in the report accompanying H.R. 12460, the Health Center Amendments of 1978. While the committee expressed support for two elements of the health initiative, the funding of new free-standing health centers and of prepaid capitation projects on a demonstration basis, it had several problems with the third aspect of the administration proposal—grants to be used for the conversion of hospital outpatient departments into health centers. The committee wanted assurances that the health centers would be separate "cost centers" in the hospitals, that federal funding for renovation and administrative costs would be limited, that physicians would work in the health centers on a full-time basis, and that services provided would meet the primary care needs of the population being served.

The committee stated that it had "concerns about the relative effectiveness of hospitals providing primary services and the difference between methods of reimbursement for hospital-based primary care and free-standing primary care centers" (H. Rept. 95-1186:16). A committee staff member said that hospital-based primary care centers could get "exorbitant cost-based reimbursement" and would add the costs of inpatient care to the primary care center as was done with hospital outpatient departments. It was feared that a hospital might view such a center as a means "to keep the hospital going, both in terms of a funnel for inpatients and a place to share overhead." In such a setting, "comprehensive, continuous, good primary health care" would not be provided as it would "in a free-standing primary care site that's made up of primary care docs" (Interview, 18 February 1980).

On July 20, two months after the CHC authorizing legislation was reported out of the House Interstate and Commerce Committee, a bill identical to the Javits bill (H.R. 13293, the Primary Health Care Act of 1978) was introduced in the House. Its sponsors were Congressmen Andrew McGuire (D–N.J.), Edward J. Markey (D–Mass.), Douglas Walgren (D–Pa.), and Henry Waxman (D–Calif.), all members of the health subcommittee of the House Committee on Interstate and Foreign Commerce. The "McGuire bill" was introduced, according to a committee staff person, to pressure the House Health Subcommittee chairman, Paul Rogers, into accepting the Senate's hospital-based care provision in the conference committee.

Congressman McGuire's interest in the primary care bill was stimulated by discussions with a physician who was on a Johnson Foundation Congressional Fellowship and who had worked on the Javits bill while spending the first six months of his fellowship in the Senate. He moved from the Javits to the McGuire staff in midyear (Interview, 18 February 1980). A coalition was organized to support the bill in the House. It included the Office of the Governor of New York, the New York City lobbying office in Washington, the AHA, and several state hospital associations. One of the efforts to get co-sponsors for the primary care center bill in the House involved phone calls by staff of the New York State governor's office to other governors whose states would benefit from the bill. They were asked to urge their congressional delegation to act on behalf of the legislation (Interview C, 25 July 1979).

Staff of the House Health Subcommittee believed, as did Senator Kennedy and DHEW officials, that since hospitals with CHC grants already operated health centers, it was unnecessary to authorize a separate program for hospitals. It was felt that such an authorization "would eventually detract from the authorization and appropriations" for the community health center programs. These staff members shared the view of the NACHC that competition with hospitals would disadvantage free-standing community-based programs. The national association had discussed their opposition to the Javits bill with staff of the House Health Subcommittee; officials of the BCHS also had informally communicated their opposition to the primary care center provision (Interview, 18 February 1980).

Samuel Beer, in the same work in which he describes the "professional-bureaucratic complex" of civil servants and congressional actors working together in a specific policy area, also discusses "the intergovernmental lobby"—organizations of local and state officials attempting to influence the federal policy process (1976:166–71). In this case, these two elements of the new "public sector politics" were acting in opposition to one another.

Another group that opposed the primary care center provision, for a very different reason from that of CHC advocates, was the AMA. In contrast to the NACHC, the AMA did not discuss the bill with Senator Javits or his staff as it was being drafted. However, about two weeks before the bill was to be considered by the House Health Subcommittee, the AMA sent a telegram to all county medical societies labeling the primary care bill as "onerous" and urging opposition to it. The AMA telegram "was not very specific," according to a Javits staff member, but the association seemed to be objecting to the salaried physician/group practice requirements of the bill. The physicians providing care would be either salaried by the hospital or be part of a group practice. This model of primary care was viewed as "another step to nationalized medicine." In spite of efforts by Javits's staff to arrange a meeting, AMA representatives would not meet with Senator Javits or his staff to discuss their specific concerns about the bill (Interview B, 10 July 1979).

The AMA did communicate their opposition to the primary care center bill to Tennessee's Tim Lee Carter, the ranking minority member of the House Health Subcommittee and a physician (Interview B, 10 July 1979). Carter had historically had good relations with the association; "the AMA comes and appeals to his brotherhood as a physician" (Interviews, 2 February 1982, 18 February 1980).

Carter had additional reasons to oppose the primary care center provision in both the House Health Subcommittee and the House-Senate Conference Committee. He believed that rural areas, like the mountainous district of eastern Kentucky that he represented, needed more community health centers and would not necessarily benefit from the conversion of hospital outpatient departments to primary care centers. Staff members of the House subcommittee told Carter that one of the unstated purposes of the Javits-McGuire bill was to provide fiscal relief for New York City hospitals. This, in the view of these congressional staffers, would consume large amounts of funds but "not really yield much in terms of results" (Interview, 18 February 1980).

Underlying the debate on the Javits proposal were two kinds of issues: questions about whether federal dollars for primary care should go to hospitals as well as to free-standing health centers with community governing boards; and distributive issues based on rural/urban and regional dimensions.

A hearing on the Primary Health Care Services bill was held by the House Health Subcommittee on August 10, 1978, but the bill was never reported out of the House committee (U.S. Code, 1978:9134). However, the issue of hospital-based primary care had to be considered in the House-Senate Conference Committee because the Senate bill reauthorizing the CHC program contained an authorization for hospital-affiliated primary care centers, while the House bill did not.

THE POLICY OUTCOME: THE ISSUE RESOLVED
During the House-Senate Conference Committee, Senator Javits argued that there was a tremendous need in cities like New York for primary health care and that it was illogical to establish new facilities to provide it when existing institutions—such as hospitals—could deliver this care. Javits was generally "influential" and was

"very persuasive in Conference." Carter argued against the Javits provision.

The House members of the committee proposed that the primary care center program be authorized as a demonstration project, to be "reexamined" in three years. This was finally accepted by the Senate conferees (Interview, 18 February 1980). In addition to making the primary care center program a demonstration, the authorization levels for the program were reduced considerably from those authorized by the Senate bill. The Senate bill had provided $35 million for fiscal year 1979, $60 million for fiscal year 1980, and $75 million for fiscal year 1981 and stipulated that not more than $500,000 could be given to a single project for planning and development. P.L. 95-626, in contrast, authorized $5 million for fiscal year 1979, $25 million for fiscal year 1980, and $30 million for fiscal year 1981. It also specified that not more than $150,000 could be used for the planning and development of any one program (S. Rept. 95-860:65).

No monies were actually appropriated for hospital-affiliated primary care centers in fiscal year 1979 because the authorizing legislation had not been passed when the House and Senate Appropriations Committees met to consider the fiscal year 1979 Department of Labor and DHEW appropriations. In October 1978, a congressional resolution was passed that provided funding only for ongoing CHCs at the fiscal year 1978 level until the appropriations bill was enacted. Such a bill was not passed and no new programs were funded in fiscal year 1979 (NACHC, *Legislative Status Report*, October 1978:1, October 1979:1). In fiscal year 1980, four rural and six urban hospital-affiliated primary care centers were funded and in the budget justifications for fiscal year 1981, the Carter administration stated that it planned to continue to support these ten programs during the fiscal year (NACHC, *Guidebook*, 1980:8–9).

THE HEALTH CENTER POLICY
NETWORK AND THE HOSPITALS

The primary care center bill originated as an attempt by hospital officials to change the requirements for health center grants so that hospitals could receive funding from the CHC program. The hospitals were not successful in this effort because most of the actors within the health center policy network were committed to maintaining the governing board provision as it had been structured in 1975. Senator Javits met with representatives from New York State health centers to reassure them of his support, and he modified his initial proposal to allay the fears of health centers about direct competition from hospital-based programs. Yet the outcome of the policy process in Congress—the establishment of a limited demonstration program—did not necessarily indicate that the narrow health center network could prevent penetration by the hospitals, key actors in other, larger health policy networks (Brown, 1978). Rather, the congressional outcome was the result of rural-urban divisions within the health center network and the influence of another "outside" political actor, the AMA.

It is not clear what the outcome would have been had competition between hospitals and health centers been the only issue. Clearly, hospitals that serve a mixed-income clientele (in contrast to those whose patients are all low-income) can draw on the political resources of their middle- and upper-class clientele, as well as members of their boards of directors, on important political issues. Hospital associations used local board members' access to members of Congress to defeat the Carter administration's hospital cost-containment bill (Califano, 1981:146). Teaching hospitals can also draw on a general reservoir of support among politicians and the public for medical research and the training of health practitioners. Even large public institutions are sometimes supported in the political arena by organized workers who depend on them for their livelihood.

Hospitals as a group are also far wealthier than are free-standing community health centers and money is a major political resource. For example, the budget of the American Hospital Association in

1974 was over $11 million, while in 1979, the budget of the NACHC was approximately $54,000 (Feldstein, 1977:133; *NACHC News*, January–February 1980:4).

This analysis of the primary care center issue, like the discussion of Medicare and Medicaid reimbursement in chapter 5, points to the limits of the political influence that can be exerted by policy networks in which the interest group component has relatively few political resources compared to other interest groups in the same policy arena. In 1978, program reauthorization was easily achieved, and the NACHC attained several of the program modifications it sought. However, program renewal and these modifications were not of major concern to any other interest group. When other providers, such as New York State hospitals, attempted to alter the CHC program to fit their needs, the potential vulnerability of the health center policy network was exposed. The resolution of the primary care center issue does not clearly demonstrate the ability of the health center network to defeat a direct challenge from other, more powerful, provider groups.

7

The Health Center
Policy Network Under Siege

Challenge and Response

One of the major themes of this book is that the institutional environments of the bureaucratic and congressional components of the health center policy network—a network in which the constituency group did not have a large amount of political resources— was critical to program maintenance and expansion at key points in time. When President Nixon attempted to end the health center program, a liberal Democratic majority in Congress was engaged in an ideological and institutional battle with the administration over the fate of a large number of Great Society programs. Congressional health center advocates were thus functioning within a sympathetic institutional environment. And during the Carter administration, bureaucratic advocates of the health center program enjoyed the support of high-level officials within DHEW/DHHS.

The institutional environments of both the bureaucratic and congressional supporters of community health centers changed radically in 1980 with the election of Ronald Reagan and the Ninety-seventh Congress. This chapter examines the specific nature of these changes, their impact on the institutional environments of health center advocates, the response of these advocates to their changed environment, and the effect on the CHC program during the first two years of the Reagan administration.

Congress

THE CONGRESSIONAL ENVIRONMENT

The Reagan administration assumed office with the goal of reversing the growth of the federal government and turning the administration of social programs over to state and local governments. During the spring and summer of 1981, the Reagan administration and the Republican congressional leadership used a budget reconciliation process legislatively enacted in 1974 to attempt to make massive cuts in funding for social programs and to replace federal categorical grant programs with block grants to the states.

The 1974 Budget Reconciliation Act required Congress to set ceilings on total spending and authorizing committees in each area of policy to "reconcile" their legislative authorizations with those ceilings. Budget committees in both the House and the Senate were then to process the recommendations of the authorizing committees before the budget went to the floor of each house. This process changed the congressional environment within which members, staff, and interest groups functioned. It greatly limited the time available for the consideration of programs, involved budget as well as authorizing committees, and focused attention on the entire budget rather than on disaggregated individual programs (Peters, 1981: 732–36; Demkovich, 1981:1806–08). It thus made previously established relationships between interest groups and subcommittee members and staff less relevant to the policy process and reversed the usually "distributive" nature of the process by which programs are authorized.

The 1980 election changed the party and ideological composition of Congress itself. Richard Nixon's social policy goals were similar to those of Reagan, but while Nixon had faced a liberal Democratic Congress, Reagan was elected with a Republican majority in the Senate and a House with a Democratic majority of only twenty-six seats (Kirschten, 1981:1533–38). In addition to the Republican party majority in the Senate, that body had fewer "moderate" and liberal Republicans than it had had in the Nixon years (*New York Times*, 29 December 1980:A14). In the 1980 election, several liberal Democrats, including Warren Magnuson of Washington, who had been chairman of the Senate Appropriations Committee, Birch Bayh of Indiana, also a member of that committee, Gaylord Nelson of Wisconsin who was on the health subcommittee of the Labor and Human Resources Committee, George McGovern of South Dakota, and John Culver of Iowa, were defeated. All of these senators had been strongly supportive of federal social programs (NACHC, *Legislative Status Report,* 6 November 1980:1–2).

The 1980 election brought to office a president whose considerable personal popularity could be used to influence voters against legislators who did not support his policies (*New York Times,* 27 October 1982:A21). In addition, many members were newly elected in 1980 and this meant that allegiance to Congress itself, which might modify partisan or other kinds of loyalty to a president, had not yet had a chance to develop.

The president and his congressional allies were successful in using the budget reconciliation process to reduce funding for many social programs but were not as successful in their attempt to restructure the nature of American federalism. While the Reagan administration proposed that eighty-eight categorical grant programs be consolidated into five block grants, Congress acted to combine only fifty-seven programs into nine block grants, some with federal requirements that modified the block grant form (Stanfield, 1982:1674). The CHC program was an extreme case of the modification of the block grant form. It was reauthorized in 1981, as the Primary Care Block Grant, but, as will be described below, was a block grant in name only. The changes in the congressional environment described above resulted in a policy process that, unlike previous health center program authorization processes, was filled with conflict and deadlock.

BLOCK GRANTS IN HEALTH

The Reagan administration proposed that twenty-six categorical grant programs that funded health services and research be combined into two large block grants, one for health services, the other for preventive health services. States would decide how each grant would be allocated among health programs and would not have to meet any federal requirements as to eligibility, services to be provided, and so forth. No state matching funds were to be required and states would be allowed to transfer up to 10 percent of the funds from any "human services" block grants to any other. In addition, the total to be spent for each block grant was to be 25 percent less than the fiscal year 1981 appropriations for all of the grant's programs (Davis, 1981:320–23). Under this proposal, community health centers, along with migrant health centers, maternal and child health services, emergency medical services, black lung clinics, venereal disease programs, and other programs were to become part of the Health Services Block Grant.

The administration's argument was that block grants in health would result in less duplication of services and greater administrative efficiency, since state officials would be able to judge local needs more accurately than had federal policymakers. Opponents of the proposal, such as Senator Kennedy of Massachusetts, argued that under the block grant system health programs serving disadvantaged populations would be competing with each other for funds, there were no assurances of the quality of programs under state administration, and in the past, local and state governments had not been concerned with the provision of services to these populations (New York Times, 3 April 1981:A18). The issue of whether specific health programs should remain categorical or become part of a larger block grant was debated in the House and Senate Health Subcommittees and ultimately resolved in a conference committee that was part of the budget reconciliation process.

THE PROCESS IN THE HOUSE

In May 1981, an administration-supported budget plan for fiscal year 1982 ("Gramm-Latta") passed the House with the support of sixty-three Democrats. This plan reduced spending by $36 billion from the fiscal year 1981 level and required that the total amount be cut by setting program authorization levels below appropriation levels for 1981. A similar plan had previously been enacted by the Senate. The authorizing committees were to have a very short time (about three weeks) to implement this budget by reducing the funding for programs under their jurisdiction (Peters, 1981:733–34).

It will be recalled that as chair of the Subcommittee on Health and the Environment of the Interstate and Foreign Commerce Committee, Congressman Paul Rogers was able to command a majority of the members in support of health services programs for medically underserved, low-income populations in spite of opposition from the Nixon and Ford administrations. In 1981, in contrast, this subcommittee was ideologically divided. (The name of the full committee became Energy and Commerce beginning in 1981.)

While six of the eleven Democrats on the Health and Environment Subcommittee (Henry A. Waxman of California, James A. Scheuer of New York, Barbara Mikulski of Maryland, Ron Wyden of Oregon, Anthony "Toby" Moffett of Connecticut, and Mickey Leland of Texas) were much more liberal on economic and social issues than the average House Democrat, two Democrats (Richard G. Shelby of Alabama and Phil Gramm of Texas) were not only more conservative than their fellow party members, but also more conservative than the average Republican members of the House on economic and social issues.[1] The average scores on both social and economic issues for all of the Democratic members of the House Health Subcommittee were about the same as for House Democrats as a whole. The Republican members of the subcommittee were, in contrast, about as conservative as were their House Republican colleagues on economic issues, while they were far more conservative than was the average House Republican member on social issues. Since Democrats in general were much more liberal than Republicans (as measured by roll-call votes on a series of selected issues) in the House in 1981, there were clearly large ideological differences on this subcommittee.[2]

The ideological diversity of this subcommittee resulted in a deadlock over whether the many categorical health programs up for reauthorization in 1981 should become a part of health block grants. The Republicans on the subcommittee, led by Congressman Edward Madigan (Illinois), the new ranking minority member, supported the president's proposals for health block grants. This support was based both on philosophical agreement and the belief that the president had a popular mandate for his program (Interview A, 5 March 1984). Congressman Henry Waxman, the chairman of the subcommittee, wanted to preserve the programs that had been "built over the years" and felt that federally administered programs targeted for specific needs were most effective in meeting health care goals. He was supported by most of the Democrats on the subcommittee (Interview A, 7 March 1984). Committee hearings were held on the block grant issue and representatives of groups served by these programs testified. They also met informally with both Democratic and Republican subcommittee members and staff (Interviews A, 5 and 7 March 1984).

Congressman Waxman developed a set of proposals for those health programs that were within the jurisdiction of the House Energy and Commerce Committee. Three block grants were to be established, one for maternal and child health, one for alcohol and drug abuse services, and one for preventive health care (APHA, Crosscurrents, Summer 1981:1; Interview A, 7 March 1984). These proposals were based on a belief that it was necessary to accommodate differences within the subcommittee by proposing some block grants in health (Interview A, 7 March 1984). Community and migrant health centers would be reauthorized as categorical programs for three years, through fiscal year 1984 (NACHC, Legislative Status Report, Primary Care Focus, July 1981:1). The family planning, venereal disease, and immunization programs would also be maintained as federally administered categorical grant programs.

Funding reductions were to be made in all of these programs in order to meet reconciliation budget levels. The funding for the maternal and child health block grant would be 18 percent less than the fiscal year 1981 amounts for the programs incorporated into the block grant. The reduction for preventive health would be 37.5 percent. Alcohol and drug abuse monies would be cut 24 percent (AHPA, Crosscurrents, Summer 1981:1). Community health centers would be funded at $248 million for fiscal year 1982, about

25 percent less than the amount appropriated for the program in fiscal year 1981 (NACHC Memo, 29 June 1981:2).

Maternal and child health and alcohol and drug abuse programs were chosen to be "block-granted" because historically these programs had included grants to state health departments to provide some or all of these services (Interview A, 7 March 1984). The argument made for keeping immunization and venereal disease as categorical was that infectious disease crosses state lines and therefore should be federally administered. A similar argument was made about the mobility of migrant farm workers. It was also argued that because migrant workers often do not vote, states would neglect their health needs when choosing among competing claims. These arguments were accepted by both the Republicans and the Democrats on the health subcommittee (Interviews A, 5 and 7 March 1984).

The structuring of the CHC and family planning programs became the most controversial issues within both the House committee and the House-Senate Conference Committee. Congressman Waxman believed that because there was no history of state interest in CHCs, this program should remain as a federally administered categorical grant program. Congressman Madigan and the other Republicans disagreed. Family planning groups, groups that Waxman supported, wanted to have that service remain a federal responsibility, while the "pro-family," antiabortion groups were divided as to whether they would have more access to family planning policy at the state or federal levels.

Phil Gramm and Richard Shelby, the two most conservative Democrats on the House Health Subcommittee, refused to support Waxman's proposals. The subcommittee was then deadlocked, nine to nine, since all seven Republicans on the subcommittee also opposed them. No formal vote was taken. At one point Republicans boycotted subcommittee proceedings and Waxman sent his proposals to the chairman of the full Committee on Energy and Commerce, Congressman John Dingell (D–Mich.). Dingell added Waxman's proposals to those which he had developed in other areas of the committee's jurisdiction.

The full Energy and Commerce Committee also became dead-locked on the reconciliation proposals. There were twenty-four Democrats and eighteen Republicans on the committee. James T. Broyhill (North Carolina) the ranking Republican on the full com-mittee, developed a substitute for the Dingell proposals which were supported by all eighteen Republicans and by three Democrats— Gramm, Shelby, and James Santini of Nevada. The committee was divided twenty-one to twenty-one.

The Energy and Commerce Committee was the only authoriz-ing committee in the House that did not approve a budget pro-posal during the reconciliation process. Instead, Chairman Dingell sent his proposals to Jim Jones (D–Okla.) the Democratic chair-man of the House Budget Committee, and Congressman Broyhill sent his Republican substitute package to the budget committee as well (Interview A, 5 March 1984). The budget committee voted to present the Democratic package on the House floor but also to ask the rules committee to allow separate consideration of the Republi-can plan. However, "Gramm-Latta II," a Republican substitute for all of the budget committee's recommendations, won full House acceptance by a close 217-to-211 vote. Ironically, the Republicans had withdrawn the Broyhill proposals from their package and the Waxman-Dingell proposals became part of the House-passed rec-onciliation bill (Peters, 1981:735–36).

The decision to withdraw the Republican health and energy proposals was made by the House leadership. Moderate Republi-cans and conservative Democrats informed the Republican leaders that they would not vote for their proposals (NACHC Memo, 29 June 1981:1) and the leadership feared that the whole package would be defeated. Republican "gypsy moths" from the Northeast and Midwest, as well as some conservatives, responded to opposi-tion voiced by the governors of their states to cuts in the federal share of Medicaid contained in the Republican health and energy proposals (Interviews A, 5 and 7 March 1984). Thus, the Demo-cratic health proposals for the relatively small health services programs survived the reconciliation process in the House because of governors' concerns with reductions in Medicaid.

THE PROCESS IN THE SENATE

Because the Senate Labor and Human Resources Committee had no health subcommittee during the ninety-seventh Congress, health issues were considered by its full membership. As a result of the 1980 election, Republicans had become the majority party in the Senate. Orrin Hatch of Utah became chairman of the Labor and Human Resources Committee, displacing Edward Kennedy, who had led the Health Subcommittee since the early 1970s as chair on health issues. The Senate Labor and Human Resources Committee, like the House committee, was ideologically diverse. Democrats on this committee were far more liberal than the average Democratic members of the Senate, while the voting scores for committee Republicans were about the same as the average for Senate Republicans on economic issues and somewhat more conservative on social issues.[3] However, two Republicans on the committee, Robert Stafford of Vermont and Lowell Weicker of Connecticut, were far more liberal than were the other Republican senators on both social and economic issues. These two senators played a key role in the politics of block grants on the Senate committee.

The committee was at first unable to act on the block grant issue. Senator Hatch and the six other conservative Republicans supported the Reagan administration's block grant proposals, while the seven Democrats, led by Senator Kennedy, opposed them. Hatch suspended committee meetings for a time (*New York Times*, 29 May 1981:A13). Senators Weicker and Stafford threatened to vote with the Democrats; as a result, a compromise was reached on the issue of block grants (Interview B, 7 March 1984). While community and migrant health centers were to be incorporated into a large health services block grant as proposed by the Reagan administration, the committee provided certain protections for these programs. These included a requirement that all existing community and migrant health centers be funded in fiscal year 1982 and fiscal year 1983; that funding had to be maintained by each state at a certain percentage of the fiscal year 1981 grant level through 1985; that some of the federal program requirements in effect in fiscal year 1981 (such as the requirement that "primary care services" be offered at all centers) be retained; and that there be a federal review and appeals procedure on state decisions (NACHC, "Update" 12 June 1981:1–2).

Senator Stafford's support for these "guarantees" for the CHC program was enlisted by the NACHC working with health centers in Vermont, Stafford's home state (Interview B, 7 March 1984). The efforts of the national association were very important to the eventual outcome of the reconciliation process as it affected health centers. Particularly in this period of very swift activity, small programs like the CHC program might have been overlooked during the "reconciliation rush."

THE SENATE-HOUSE CONFERENCE COMMITTEE
The House-Senate Budget Reconciliation Conference, which took place in July 1981, was the largest conference ever held. It involved fifty-eight mini-conferences and thirty congressional committees. It was also a process in which a huge number of program and funding decisions were made in a very short time (Peters, 1981:736). The conferees from the Senate Labor and Human Resources and House Energy and Commerce Committees were the last to resolve their differences. Their conference was "unusually controversial" (Interview B, 7 March 1984).

Although there were "fights over everything," the main issues of contention were CHCs, family planning, and the National Health Service Corps (Interview A, 7 March 1984). Congressman Waxman was adamant about keeping these programs categorical; Senator Hatch was equally committed to having them in a "real block grant" (Interview A, 5 March 1984; Interviews A and B, 7 March 1984). Senator Kennedy supported Waxman's position; Congressman Madigan usually supported Senator Hatch (Interview A, 5 March 1984). The family planning program was the most controversial issue because of pressure from antiabortion groups, but Senator Hatch also had special concerns about CHCs and the NHSC.

Senator Hatch believed that the Carter administration had intended to use these two programs as the core of a national health insurance scheme in which a significant portion of the population would receive health services at federally run clinics staffed by federally salaried physicians. This had been clearly expressed in papers produced by DHHS Office of the Assistant Secretary for Planning and Evaluation, which projected funding between 750 and 1,000 new health centers over a five-year period. Hatch believed that this program was being managed for "ideological purposes" and as a result inappropriate areas were being designated as medically underserved; health centers were being funded in areas where they were not necessary; other centers were too large and were inefficiently managed (Interview B, 7 March 1984).

The same view of the CHC program was expressed by the Heritage Foundation, which criticized both the Health Services Administration and the BCHS during the Carter administration for changing their original "mission" of "gap-filling in the existing health care delivery system" to that of "the development of an alternative health care delivery system." The BCHS should change its goal "to assure services that are truly needed to be provided in a cost efficient manner without interfering with the ability of the private sector to provide such services and without using these programs as a bootstrap to a national health service program" (Winston, 1981:275, 286).[4]

In spite of the distance between the Republicans and Democrats on the block grant issue, a compromise was eventually reached. While the Republicans were being pressured by their leadership and by the administration to hold out for an "ideologically pure" policy, at the same time they were being asked to complete action on the health proposals so that the whole budget package could be enacted (Interview B, 7 March 1984). The Democrats "didn't have the ability to refuse all changes." The Democrats finally proposed that CHCs be placed in a "primary care block grant." This would be the only program in the block grant and there were to be a series of provisions to assure that a state would accept the block grant only if it really intended to continue the health center program rather than to fund other health department programs (Interview A, 7 March 1984). The Republicans felt it very important to have the "principle" of primary care programs in a block grant even if it were voluntary rather than mandatory for a state to accept the grant (Interview B, 7 March 1984). The primary care block grant was a "symbolic gesture . . . the necessary political act so that we could reach a resolution" (Interview A, 7 March 1984).

THE OUTCOME
The primary care block grant created by the 1981 Reconciliation Act provided that the health center program would remain a federal grant program during fiscal year 1982. Beginning in 1983, individual states would have to apply to take over its administration. If they did not do so, the federal government would continue to administer health centers within the state. This provision is unique to the primary care block grant. In addition, states choosing to administer the program would have to fund each health center that received a federal grant in fiscal year 1982 at the same grant level, match a proportion of federal funds, and meet other previously established program requirements, including the requirements that every center provide primary care services and have a consumer-dominated governing board (NACHC, *Guidebook*, 1982:II-5). These were, in effect, legislative disincentives for state administration of the program. Funding for the CHC program was at the same level proposed in the House bill (NACHC, Memo, 28 July 1981:1).

In addition to the primary care block grant, the three other block grants proposed by Congressman Waxman were approved by the Senate and House conferees. The family planning, venereal disease, migrant health center, tuberculosis, immunization, and black lung programs, all of which President Reagan had included in his block grant proposals, were to remain as categorical grants for fiscal year 1982 (AHPA, *Crosscurrents*, September 1981).

THE ROLE OF THE NATIONAL ASSOCIATION
Although some accounts of the budget reconciliation process suggest that "the lobbying community found itself literally shut out" of the conference committees (Peters, 1981:736; see also Stanfield, 1982:1673), representatives of the NACHC worked closely with

Democratic House members and staff in drafting the language creating the primary care block grant (Interview A, 7 March 1984). Both Democratic and Republican health committee staff persons assessed the national association as being "very effective" in making its views known to Congress during the budget reconciliation process (Interviews A and B, 7 March 1984).

Thus, the interest group component of the health center policy network was very active during the budget reconciliation process. Representatives of the association talked to Congress members and staff about the negative impact of budget cuts and the block grant form on the health center program. In contrast, officials of the BCHS were not active during this period. As I will discuss below, BCHS officials responded to their new administrative environment by not initiating any communication with members of Congress or congressional staff. This reversed the pattern of earlier years, when bureaucrats were as active or more active than was the national association in working with Congress. This reversal was not only a result of the changed policy environment of the Reagan administration but also a consequence of the development of the national association as a very effective program advocate. While the CHC program did sustain a very large cut in funding, some of this money was restored in a supplemental appropriation bill enacted the next year. In addition, the national association played a major role in preventing the inclusion of the program in a health services block grant. It has been argued that such a structural shift from a categorical to a block grant would have been ultimately more serious than large funding cuts since once a federal program was dismantled it would be very difficult to reestablish it, whereas an increase in funding levels could be achieved far more easily (Stanfield, 2 October 1982:1674).

PROGRAM FUNDING FOR 1982: CONGRESSIONAL AND INTEREST-GROUP ADVOCACY

During fiscal year 1982 (1 October 1981 to 30 September 1982), the community health center program was funded under a continuing resolution because President Reagan had threatened to veto the fiscal year 1982 appropriations bill for the Departments of Labor, Education, and Health and Human Services. The President opposed the regular appropriations bill because both the House and the Senate had approved funding levels for most programs that were higher than the amounts proposed by the administration. The continuing resolution provided $248.4 million for the community health center program, approximately the level set during the budget reconciliation process and about 25 percent less than the appropriation of $325 million for the program for fiscal year 1981 (NACHC, *Washington Update*, 5 April 1982:1).

However, in July 1982, the president signed an urgent supplemental appropriation for fiscal year 1982 (P.L. 97-216) that contained $33.85 million in additional funding for CHCs and $24.4 million for maternal and child health programs. President Reagan had vetoed similar bills twice during the month of June in a dispute over housing programs (NACHC, *Washington Update*, 26 July 1982:1, 12 July 1982:1-2).

This supplemental funding was not to be used to refund projects that had lost their federal grants but rather to enable health center projects whose funds had been cut to restore some of the eliminated services. Most of the money was to be used for "health prevention" and "health promotion" activities (NACHC, *Washington Update*, 26 July 1982:1, 7 September 1982:1). As will be discussed below, BCHS officials had identified "health promotion and prevention" as an area of activity in which Reagan administration goals and health center capabilities were compatible.

Many programs were in competition for this supplemental funding (NACHC, *Washington Update*, 5 April 1982:3). Three liberal Democratic congressmen, Joseph Early (D–Mass.), Louis Stokes (D–Ohio), and David Obey (D–Wis.), were advocates of the CHC program on the House Appropriations Committee. Two members of the Senate Appropriations Committee, Senator Ernest Hollings (D–S.C.) and Senator Patrick Leahy (D–Vt.), worked very actively for CHC funding under the urgent supplemental appropriation on the Senate side (NACHC, *Washington Update*, 22 February 1982:5, 5 April 1982:2, 12 July 1982:1-2, 7 September

1982:2). Senators Hollings and Leahy co-sponsored an amendment providing additional funds for the program and "lobbied" their congressional colleagues on the Senate Appropriations Committee (Interview B, 5 March 1984). Senator Leahy was also the chief advocate for the CHC program during the House-Senate Conference Committee on the appropriations bill (NACHC, *Washington Update*, 14 June 1982:1, 8). Again, the NACHC was central to this effort. NACHC staff supplied Hollings and Leahy with detailed information (on very short notice) about health centers in each of the states of the senators who were members of the Health Appropriations Subcommittee—information used successfully by these senators to persuade their colleagues to support additional appropriations for CHCs (Interview B, 5 March 1984).

The Bureaucracy

THE BUREAUCRATIC ENVIRONMENT

To a greater extent than ever before, the Reagan administration implemented a policy of appointing cabinet officers and other bureaucratic policymakers who shared the president's domestic philosophy and were committed to carrying it out. Ideological purity was the most important factor in filling such positions— there were "few pragmatists floating around" (Nathan, 1983:71, 73). Many subcabinet officers were "more doctrinaire Reaganites than their cabinet superiors. . . . This use of lower-level personnel to teach and extend the gospel is the same approach Reagan used as governor of California" (Nathan, 1983:76). These appointees immediately changed the direction of many existing projects, stopped others entirely, and dismissed or transferred career civil servants believed to be ideologically incompatible with administration policy through "reductions in force" (RIFs) (Nathan, 1983:73–77).

The first secretary of DHHS, Richard Schweiker, had been a Senator from Pennsylvania and the ranking minority member on the Senate Labor and Human Resources Committee. Although he was personally more moderate than some of his cabinet colleagues, Schweiker was viewed within DHHS as especially sensitive to the ideological and political leadership of the White House on health and welfare issues. The health and welfare portions of the 1983 budget were shaped by OMB and the White House, with little effective input from DHHS. One of the results was said to be a "morale crisis" within the department and the departure of career civil servants not already "RIF'd" to positions in Congress or outside of government.

Career civil servants who remained in the bureaucracy were severely limited in their ability to make autonomous decisions and constrained in their relationships with outside interest groups (Nathan, 1983:73–77). "In many instances they have to get clearance from their secretary to be interviewed by the press or by other groups where the information would be made public," according to one observer, "so there's almost a sense of paranoia in every area of government about what they say, how they say it, what they write, how they write it, perhaps more so in this than in any other administration." This "fundamentally changed tone and approach to domestic policymaking and its execution" (Nathan, 1983:78) altered drastically the bureaucratic environment within which administrators of the community health center program had to function.

First, the administration's personnel policies affected staffing in both the Washington office of the BCHS and the regional offices administering federal primary care programs. As a result of the reductions in force, civil servants dismissed from other parts of the government "bumped" BCHS personnel in both the central office and at the regional level. In the central office, three of the five heads of program divisions within the bureau lost their positions and were replaced with branch chiefs who had had no prior experience with the community health center program or with primary care (Interview, 6 March 1984). At the regional level, young professionals with field experience working with community groups (many of whom were female and/or black or Hispanic) were replaced by (white, male) veterans of the Public Health Service who had had little experience working with primary care programs (Interviews, 4 August 1982, 6 August 1982, 6 March 1984).

Second, although the CHC program accounted for a minuscule portion of the DHHS budget, its assumptions—that the federal government should take the responsibility for delivering health care to medically underserved populations—were diametrically opposed to those of the Reagan administration and to the individuals in policymaking positions within the PHS. The subcabinet officials sympathetic to the CHC program during the Carter years—Richmond, Hanft, and Davis—had departed. The assistant secretary for health under Schweiker, Dr. Edward N. Brandt, Jr., came to his position from the University of Texas at Austin where he was vice-chancellor for health affairs. Prior to that, he had been dean of the medical school. His candidacy was sponsored by both the AMA and the American Association of Medical Colleges. His assistant secretary for planning and evaluation was Dr. Robert J. Rubin, a nephrologist (New York Times, 19 May 1981:C3). Rubin had been a legislative aide to Schweiker when he was on the Senate Labor and Human Resources Committee. Rubin did not support the CHC program (Interview, 18 August 1982).

Under the leadership of Dr. Karen Davis, the Office of the Assistant Secretary for Planning and Evaluation during the Carter administration had been very involved in primary care policy. Her staff had worked on the planning for expanded community health center and National Health Service Corps programs. During Dr. Rubin's tenure, primary care received little attention. There was a major shift in the agenda of this office from the Carter to the Reagan administration (Interviews, 18 August 1982, 6 March 1984).

The top administrators of the BCHS retained their positions during the first year and a half of the Reagan administration. This was a period of administration scrutiny of these officials and their policies, policies that had been criticized in the Heritage Foundation Report, quoted above. Authors of the report had also served on the Reagan administration's transition staff in 1980–1981 (Interview,

6 March 1984; Interview B, 7 March 1984; NACHC, *Legislative Status Report*, 7 January 1981:4).

THE RESPONSE OF BUREAU OFFICIALS:
DEFENSIVE STRATEGIES

During the first years of the Reagan administration, officials of the BCHS related very differently to their superiors in the Public Health Service and DHHS, to members of Congress, and to staff and members of the NACHC than they had during the Carter, and even the Nixon and Ford, administrations.

First, in response to their dramatically changed environment, officials of the bureau made a conscious decision to "keep a low profile" and to "go into a period of public hibernation" (Interview, 6 March 1984). They did not initiate contacts with staff in the Office of the Assistant Secretary for Health or the Office of the Secretary of DHHS. They did, of course, respond to questions or requests from officials above them. Informal communication between congressional staff and bureau officials and staff was ended. Instead, communication with sympathetic members of Congress and congressional staffers took place through the NACHC. However, the bureau terminated its technical assistance contracts with the national association. The Heritage Foundation and the Reagan transition team had compiled a list of groups that had received federal money and also did advocacy work for social program constituencies. The national association was on that list. "They were a targeted group as we were a targeted bureau. So you don't continue then to throw salt on an open wound" (Interview, 6 March 1984). Grants could no longer be given to a group now perceived as "fighting the administration" (Interview B, 17 August 1982). In addition to this generally defensive posture, officials of the bureau engaged in a number of specific defensive strategies in the day-to-day operation of the health center program.

As a result of the Omnibus Budget Reconciliation Act of 1981, the bureau had to implement a cut of about 25 percent from the amount appropriated for the CHC program during fiscal year 1981. This was done in a way that bureau officials felt would give the most protection to the program as a whole. Instead of cutting funds for all programs equally, the budget reduction was implemented by completely defunding about one-quarter of the health center projects, "significantly" reducing the funding of another 50 percent, while funding another quarter of the programs at 90–100 percent of their 1981 level (NACHC, *Washington Update,* 6 April 1982:4). As of May 1982, 186 health center projects had been defunded (NACHC, *Washington Update,* 17 May 1982:3). A specific set of criteria was developed by the bureau to guide the decision-making process on defunding. These criteria were: (1) the relative need of the grantee's service area; (2) the center's performance on indicators of administrative efficiency; (3) its billing and revenue collection performance; (4) the status of its most recent financial audit; and (5) comments on individual health center programs from governors, state health departments, and state medical societies (NACHC, *Washington Update,* 5 April 1982:5). In his address to the members of the NACHC at the organization's 1982 Policy and Issues Forum on February 5, 1982, the director of the bureau stressed the importance of developing good relationships with local elected officials, local and state health departments, and local medical societies. He also emphasized the centrality of effective financial and program management.

The financial and managerial criteria were used by the bureau to defund badly managed programs (Interviews A, 17 and 18 August 1982, 6 March 1984). Such projects could be "an embarrassment" to the CHC program as a whole if opponents chose to publicize their failings (Interview B, 17 August 1982). The solicitation of comments by state medical societies, state health departments, and governors was a way of eliciting support, or at least neutrality, from providers and elected officials with increased access to the federal policy process. The AMA had far greater access to the Reagan administration than to previous administrations. Pressures to involve state health officials and governors in primary care programs had been felt even during the last years of the Carter administration.

Both local medical societies and the AMA had become concerned about the expansion of the CHC and NHSC programs during the Carter administration. Local medical societies reacted to the presence of new projects in their communities, and the AMA to the further program growth that was being advocated in 1979 and 1980 by the Office of the Deputy Assistant Secretary for Health Planning and Evaluation in DHEW/DHHS. The AMA, like conservative senators such as Orrin Hatch, feared that a major expansion of the program would create a national health service in the United States (Interview, 6 March 1984).

It was therefore strategically important within this political environment to elicit written support or specific criticism about health centers from local providers. Although there were a few cases where state medical societies were engaged in battles against individual health centers (for example, in Alabama and in South Carolina), the responses from medical societies to the bureau's solicitation of comments on the health center program was "overwhelmingly positive" (Interview A, 17 August 1982).

Another defensive strategy engaged in by Bureau officials was to increase the involvement of the Washington office in the awarding of health center grants. This was done through a system of "concurrence" in which all funding decisions had to be approved by the director of the BCHS. This reversed the policy, in effect since the Nixon administration, of having the regional offices make the final decisions on grant awards. Such a centralization of decision making within the bureau was a response to the presence of new, inexperienced personnel in both the regional and national offices and reflected the desire of the few top remaining BCHS officials to maintain firm control over the process of "targeting" funding cuts (Interviews, 4 and 6 August 1982; 6 March 1984).

In addition to instituting the system of "concurrence" and "targeting" funding cuts, BCHS officials encouraged the regional offices to involve state health departments in joint planning and evaluation of health center programs in their regions. The primary care block grant, as discussed earlier, provided that beginning in 1983 states could apply to take over the administration of community health centers within their boundaries. From the perspective of the Reagan administration, one of the bureau's tasks was to implement the block grant by giving states assistance in preparing to undertake this responsibility. It was a peculiar position for federal bureaucrats because, especially at the regional level, they would be working toward the abolition of their jobs. Nonetheless, the view of bureau officials was that without the establishment of cooperative agreements with states, the bureau would not be viewed as following administration policy and this would be as great a threat to its existence as the decentralization of the program itself. So the central office "pushed" the "reluctant regional people" to work with states to implement the block grant concept (Interview, 6 March 1984). However, while "memoranda of agreements" were written in 1981 that specified the role of states in reviewing and evaluating CHC programs, only one state, West Virginia, actually elected to take over its program (NACHC, *Washington Update*, 17 May 1982:4–5, 3 March 1984:1).

THE "SUCCESS" OF THE BUREAUCRATIC STRATEGY
Top officials of the BCHS thus responded to their drastically changed environment by adapting in order to preserve the bureau and its programs. The one area in which a bureaucratic initiative was undertaken during the first eighteen months of the Reagan administration was a proposal that health centers be a part of Secretaries Brandt and Schweiker's program of "health promotion and disease prevention." This initiative, however, was clearly in response to a policy stated publicly by these Reagan administration officials. Along with this additional funding to individual programs, the NACHC received a federal grant for an eighteen-month technical assistance program called the "Community Health Connection." Staff employed under this grant would provide technical assistance to health centers in implementing their health promotion and disease prevention programs. This grant was "cleared" with Brandt before it was awarded (Interview, 6 March 1984). Thus, a contractual relationship between the bureau and the national association was reestablished.

The defensive, adaptive posture toward the Reagan administration of bureaucrats within the health center policy network was successful in terms of the bureau's own survival. During the spring and summer of 1982, two PHS agencies, the Health Services Administration and the Health Resources Administration, were combined into a new Health Resources and Services Administration (HRSA). The BCHS (previously under the Health Services Administration) was renamed the Bureau of Health Care Delivery and Assistance (BHCDA) and was to administer the National Health Service Corps as well as community and migrant health centers, family planning, and maternal and child health programs (NACHC, *Washington Update,* 3 May 1982:5, 17 September 1982:2). Dr. Edward Martin, who had been the director of the BCHS since 1975, became director of the new BHCDA in February 1983.[5] By the beginning of 1984, the top officials of the new bureau were viewed by their superiors in DHHS as "credible, competent program managers" who had worked within the administration's priorities. The assistant secretary for health began to consult with bureau officials, a reversal of the situation during the first eighteen to twenty-four months of the Reagan administration (Interview, 6 March 1984).

The National Association of Community Health Centers

THE POLITICAL ENVIRONMENT

In 1981, health centers were being funded by an administration dedicated to severely limiting or ending the role of the federal government in providing health and other social services to populations not served by the private sector and using market forces to provide appropriate and cost-effective health care. Reagan administration health policy was based on assumptions antithetical to those that had led to the establishment of federally supported, community-based health services provided by salaried physicians. In addition, the administration in power had won the election without the support of liberal or minority constituencies and had no political debts to pay to these groups. Also, as noted previously, the NACHC had been on a list of groups whose advocacy behavior had been criticized as inappropriate by Reagan administration policy analysts. It is not surprising therefore that during the first eighteen months of the new administration, top health policy officials were not willing to communicate with the national association's representatives.

Attempts to make appointments with the secretary of DHHS and the assistant secretary for health were unsuccessful. In all previous administrations, including those of Presidents Nixon and Ford, representatives of the national association had been able to see the secretary of DHEW/DHHS, even if that administration and the national association did not agree on policy issues. Also in contrast to previous administrations, high-level Reagan administration health officials were unwilling to address conferences or meetings sponsored by the national association. Both Secretary of Health Brandt and DHHS Secretary Schweiker were invited to address the organization's annual meeting. Both refused to come or to send a representative (Interview A, 17 August 1982). (Secretary Brandt did speak later, at an association conference in 1983). The experience of other health-provider groups was quite different. A staff person with the AMA stated that his organization's access to health policymakers had greatly increased under the Reagan administration (Interview, 14 July 1982).

RELATIONSHIPS WITHIN THE POLICY NETWORK

This absence of dialogue between administration policymakers and the NACHC did not extend to the level of the health center policy network. In fact, during the process of the implementation of health center budget cuts, the national association and BCHS staff and officials worked together very closely. The national association communicated the general concerns of its membership about some of the "defunding criteria" established by the bureau and acted on behalf of specific health centers during the defunding process.

One of the defunding criteria was the relative need of the grantee's service area. The first part of this criteria was that the service area be designated as a medically underserved area (MUA). (This requirement, promulgated previously as a regulation, was written into the 1981 Omnibus Budget Reconciliation Act). In the fall of 1981, the bureau published a list of areas that had been MUAs but were not to be redesignated as medically underserved. There were approximately eighty such areas. The national association clarified the right of centers to appeal these de-designations based on updated census data, and about 70 percent of the centers that appealed won their cases.

The demonstration of "relative need" also required that each center submit a "needs assessment demand analysis" along with its annual grant application. This required the collection and analysis of an additional set of data about the center's catchment area. Such a process required using either staff or outside consultants during a period when grants were to be reduced. The instrument to be completed also required that data be handled in a very specific way and the instructions offered by the bureau were not always clear. Representatives of the NACHC discussed these problems with bureau staff. Officials of the bureau asked the national association to write an instructional manual for the needs assessment demand analysis to be used by health centers. Association staff also provided technical assistance to the staff of individual health centers working on the analysis.

In addition, NACHC staff monitored the funding decisions made by the bureau. In cases where it was felt that programs were being unjustly defunded, association staff helped the centers to appeal to the bureau for the reconsideration of the original decision (Interview, 16 August 1982).

It might be expected that the relationship between BCHS and NACHC officials would be strained during this budget reduction process, and that officials of the national association would express hostility toward the administrators who were cutting the funds of the association's constituency. While the executive director of the national association did note the organization's initial opposition to the requirement that state health departments and medical societies comment on health center performance, she also indicated that the criteria of administrative and fiscal efficiency were reasonable standards for judging health centers. In addition, she talked sympathetically about the difficulties experienced by bureau staff and officials, within the Reagan administration, including the great personal pressure on them. She suggested that some who chose to remain in the bureaucracy rather than to leave did so out of a desire to preserve the CHC and other primary care programs to the greatest extent possible. Such individuals, she said, were trying to ensure "at least some efficiency and continuity" in program administration.

> I would hate to think what happens to these programs if some of the people who were very involved with their development and their growth were just not around any more, just totally disappeared and turned over every single aspect of the program to someone who has no knowledge and no more understanding of the program than a wall. . . . A lot of people have just tried to hang in there to see that there is some level of objectivity given to the program and that the program is administered appropriately. (Interview, 16 August 1982)

Bureau officials also described the relationship between themselves and NACHC staff as very cooperative and discussed the work of the national association with admiration.

THE RESPONSE OF THE NACHC TO
A CHANGED POLITICAL ENVIRONMENT
Officers and staff of the NACHC, like BCHS officials, assessed the radically changed political environment and took a series of actions in response. In early 1980, a Blue Ribbon Commission on Association Restructuring was appointed by the president of the association to examine how the NACHC should respond to new developments in national health policy. This commission recommended that the association's board of directors work to develop primary care associations at both the state and regional levels and restructure the association so that these associations would be part of the national organization. This proposal was circulated to the

membership and then adopted by the house of delegates at the association's annual meeting in September 1980 (Interview, 16 August 1982).

It was clear that state governments were becoming increasingly involved in health policy. If health centers were to survive, they would have to establish relationships with state health department officials (since these agencies both license health institutions and set rates for Medicaid reimbursement) and state legislators. A need for organization at the regional level was also identified. Regional groups could deal with regional funding allocations and other policies that were the responsibility of DHHS regional offices (NACHC, "Restructuring," p. 1; Interview, 16 August 1982).

Once the national election occurred and the Heritage Foundation Report on social policy was released, elected officials and NACHC staff knew that the Reagan administration would make every effort to end federal responsibility for health services and that the restructuring proposals were very appropriate. During 1981, they were implemented (Interview, 16 August 1982). Changes were made in the composition of the board of directors and new procedures were instituted for dues allocation and the chartering of state and regional chapters.

The new board of directors is composed of eight elected officers and two representatives from each of the association's ten regional chapters—the ten regions correspond to DHHS regions. Each regional chapter consists of chartered state chapters formed by health centers and other primary care projects. State organizations are chartered for a two-year period, and each state and regional chapter must make an annual report of all chapter activities and a semiannual financial report to the national association. Health centers are entitled to membership in all three levels of the association; the association provides a percentage of dues to the state and regional chapters (NACHC, "Restructuring," pp. 2–8).

Along with restructuring, the leadership of the association planned to assist health centers to develop or strengthen primary care associations in their states. Under a three-year, $378,000 grant from the Robert Wood Johnson Foundation, which began in January 1982, NACHC staff gave technical assistance in grant writing, legislative and policy analysis, and organizational development to twelve state primary care associations in 1982, eighteen in 1983, and another twenty in 1984. In preparation, national association staff did an update of a study of whether and how health centers are reimbursed by Medicaid in each state. An assessment was also made of the extent of health center organization at the state level and the degree to which existing state primary care associations had developed contacts with state legislators and health departments (Interview, 16 August 1982). This strategy of state level organizing, both to increase grass-roots support for efforts in Washington and to work directly in the states, was one of a number of new strategies pursued by advocates of human service programs during the Reagan years (Stanfield, 2 October 1982:1673–76). As of summer 1986, nine regional and forty-two state primary care associations had been chartered by the NACHC (NACHC, Communication, 11 July 1986).

The national association's application to the Robert Wood Johnson Foundation for financial support was part of its effort to become less dependent on government monies as a source of organizational funds. In 1979, approximately 85 percent of the association's budget came from federal contracts; by 1986, only 63 percent came from this source. In addition to the grant from the Johnson Foundation, the national association has increased its revenues from conferences, dues, and the sale of technical assistance manuals it has produced (NACHC, Communications, 8 November 1983 and 5 September 1986).

In its study of state Medicaid policy, the NACHC identified potential prepayment or capitation arrangements between states and health centers as one of the financing-reimbursement strategies that could be very significant for the future survival of CHCs. The 1981 Budget Reconciliation Act provided for federal waivers for states to establish demonstration projects for prepaid plans with Medicaid populations, but little information had been collected by either health centers or state officials about the technical aspects of such arrangements. Accordingly, the executive director of the national association established a Task Force on Medicaid Capitation. It included representatives of state health departments and health centers and representatives of the Health Care Financing Administration and the BCHS.

This task force developed a technical assistance document for health centers and state officials interested in establishing new reimbursement arrangements under Medicaid. It included an analysis of changes in health center operations required under a capitation plan, model contracts between health centers and states, and a discussion of different reimbursement options. For example, a health center could be involved in capitation arrangements for all or part of the services it provided; it could subcontract through an existing HMO to provide certain services; or a group of health centers could provide services as subcontractors to a state primary care association that would have a contract with the state (Interview A, 17 August 1982).

Thus, the NACHC's response to the Reagan administration's policies of "new federalism" and "competition" in the health care sector has included an effort to create the conditions necessary for the development of health center policy networks at the state level and for its own financial independence from federal funding. The association has also assisted health centers in entering into a new financial-organizational mode—that of prepaid financing. In 1981, it worked successfully to prevent the health center program from being included in a health services block grant. It then helped affiliated organizations to prevent the implementation of state administration of health centers under the primary care block grant. State primary care associations argued against state takeover of the health center program at state health departments and with state legislators (Stanfield, 2 October 1982:1673). As noted earlier, only one state, West Virginia, opted to take the block grant. The governor of West Virginia returned it to the federal government less than a year later (NACHC, *Washington Update*, 3 March 1984:1).

Both the CHC program and the health center policy network

survived the first years of the Reagan administration. The NACHC has clearly emerged from this period with new strength. Both the bureaucratic and congressional actors within the health center policy network regard the national association as a very effective advocate for the program.

The health center network, has however, operated within a political environment in which conservative forces are entrenched in the White House and are far stronger in Congress than they have been for the past twenty-five years. The cost of program survival has been a large reduction in the number of people served and the scope of services provided. Even those centers hurt least by the defunding process have had to cut back substantially in both of these areas (Interview A, 17 August 1982); those receiving care at health centers have also suffered from reductions in funding for other health, income maintenance, and social service programs.

Update:
The Community Health Center Program in 1987

The major factors in the policy environment of the health center program during the early years of the Reagan administration have continued to characterize the first half of Ronald Reagan's second term in office. The administration has remained committed to decreasing the federal role and increasing the involvement of states in the provision of health care for the medically underserved. At the same time, the health policy network has functioned within an environment of great concern about the size of the federal budget deficit and congressional efforts to reduce federal spending in order to reduce the deficit. Finally, the health policy environment has become increasingly structured for competition. Health center administrators and governing boards are expected by federal and state officials to organize their centers to compete with other health services organizations in providing cost-efficient, "managed" health care.

FEDERAL VERSUS STATE RESPONSIBILITY
FOR PRIMARY CARE:
THE 1986 REAUTHORIZATION OF THE CHC PROGRAM
Every year since 1981, President Reagan has proposed to Congress that the community health center program be included, along with several other health programs, in a health services block grant to be administered by the states. The administration has held to this position even though health centers were funded as a primary care block grant by the 1981 Budget Reconciliation Act. This legislation, it will be recalled, allowed states to apply to administer health center programs, but also required them to provide matching funds and meet certain other program requirements. As noted above, only one state (West Virginia) applied for the block grant and kept it for only one year. In 1984, 1985, and 1986, Congress rejected the block grant idea and affirmed that the health center program was to be administered federally.

In 1984, legislation authorizing the community health center program was unanimously passed by both houses of Congress. It was then pocket vetoed by President Reagan. Essentially the same legislation was again passed unanimously by the Senate on July 19, 1985 (NACHC, *Guidebook*, 1985:I-1) and by the House on March 5, 1986, with more than enough votes to override a presidential veto. The Senate unanimously passed the House version of the bill on April 11, and it was signed into law by President Reagan on April 24, 1986, as P.L. 99-280. This law repealed the primary care block grant entirely and authorized funds for community and migrant health centers as separate categorical grant programs through fiscal year 1988 (NACHC, *Washington Update*, 10 March, 14 April, 25 April 1986:1). This clear rejection of the Reagan administration's position is an echo of the sharp disagreements ten years earlier between Congress and the Nixon administration on health care policy for the underserved.

While it rejected the block grant approach, Congress approved the concept of greater state involvement in the administration of the community health center program. First, P.L. 99-280 authorizes the secretary of DHHS to enter into memoranda of agreement

(MOA) with state governments. These agreements outline the state's role in assessing primary care needs, planning and developing new health centers, evaluating existing centers, and providing technical assistance to the centers. Second, the legislation would allow state governors to recommend criteria for designating medically underserved areas and other special need areas if they do not meet existing MUA criteria (NACHC, *Washington Update,* 25 April 1986:2; S. Rept. 99–104:14–15).

The continuing activism and effectiveness of the NACHC in protecting the existing program is seen in the fact that state primary care associations ("a statewide organization representing the majority of CHCs in a given state") are to be "a party to the MOA" and are to have "a clearly defined role in each aspect of the MOA for involvement and consultation" (S. Rept. 99–104:14). Under such agreements, the state health department and the state primary care association are to work together to develop a plan for primary care in that state (NACHC, *Guidebook,* 1985:IV-16–22).

In addition, statewide primary care organizations shall also be consulted, along with governors and local officials, on the criteria for the designation of medically underserved areas (S. Rept. 99–104:15; H. Rept. 99–157:10). The BHCDA began providing funding for state associations to participate in primary care planning with state governments in 1985 (NACHC, *Washington Update,* 15 July 1985:2–3).

PROGRAM APPROPRIATIONS
AND BUDGETARY POLITICS
CHC Program Funding   As we have seen, the CHC program's initial appropriation for fiscal year 1982 was about 25 percent less than the level at which the program was funded in fiscal year 1981 (the last year in which a budget was prepared by the Carter administration), but the centers received $33.85 million in additional funding under an urgent supplemental appropriation. This pattern, presented in table 1, was repeated in fiscal years 1983 and 1984. In fiscal year 1983, $65 million was added to an initial appropriation of $295 million as part of the Fiscal Year 1983

Urgent Supplemental Appropriation Act (the "Jobs Bill"); $10 million was added to an initial appropriation of $327 million under similar supplemental legislation for fiscal year 1984. In addition, in fiscal years 1984, 1985, and 1986, additional money was appropriated to enable health centers to replace physician positions previously provided by the National Health Service Corps, a program that will no longer be placing professionals in CHCs. Thus, while the program was cut 25 percent as a consequence of the 1981 budget reconciliation process, the actual amounts appropriated to the program have been higher.

Table 1. Community Health Center Funding, 1981–1986
(in $ millions)

Fiscal Year	Initial Appropriation	Additional Appropriations	Total
1981[a]	—	—	325.0
1982	248.4	+33.8 Promotion and disease prevention	282.2
1983	295.0	+65.0 "Jobs Bill"	360.0
1984	327.0	+10.0 "Jobs Bill" +14.3 NHSC conversion costs	351.3
1985	360.0	+23.0 NHSC conversion costs	383.0
1986	400.00	− 4.0 Gramm-Rudman cut +10.4 NHSC conversion costs −15.0 NHSC replacement costs[b]	391.0

Source: Department of Policy Analysis, NACHC, Communication, 26 August 1986.
  a. Last year of Carter administration budget.
  b. $15 million was subtracted from the 1986 appropriation to reflect the proportion of funds used to replace NHSC personnel. Funding for these personnel did not previously come from CHC monies but from a separate NHSC budget.

However, the real value of health center appropriations declined by 20 percent between fiscal years 1981 and 1986. While the appropriation in 1986 was 20 percent higher than it was in 1981, medical care inflation increased 50 percent during that same period.[6]

Budget Deficit Politics   In 1985 congressional concern about the large size of the budget deficit resulted in the enactment of the Balanced Budget and Emergency Deficit Control Act of 1985, P.L. 99-177 (the Gramm-Rudman law). This legislation establishes annual reductions in the federal budget deficit beginning with $171.9 billion in fiscal year 1986 and declining to zero by 1991. If the president and Congress cannot agree on how to meet the deficit reduction figure specified for a given fiscal year, then the legislation provides that spending for all federal programs be reduced by the same proportion in that year.

Some exceptions to the "across-the-board cuts" are specified in the legislation. A number of programs, including social security, interest payments on the debt, a large number of defense programs, AFDC, Medicaid, food stamps, and WIC are excluded from these automatic reductions entirely, while reductions in another group of programs are limited to 1 percent in fiscal year 1986 and 2 percent in each of the years after that (NACHC, *Washington Update,* 30 December 1985:2). Further evidence for the continued successful functioning of the health center policy network within this environment of funding cutbacks is the fact that community and migrant health centers, along with Medicare and Indian and veterans' health care, are the only programs in this category. (As noted earlier, many migrant health centers belong to the NACHC and advocates of the two programs act together in supporting funding for them. The migrant health center program is discussed briefly in chapter 8.)

"STRATEGIC PLANNING"
IN A COMPETITIVE ENVIRONMENT
Many policy analysts believe that the U.S. health care system is "about to undergo a radical transformation" (Abramowitz, 1985:11). The traditional fee-for-service system of plural providers will be replaced by large "for-profit" corporations delivering care via HMOs

and preferred provider groups to the "vast majority" of the population. A 1985 financial management study predicts that all public sector reimbursement will be prospective, favoring health care organizations that can control costs (12–15). In a December 1985 address to health center administrators and board members at a NACHC health policy seminar, Richard Bohrer, director of the Primary Care Services Division of the BHCDA, referred to this study as a useful guide to the future environment in which health centers would have to function. Health centers could operate in such an environment by practicing "strategic management" and by "marketing" themselves to both consumers and clinicians while they maintained "strong community-based boards" and other unique aspects of the CHC model.

One specific competitive strategy supported by the BHCDA is participation in prepayment plans. While the bureau does not encourage health centers to undertake the financial risk involved in creating an HMO, it strongly supports arrangements in which a CHC enters into a contract with an existing HMO, or a state or other organization, to provide outpatient services on a prepaid basis. The bureau provides technical assistance for establishing such arrangements through several different sources (BHCDA, Memorandum, 1985:1–7). Health centers are urged to respond to competitive pressures at the state level: "BHCDA strongly encourages CHCs to participate in prepaid health programs. This is particularly critical to community health centers in states where Medicaid programs are aggressively encouraging or mandating recipients to enroll in prepaid, capitated systems. In these situations CHCs must participate in this prepaid program or risk losing their Medicaid patients" (BHCDA, Memorandum, 1985:1).

As noted above, the Task Force on Medicaid established by the NACHC in the early 1980s produced a document that provided health centers with technical information needed to enter into prepaid arrangements. Legislation proposed by the national association and passed as part of the Consolidated Omnibus Budget Reconciliation Act of 1986 would facilitate contract arrangements between health centers and state Medicaid agencies for the provision of-health services on a capitated basis. The 1986 law exempts community, migrant, and Appalachian health centers from a requirement (which HMOs must meet) that they have a non-Medicaid/Medicare enrollment of 25 percent. (Such centers must be receiving federal grants of at least $100,000 and have received this size grant for at least two years before entering into a contractual arrangement.) It allows states to continue the Medicaid eligibility of patients enrolled in a health center capitation program for up to six months even if technically they should lose their Medicaid eligibility during this time. It also allows states to bar Medicaid enrollees in such a program from leaving the program for six months without cause (the "lock-in" provision). Until this legislation was passed, states had to apply for special waivers from the Health Care Financing Administration in order to contract with health centers for prepaid services (NACHC, *Washington Update,* 14 April 1986:2–3).

In August 1985 the NACHC received a $120,000 grant from the Robert Wood Johnson Foundation to work with a private market research and consulting firm to do "strategic planning" with four CHCs over a three-year period. The purpose of this demonstration project is to help these centers to develop research, business, and marketing plans to attract "private," that is, non-grant, dollars by providing services to new populations. These new markets can be middle-class insured patients, groups of Medicare or Medicaid patients to be enrolled in prepaid plans, or populations in new geographic areas (NACHC, Communication, 5 September 1986). This is meant as a demonstration of "competitive strategies" that other health centers can follow.

Information on such competitive strategies is a very prominent part of the educational offerings at the NACHC, regional, and state primary care association conferences. Almost half of the forty-six educational sessions offered at the NACHC's 1985 convention dealt with issues related to increasing health center revenues from sources other than federal grants and making center operations more cost-effective. These included workshops on "Diversification Opportunities for CHCs," "Exploring Revenue Potential," "Prepayment Arrangements . . . Alternatives for Health Centers,"

"Consortia Development . . . Strategies and Implications," and "Strategic Planning for Boards of Directors." The other two categories of topics discussed in these workshops are issues related to grant requirements, such as "Assuring Compliance and Effectiveness of Boards of Directors," and clinical issues relevant to the delivery of care to medically underserved populations, such as "Preventive Dentistry" and "Community Responsive Practice." Similarly, at the 1986 Conference of Community and Migrant Health Centers in Federal Region II, which includes New York, New Jersey, Puerto Rico, and the Virgin Islands, sessions were held on "Prepayment," "Capital Formation," "Marketing Strategies for Primary Health Care Programs," and "Strategies for Corporate Restructuring and Diversification," as well as on internal administrative and clinical issues.

One of the central questions about the future of health centers is whether it will be possible to compete effectively for "new markets" and at the same time to deliver comprehensive primary care to low-income populations — to provide "community responsive practice." The community health center program's future, like its present, will depend on a constellation of forces in the larger health policy and political arenas.

The next two chapters will be concerned with two sets of conclusions drawn from this study: first, ideas about the nature of policy networks in social welfare policy which provide a direction for future research in this area (chapter 8); and second, lessons from the community health experiment that are relevant to current and future planning for health care delivery in the United States (chapter 9).

8

Networks in Social Welfare Policy

Models of Policy Networks and the Health Center Case

In order to examine the question of whether the policy network relating to the neighborhood/community health center program fits the subgovernmental model described in the literature, we need to restate the major characteristics of that model. In discussing the concept of subgovernment in relation to empirical data on interest-group politics, John T. Tierney presents three propositions that faithfully represent the central elements of this concept as it has been used in the literature.[1]

Proposition 1 is that "triangulated subgovernments are bounded and close-knit communities made up of the administrators of an agency, members of Congress who have committee jurisdiction over that agency, and lobbyists from organized interests especially attentive to the programs and policies of the agency—all working cooperatively with one another to advance their mutual interests" (Tierney, 1985:6).

This proposition identifies the institutional positions of political actors in subgovernments and characterizes their relationships as close and cooperative. The policy network supportive of the neighborhood/community health center program has been a close and cooperative one for more than two decades. However, for the

200

first part of its existence, it was not "triangulated." The political actors responsible for the survival of the program in its earliest years were bureaucratic and congressional actors. The interest group component of the network developed later, with support from bureaucrats. The creation of the NHC program fits Beer's description of the initiation of social welfare policy by members of a professional-bureaucratic complex.

It began with a close working relationship between the staff of Senator Edward Kennedy and OEO officials, who together wrote the Health Center Amendments to the OEO Act in 1966 and 1967. It continued during the Nixon administration, when staff of the Senate and House health subcommittees (the Senate Health Subcommittee of the Committee on Labor and Public Welfare and the House Subcommittee on Public Health and the Environment of the Committee on Interstate and Foreign Commerce) worked with the BCHS to write new legislation that authorized funding for CHCs as a separate categorical grant program. This interaction occurred in spite of the Nixon administration's attempt to prevent communication between civil servants and Congress without the presence of administration "loyalists." When the CHC authorizing legislation expired in 1978, the Carter administration was in office and this close, cooperative relationship between civil servants and congressional actors working on health center legislation had the full support of political appointees within DHEW.

Representatives of individual health centers were in contact with both bureaucratic and congressional actors during the program's earliest years, but regional and national organizations of health centers were not formed until the early 1970s. During its first several years, the National Association of Neighborhood/ Community Health Centers was primarily concerned with the education and training of health center staff and consumer board members. Beginning in 1975, its resources were focused on the policy process and how it affected health centers. The national association was not a central participant in the process that resulted in the enactment of legislation authorizing the community health center program in 1975, but it was a highly visible actor in the reauthorization process that took place in 1978.

When the Reagan administration proposed in 1981 that the CHC program be included in a large health services block grant to the states, the NACHC worked closely and successfully with congressional allies to oppose this policy change. While the Reagan administration was more successful than the Nixon administration in constraining established relationships between civil servants and liberal members of Congress and between bureaucrats and outside groups (Nathan, 1983:73–77), informal communication between bureaucratic officials administering the CHC program and representatives of the national association continued. Communication between congressional supporters of the program and bureau officials took place "through" the NACHC.

Proposition 2 states, "The policy demands of interest groups in subgovernments typically do not face effective opposition from other groups. That is, the organized interest participants within these policy communities are not in fundamental conflict with each other. In fact, interest groups in a mature subgovernment should seldom be directly challenged by hostile groups fundamentally opposed to their interests" (Tierney, 1985:8). In Ripley and Franklin's terms, subgovernments are involved in distributive policymaking that is quiet and nonconflictual. The absence of conflict is due to the fact that no group capable of political action perceives itself as being hurt by the outcome of the policy process (1987:21).

As discussed in chapter 3, the neighborhood/community health center program did not face opposition from national interest groups in its earliest years. This was because program advocates engaged in strategies of co-optation. Private practitioners were assured that health centers would not compete for valued patients and the centers were encouraged to include private physicians in their operations. Hospitals and medical schools received a large proportion of the health center grants administered by the OEO. In 1974 and 1975 the AMA stated its opposition to legislative authorization of a separate health program at congressional hearings but did not press this opposition actively. The program's small size made it a low priority for the AMA. Since neither organized interest groups nor the general public viewed it as a salient issue, few in Congress were attentive to health center policy. The policy network that related to the program was, like a traditional sub-government, quiet and noncontroversial.

In 1978, when support from both the administration and Congress meant that the program's survival was no longer at issue, questions about the allocation of program resources surfaced. There was some conflict between rural and urban groups and between hospitals and free-standing health centers. A proposal introduced by Senator Jacob Javits at the request of hospitals in New York State would have allocated health center monies to hospital-based "primary care centers" operating without governing boards. Substantial changes in the original proposal were made by Javits in response to the concerns of the NACHC, but advocates of maintaining the governing board requirements for all programs did not prevail in the Senate subcommittee. As in the typical subgovernment, compromise was the result of negotiation within the policy network (see Ripley and Franklin, 1987:8–9).

However, the compromise on the Javits proposal was not to be the final outcome of the congressional policy process. The AMA objected strongly to primary care centers because they were a form of hospital-based group practice. This objection was voiced in the conference committee dealing with the health center legislation and the hospital-based primary care program was reduced to a demonstration program. While Senator Javits had a long history of support for the health center program and can clearly be regarded as part of that policy network, the AMA was not. Yet the AMA had substantial influence on the issue of hospital-based primary care. The boundaries of the health center policy network were clearly more "elastic" than those of the subgovernments described in the literature.

The final proposition refers to the characteristic of subgovernments suggested by the term *iron triangle* —their independence of higher-level political actors. Proposition 3 states: "Subgovernments are capable of developing and administering public policy within their narrow realms without significant opposition from or penetration by other political actors. Moreover, mature subgovernments are relatively impervious to changes in partisan control of the presidency or to shifts in the partisan balance in Congress" (Tierney, 1985:10).

Decisions about the NHC/CHC program were generally made in a quiet, routine way by members of the policy network without the intervention of higher-level political actors such as congressional leaders or the president. The major policy change in the program—the 1975 shift from funding large urban programs to establishing many small ones—was initiated by officials of the BCHS who persuaded their superiors within the PHS of its merit. Thus, the health center policy network functioned with a certain amount of independence. Yet the source of that independence was different from that attributed to political actors within a subgovernment.

In the typical iron triangle, the political resources of the interest group afford congressional and bureaucratic actors independence from their institutional environments. Such independence is the source of the difficulties of "political executives" who attempt to impose policy direction on the career civil servants below them (Heclo, 1977; see also Seidman, 1975). This was not true in the health center case. The NACHC had few resources that could be used on behalf of other actors within its policy network. It did not contribute large sums of money to members of Congress, as did the AMA and American Dental Association; its membership did not include the prestigious scientists found in the medical research subgovernment nor the "prominent local figures" who sit on the boards of hospitals that belong to the AHA (Drake, 18 December 1979:16). In fact, until the early 1980s the national association depended on technical assistance contracts with the BCHS for more than three-quarters of its revenue. In the health center case, the absence of intervention by political actors from outside of the policy network was due to the low saliency of the issue to such actors, not to the political resources available to interest groups within the network.

There is yet another way in which the statements made in Proposition 3 do not accurately describe the policy network supportive of CHCs. While policymaking was done by political actors at the bureau and subcommittee level, the larger political environment, including changes in presidential administrations and congressional majorities, affected the behavior of these actors and was crucial to the fate of the program. The history of health center policy is one of program change in response to changes in the larger congressional and administrative environments. Adaptability rather than autonomy was, and is, characteristic of this policy network.

The initiation of the program, a model for health care reform, was made possible by the experimental environment within OEO in the mid-1960s. When the Nixon administration took office in 1969, bureaucratic advocates of the program found themselves in a hostile environment. The president opposed the authorization of a separate health center program and had appointed political loyalists to program positions within the bureaucracy. Communication between agency staff and Congress was restricted and monitored. This attempt to disrupt networks that supported social programs was intensely resented by Congress members and staff as well as bureaucrats and contributed to the larger conflict between the president and Congress.

Yet the conflict between a Republican administration that wanted to reduce federal support for social programs and a liberal Democratic Congress that wanted to continue them was ultimately beneficial for the health center program. The very specific provisions of the 1975 community health center authorizing legislation were intended by congressional actors to "protect" the program from the administration.

The rural health initiative was a response by BCHS officials to an environment of funding constraints imposed by the Ford administration and congressional concern about the lack of health services in rural areas. In contrast, during the Carter administration there was support for the health center program from high-level officials of DHEW, and the program was expanded during these years.

Both the administrative and the congressional environments of the actors within the community health center policy network were drastically altered by the election of Ronald Reagan and the Ninety-seventh Congress. The Reagan administration was more consistent than the Nixon administration had been in filling the bureaucracy with appointees who would carry out its policies and Congress was more conservative than it had been during the Nixon, Ford, or Carter years. In the atmosphere of budget cutting as a popular mandate after the election, liberal Democrats could no longer command a majority of votes in support of maintaining social programs at previous funding levels. One-quarter of all existing health center programs were defunded as a result of budget cuts in 1981.

The health center policy network was clearly not as autonomous as is a subgovernment; yet it also does not fit the description of an "issue network" as discussed by Hugh Heclo. Issue networks contain large numbers of political actors from the bureaucracy, Congress, and private organizations who share expertise and interest in a policy area. But these political actors do not necessarily agree on policy direction or work together to achieve a common goal (see Heclo, 1978:102–4). The community health center policy network is comprised of bureaucratic, congressional, and interest-group actors who have consistently acted together to achieve policy objectives.

The findings of this study suggest that policy networks should be conceptualized on a continuum in terms of the mutuality of position of the participants and their ability to act autonomously within a policy area. At one end of the continuum is the traditional subgovernment, or iron triangle, in which bureaucratic, congressional, and interest group actors are in basic agreement on policy and are able to maintain hegemony within a specific policy area. At the other end of the continuum is the open issue network based on expertise rather than mutually supportive activity. The

CHC case represents a third kind of policy network in between these two. It includes actors who work together on behalf of common policy goals but who must be far more sensitive to the larger political environment than are those actors within a sub-government. In the health center case, one of the reasons for this sensitivity is that centers and their clientele do not enjoy the independent resources available to business, labor, and professional groups. This kind of policy network can be called an "elastic net."[2]

Given such a continuum of policy networks, it is important to examine other cases in the area of social welfare policy in order to test the usefulness of this idea.

Policy Networks Compared:
Health Centers and Food Stamps

As noted in chapter 1, only one published study done to date has both analyzed a policy network longitudinally, during several administrations, and also focused on theoretical issues about the nature of policy subsystems. Jeffrey M. Berry's *Feeding Hungry People* is a study of federal rule-making in the food stamp program. I will compare Berry's findings about the food stamp policy network to the analysis of the CHC policy network presented above. Then, to broaden the empirical data base further, I will examine four other cases in relation to ideas about social welfare policy networks developed from the first two.

The food stamp policy network, like the community health center program network, was far more directly affected by the larger political environment than is true of the iron triangles described in the literature. According to Berry, "The history of the food stamp program reveals a policy subsystem that is far less autonomous than either Cater or Heclo contend is typical. At times, of course, members of the subsystem have made food stamp policy with minimal outside interference. Overall, though, the food stamp issue network has not been an autonomous force impervious to White House influence or swings in the nation's ideological pendulum. . . . The differences for food stamp policy making between a Butz and a Bergland or a Carter and a Reagan have been dramatic" (1984:134–35).

Although the food stamp and CHC policy networks are both considerably less autonomous than are traditional "subgovernments," and although both are federally funded social programs that serve essentially the same populations, there are significant differences between them. The policy network relating to the CHC program involved mutual support among participants on behalf of a common goal—the continuation of the program. This is one of the characteristics of subgovernments and of "elastic nets." In contrast, the relationships among participants in the food stamp policy network were based primarily on "expertise" rather than "unity of purpose." "A common outlook and cooperative working relationship among the committees, USDA, and the lobbyists has been the exception and not the rule during the life of the program. Sometimes two sides of the triangle have worked against a third" (1984:135). It is for this reason that Berry calls the food stamp subsystem an "issue network." The difference between the CHC and the food stamp policy network can be seen most clearly if the three sets of relationships that comprise them— bureaucratic-congressional relationships, bureaucratic-interest group relationships, and congressional-interest group relationships—are longitudinally compared.

BUREAUCRATIC–CONGRESSIONAL RELATIONS
Beginning with Senator Edward Kennedy's advocacy of OEO funding of neighborhood health centers, bureaucratic actors worked with members of the congressional health subcommittees and their staffs in support of federal sponsorship of health center projects. This relationship continued until the Reagan administration. In contrast, there was little cooperation between food stamp program administrators and congressional actors during these years.

The food stamp program was established by the Roosevelt administration in 1939 with the dual purpose of feeding the poor and reducing farm surpluses. It ended in 1943 as the economy improved and crop surpluses declined. During the 1950s, a few congressional liberals and former program administrators advocated a new food stamp program, but the Eisenhower administration was not supportive. When John F. Kennedy became president, after a campaign in which he had seen and discussed malnutrition in America, a food stamp "pilot program" was initiated. In 1964 Congress passed legislation that legitimized the ongoing program.

During most of the 1960s, program administrators operated without consulting members of Congress. Most members of the agriculture committees, those with jurisdiction over the program, were not interested in food stamp policy. As the program expanded, participation decreased. The program regulations, which reflected the views of its administrators, were not designed to assure poor families an adequate diet, but rather to expand food buying and to prevent cheating. Many families found that they could not afford to buy food stamps (Berry, 1984:21–37).

In 1967, hunger became a political issue. A few liberals on the Employment, Manpower and Poverty Subcommittee of the Senate Committee on Labor and Public Welfare focused congressional and public attention on the food stamp program through a series of trips to poverty areas and congressional hearings. As a result of these efforts, the Senate Select Committee on Nutrition and Human Needs was established in 1968. The members of the select committee and the committee staff pressured the bureaucracy as well as Johnson and then Nixon administration appointees to liberalize the food stamp program. This was done by using hearings to reach the media and thus public opinion. Food stamp program administrators were defensive in response to this criticism. (During this period legislative liberalization of the program was opposed by the chairpersons of the Senate and House agriculture committees and other powerful legislators.)

Significant reforms were achieved in the program during the Nixon administration through regulations issued by the secretary of agriculture as a consequence of the efforts of these liberals in

Congress, journalists, and the "antihunger lobby" (Berry, 1984: 46–64).

Because of these changes in program regulations, increased unemployment, and inflation in food prices, participation in the food stamp program and its costs grew tremendously during the first part of the 1970s. The media, conservatives in Congress, President Ford, and several of his cabinet officials attacked the program. The Ford administration attempted to reduce spending on food stamps through administrative changes, but first Congress blocked the proposed regulations and then antihunger groups sued in court and won an injunction preventing the implementation of a second set of regulations (Berry, 1984: 80–90). Thus, instead of cooperation and consultation between bureaucrats and members of Congress, there was congressional criticism of food stamp program administration throughout the 1960s and 1970s, first from liberals and then from conservatives.[3] In addition, the debates on food stamp policy were often *public* debates, carried on through the media. In contrast, CHC policy received little public attention; it was almost never discussed in the mainstream media after the OEO years.

INTEREST-GROUP RELATIONSHIPS WITH
THE BUREAUCRACY AND CONGRESS
As discussed above, NACHC officials and staff of the regional health center organizations developed cooperative working relationships with officials and staff of the BCHS and with members of congressional health subcommittees and their staffs. By the end of the 1970s, the national association could be said to be an "institutionalized group," a group consulted "regularly" by program administrators and viewed by them as representing program constituents (Berry, 1984: 127–28).

This was not true of the interest groups that became the primary lobbyists for the food stamp program during the 1970s, the Community Nutrition Institute (CNI) and the Food Research and Action Center (FRAC). The relationship between these groups and the administrators of the food stamp program was "contentious" except for the period of the Carter administration (Berry, 1984:128). The

CNI and the FRAC were critical of bureaucratic actions and used the media to make their criticism public. They also used a strategy of litigation, obtaining an injunction against food stamp regulations issued by the Ford administration.

Neither the CNI nor the FRAC had a cooperative relationship with the agriculture committees that had legislative jurisdiction over the food stamp program. Instead, these groups worked with the liberal Congress members and staff of the Senate Select Committee on Nutrition and Human Needs in their efforts to expand the program (Berry, 1984:56, 100).

When the Carter administration took office, food stamp advocates were appointed to positions within the agencies and bureaus responsible for the program. The "outsiders" thus became "insiders." "After years of hostile treatment from USDA, public interest groups were now on the inside running the program"; these groups now had access to program administrators and were consulted when new program regulations were drafted (Berry, 1984:94–96).

After a food stamp bill was passed in 1977 with many of the reforms sought by liberals, congressional actors paid little attention to the process of writing regulations. Liberals were happy with the administration of the program; conservatives were not active on the issue. Food stamp advocates who had worked in the Carter administration were again "outsiders" when the Reagan administration came to power (Berry, 1984:96, 99). It was only during the Carter years, then, that food stamp policy was made quietly by bureaucrats and interest groups with similar views in the way characteristic of a subgovernment or an "elastic net."

Explanations for Variation in the Policy Networks

The differences in the nature of the relationships among political actors in the food stamp and health center policy networks are related to the origins of each program within the bureaucracy, the extent to which bureaucrats acted as program advocates, the location of each program within a congressional committee's jurisdiction, and variation in the type of policy issue.

The NHC concept was developed by activist physicians and OEO officials dedicated to improving health care for the poor. The earliest projects embodied the ideas of "social medicine"—that health status was a product of the social and physical environment and "treatment" included intervention in that environment. As a form of group practice employing salaried physicians and using health care teams for the delivery of primary care, health centers were also viewed as a catalyst for broader health system reform. Many of those recruited to administer the program shared this desire to provide greater access to care and to effect other changes in the health care system. The commitment of bureaucrats to the health center program continued after the War on Poverty had ended. Individual bureaucrats acted consciously to create a network of support for the program both in Congress and outside government. This included a role as "patrons" of the health center constituency organizations (Walker, 1983:404).

In contrast to the bureaucratic actors who created a support network for the health center program, food stamp program administrators during the Johnson years preferred to operate "autonomously," without consultation with political appointees or congresspersons (Berry, 1984:20–28). While the neighborhood health center "experiment" was developed by bureaucrats within OEO interacting with reformist physicians, changes in the food stamp program in the early 1960s were initiated by President Kennedy. The civil servants whose task it was to revamp the food stamp program were not acting as "policy entrepreneurs" as were the administrators of the NHC program. They thus did not need to reach out to congresspersons or others outside the bureaucracy for support.[4]

Had these civil servants been interested in initiating cooperative relationships with Congress, the task would not have been as easy as it was for the health center advocates. In the health center case, the key committee chairmen, Kennedy and Rogers, were sympathetic to health program innovation and to programs for the poor. In contrast, the food stamp program, aimed initially at reducing farm surpluses as well as hunger, fell within the jurisdiction of the Agriculture Committees in the House and Senate. Their members were concerned with price supports. Food stamps were not a salient issue (Berry 1984:37).

Ripley and Franklin, building on Theodore Lowi's typology, argue that subgovernmental relationships are characteristic of noncontroversial, "distributive" policymaking. When issues are controversial, involving the perception that resources will be allocated to the disadvantaged ("redistributive policy"), "higher-level" political actors such as the president and coalitions of interest groups will become involved (1987:21–26). While Berry describes conflict over food stamp policy as being confined to an issue network (as opposed to generating redistributive conflict between "peak associations"), the food stamp issue was far more controversial than was federal support of CHCs. Put in another way, food stamp policy was made by an issue network of actors who fundamentally disagreed with one another on the direction of policy, while participants in the health center policy network generally supported program expansion. One reason the food stamp program was controversial, while the neighborhood/community health center program was not, is the difference between "welfare" and "health" as issues.

The limited data available shows greater support among the American public for spending on health than for spending on welfare programs. Between 1961 and 1973, support for spending on welfare declined while support for spending on hospitals and medical care increased slightly (Converse et al., 1980:387–97). In a 1975 Gallup poll that asked those interviewed what areas federal money should be spent on, "health care" was one of the top three choices for 53 percent of those interviewed, while "welfare and aid to the poor" was the first, second, or third choice of 32 percent (Gallup, 1978:656).

It can be hypothesized that health care programs for the poor are viewed more positively than are income or in-kind distribution programs. Welfare has had a traditionally negative connotation—the notion that recipients are avoiding work—while those seeking health services are regarded more benignly. In addition, food stamps become a "public issue" since people using them shop in the same supermarkets as people who do not (Berry, 1984:98–99). Community health centers, in contrast, are separate institutions, apart from the private medical system and used only by the poor.

These differences in the nature of the issues do not, however, fully explain the large difference in the amount of controversy related to them. Beginning with a campaign against "dispensary abuse" in the 1890s, private practitioners have raised the issue of "abuse" of the provision of free health care by the nonpoor when they felt economically threatened by such services (see chapter 2). In addition, government funding of health services raises the spectre of socialized medicine, a label used very successfully by organized medicine in its fight against national health insurance in the 1940s and Medicare in the 1950s. Clearly, neighborhood/community health centers could be so labeled; in fact, they have been by conservative congressional actors during the Reagan administration.

The absence of active opposition from established health providers at the national level throughout most of it history was central to the noncontroversial nature of the health center program. This was at least partly related to "preventive" action taken by bureaucratic advocates of the program when the first health centers were funded. Food stamp administrators did not take similar action to protect their program.

Neither the CHC nor the food stamp policy network is a traditional "subgovernment." They are both far less autonomous than other subgovernments described in the literature. Yet in many ways, discussed above, they are quite different from one another. "Bureaucratic advocates" acted to create a policy network supportive of the health center program while food stamp administrators did not and, instead, had generally hostile relationships with congressional and interest group actors. Once the constituency group representing health centers developed as an effective interest group, the health center policy subsystem began to resemble a more traditional subgovernment, while with the exception of the

Carter years, the food stamp policy network did not. Thus, participants in the making of food stamp policy appear to be part of a more open issue network while those involved in policy relating to CHCs have closer, more supportive relationships—a type of policy network that has been called an "elastic net."

The similarities and differences between two policy networks have been analyzed. It would now be logical to expand the analysis to other cases. Unfortunately, there have been no other studies that examine social welfare policy networks over time in relation to the subgovernment and issue network models. However, some discuss various phases of policymaking related to social programs initiated since the 1960s. These include *The Dance of Legislation* by Eric Redman (1973), a description of the process leading to the creation of the National Health Service Corps, as well as studies of the implementation of that program by Frank J. Thompson (1981) and Fitzhugh Mullin (1984); a study of the politics and policies relating to federal health care for migrant workers by Budd Shenkin (1974); Henry A. Foley's study (1975) of the creation of the community mental health center program in the early 1960s; and several discussions of the federally funded legal services program.

The books by Redman and Shenkin are first-person accounts of the policy process by participants and thus describe the interactions and relationships among political actors that constitute policy networks, even though they do not label them as such. Foley's study of the development of the community mental health center legislation was one of the primary sources of Beer's discussion of the concept of the professional-bureaucratic complex. Data on the legal services program are included because the other three cases being reviewed are all health programs. If, as argued above, the nature of the issue is a critical variable, then it would be important to examine another "nonhealth" case.

Since none of these studies focuses directly on policy networks, it is not possible to compare the nature of such networks—including the degree of their mutuality and autonomy—to the food stamp and the health center cases. However, several aspects of the policymaking processes relating to these programs suggest important similarities to the dynamics of policymaking found in the two cases analyzed above.

A Broader Comparison of Policy Networks

PUBLIC SECTOR POLITICS: BUREAUCRATIC ADVOCACY
All of these programs served, at least in part, economically and socially disadvantaged populations and all were initiated by public sector actors, participants in the kind of professional-bureaucratic complex described by Beer, rather than by higher-level political actors such as the president or by private organizations outside of government. In all but one case, that of the NHSC, policy innovation came from within the bureaucracy rather than from Congress.

The authorization of the community mental health center program was the result of a process very similar to the one that established the NHC program. In both cases bureaucratic entrepreneurs created a policy network supportive of a new kind of federal health program. Program initiation represented a major shift in treatment philosophy and the role of the federal government in treatment services.

Foley traces the process by which public and congressional opinion about the treatment of mental illness was changed over a twenty year period by the work of Dr. Robert H. Felix, the director of the National Institute of Mental Health (NIMH). By cooperating with the "health syndicate," the network of bureaucrats, Congress members, and philanthropists who lobbied to expand medical research by the federal government during the 1950s, Felix got large increases in his agency's budget. He used this money to fund research and training programs that provided grants to local governments, universities, and service institutions. These institutions then became supportive of the agency and later became allies in the effort to persuade Congress to sponsor mental health services in community settings (Foley, 1975:6–22). In this case the medical research subgovernment was acting as a "patron" of what was to become a network supporting community mental health services.

In 1963, this "mental health elite," composed of NIMH officials, professional associations, and service institutions, succeeded in convincing Congress to provide federal funding for the operation of community mental health centers. Potential opposition from the administrators of state mental hospitals was prevented through a strategy of cooptation, but opposition from the AMA prevented the authorization of monies for staffing these centers until the enactment of the second Community Mental Health Act in 1965 (Foley, 1965: chs. 3, 5).

Policy entrepreneurship by bureaucratic actors was central to program initiation in both the community mental health and health center cases, but the level of the bureaucracy from which the entrepreneurs operated was different. Felix was director of the NIMH; neighborhood health centers were initially proposed by program staff within OEO's Community Action Agency who then received the support of Sargent Shriver, director of OEO. Felix also mobilized broad support for the concept of community treatment from the "mainstream" mental health community and from local government. Active support for the neighborhood health center program was not as widespread within the general health services policy community. Clearly its advocates did not possess the level of resources enjoyed by the director of NIMH.

The legal services program, like the community health and community mental health center programs, was not initiated by the potential recipients of these services, but by professionals and bureaucrats working within a specialized policy area. Legal services, like health services, were not mentioned specifically in the 1964 legislation authorizing money for antipoverty efforts (Hollingsworth, 1977:294–95). And like the neighborhood health center program, the legal services program was funded first by the Community Action Agency within OEO. The establishment of federally sponsored legal services offices in low-income neighborhoods was proposed by two attorneys, Edgar and Jean Cahn, who were advisers to Sargent Shriver. The Cahns envisioned these neighborhood offices as advocacy centers for the poor in their relationships with unresponsive social institutions, including other antipoverty agencies. Jean Cahn became the first administrator of the program (Stumpf, 1972:268; Pious, 1972:418–19).

Bureaucratic initiation of policy change within an already established program occurred in the case of migrant health care. Here a shift in the type of services to be provided was initiated by bureaucrats who belonged to a "change agent group" within the Public Health Service (Shenkin, 1974:122).

The migrant health program had been established in 1962 after considerable media and public attention was focused on the living conditions of migrant workers. The program did not challenge the interests of growers or local medical care providers, including local and state health departments. Three-quarters of the funds appropriated for migrant health went to health department programs that did not provide comprehensive primary care. Migrant workers themselves had no role in the creation of this program (Shenkin, 1974:144–49, 163).

In 1969, a new set of program guidelines was issued which allowed for the funding of migrant projects that used the NHC model of comprehensive primary care and consumer involvement in program governance. In 1970, such projects received funding for the first time. This policy shift was made by a group of health care reformers who gained control over policy decisions on migrant health for a short period of time as a result of the reorganization of the PHS in 1969 (Shenkin, 1974:120–23). This group included a small number of career bureaucrats within the PHS who were committed to health care innovation, along with the young physicians and health administrators serving for two years in the PHS as an alternative to the draft (Shenkin, 1974:111,118). Shenkin himself began his career in the PHS as such a "two-year" person and later became the administrator of the Migrant Health Program. Although the political ascendancy of this "change agent group" was short-lived, the innovations they initiated resulted in major changes in the health program for migrant workers (Shenkin, 1974:xiii, 133–34). In 1974, after he left the PHS, Shenkin worked on migrant health center legislation with the congressional staffers who also were working on the community health center legislation. He describes sharing a commonality of age, background, and point of view with these individuals (1974:213–19). Shenkin was part of the network of physicians and other young professionals in government during the 1970s whose policy commitments had been shaped by the social events of the 1960s (see chapter 4). The impact of these individuals within government is an important issue that has not yet been addressed in the literature on policy entrepreneurship.

Policy initiation also came from within government in the case of the NHSC. The idea of a federal doctor corps to provide medical care in areas without physicians was suggested to Eric Redman, a very junior member of Senator Warren Magnuson's staff, by a Seattle pediatrician who was an "unofficial adviser" to the senator (Redman, 1973:38). In contrast to the other cases of policy innovation discussed above, the 1970 legislation establishing the NHSC was a result of lobbying for the program within Congress by Magnuson's staff, not by bureaucratic actors. Neither the health officials of the Nixon administration nor the health bureaucracy supported the legislation (Redman, 1973; Thompson, 1981:86–87).

PROGRAM ADVOCACY BY A "THIRD PARTY"[5]
Although the legal services program was initiated within the bureaucracy in much the same way as was the NHC program, its subsequent political history was quite different. An early struggle for control among the advocates of independent neighborhood legal services offices (the Cahns among others), officials of the Community Action Program, and the American Bar Association (ABA) and other lawyers' groups was won by the national bar associations (Pious, 1972:420–22). The primary supporter of the legal services program during most of its existence was the ABA, a professional group outside government with substantial political resources.

Although technically part of the Community Action Program (CAP) the legal services program was essentially independent of its bureaucratic home. Grants and program guidelines needed ABA rather than CAP approval. Representatives of the ABA, rather than bureaucratic officials, attempted to mobilize support for the legal services program from local bar associations and legal aid societies, groups initially cautious about the program. National bar leaders lobbied successfully with their fellow attorneys in Congress for legislation to increase the independence of the program from OEO (Pious, 1972:422–30; Stumpf, 1972:269–70). Support from the ABA was critical to the survival of the OEO legal services program and its antecedent, the Legal Services Corporation (Hollingsworth, 1977:297–99). "The elite bar (the American Bar Association for the most part) came to view Legal Services as an institution to be defended. . . . Friends in OEO, like Sargent Shriver, had long gone; political enemies abounded on all levels . . . and client groups had neither the strength nor the will to defend programs" (Hollingsworth, 1977:297–98; see also Pious, 1972:431).

In spite of the fact that the legal services program had an influential professional group as its advocate, continued federal sponsorship of legal services was often controversial. Program supporters met with strong opposition throughout the history of the program and this opposition generated considerable public debate.

THE NATURE OF THE ISSUE

A major source of dispute about the legal services program was the type of cases that legal services lawyers should be allowed to handle. The national, but not necessarily the state and local, bar groups supported legal services involvement in class action suits to establish the rights of large groups of people. In 1967 and in 1969 conservative members of Congress attacked the program in response to the successes of the California Rural Legal Services Program in broadening the rights of migrant farm workers and Medicare recipients (Stumpf, 1972:281–87; Pious, 1972:427–31). One author called the legal services program "the most praised and the most vilified unit in the now defunct War on Poverty" (Stumpf, 1972:267).

The debate over "law reform" as a proper sphere of activity for federally funded lawyers was carried on in the national media. The ABA prevailed in its opposition to efforts by Congress to prohibit suits against government agencies and to give state and local governments veto power over the funding of local projects (Pious, 1972:427–31). However, the 1974 legislation establishing a Legal Services Corporation prohibited lawyers from handling "political" cases such as those involving school desegregation, the selective service, and abortion (Hollingsworth, 1977:298).

At least twice in its history, the legal services program became a "redistributive issue" on which national political leaders and coalitions of national organizations were active. The Nixon White House was directly involved in conflict with the ABA and congressional leaders over the structure of the Legal Services Corporation in the early 1970s (Pious, 1972:438–45). In 1981, a presidential proposal to replace the Legal Services Corporation with block grants to the states resulted in the mobilization of two ideologically opposed coalitions. The one organized by the ABA included state and local bar associations, judges, and liberal groups such as the United Auto Workers, the National Council of Churches, the League of Women Voters, and the NAACP. The block grant proposal was supported by ideologically conservative groups such as the Moral Majority, the U.S. Chambers of Commerce, the Conservative Caucus, and the National Conservative Political Action Committee (Peirce and Steinbach, 1981:1025). A *New York Times* article called the controversy over legal services for the poor "the longest-running political brawl since President Reagan came to town" (8 June 1984:A16). Clearly, policymaking about federally supported legal services was not confined to a quiet subgovernment or an "elastic net," but was even more open in terms of the number of diverse groups involved than was the food stamp issue network.

In contrast to legal services, the three other health programs reviewed here were much "quieter" issues. Migrant health, like the community health center program, was an issue of low salience to the general public and generated little interest outside of government (Shenkin, 1974:204). The NHSC was supported by a broad coalition within Congress—conservative and rural Congress members from areas with few physicians, as well as liberal members of Congress committed to restructuring American health care. There was conflict within this policy network after 1976 when corps doctors were placed in other federal programs such as community health centers. Conservatives viewed the corps as a device to stimulate private practice in underserved areas and opposed the idea of a federal doctor corps (Mullin, 1984:189). Nonetheless, this policy did not generate much public debate nor did it involve interest groups from outside the health services policy community (see Thompson, 1981:88–90). Compared to legal services and food stamps, the community mental health center program was also not a controversial issue.

Further Explanation for Variation in Policy Networks

This analysis of four additional cases in the area of social welfare policy confirms the fact that such cases do not fit the traditional subgovernmental model of policymaking. At the same time, there is variation in the autonomy of these policy networks; they are on a continuum of openness to outside actors. The two variables that appear to be central in determining where on the continuum such networks operate are the amount of resources available to program advocates and the nature of the issue itself. (These are of course interrelated, since one form of power is the ability to shape the way in which an issue is perceived.)

As these cases suggest, the greater the resources enjoyed by private or public sector advocates of a policy, the greater the autonomy of the policy network. For example, the policy network supportive of the community mental health center program appears to have been more autonomous and closer to the traditional subgovernmental model than was the network relating to the neighborhood/community health center program. The director of

NIMH had far more resources to use in mobilizing mental health agencies and professional groups on behalf of community-based care than did the advocates of neighborhood/community health centers.

At the same time, the history of the legal services program makes it clear that if an issue provokes conflict, the policy network relating to that issue will be more open, even if it includes political actors enjoying large amounts of political resources. The policy networks relating to the migrant health, community health center, and National Health Service Corps programs appear to have been more autonomous than was the network concerned with the legal services program. This was in spite of the fact that the latter program always had the support of the ABA, a prestigious and influential professional group.

As noted earlier, the provision of health care to the poor was less controversial than efforts to provide food stamps or legal services. Increasing access to health services does not appear to arouse negative feelings among the public about the receipt of benefits by the "unworthy" as readily as do the food stamp or AFDC programs. Possibly this is because ill health is regarded as a situation in which seeking help is acceptable. In addition, these federal health programs remained small enough so that the traditional arrangements between private and public medicine were not challenged on a widespread basis. Opposition to these programs from existing providers did not have a national impact. In the case of legal services, a program supported by a national provider group, opposition came largely from outside the legal community. Law reform and social advocacy were challenging to existing institutional structures in a way in which health services for the poor were not (see Stumpf, 1972:282).

The direction of future research is clear. More studies are needed to analyze the nature of policy networks relating to social welfare programs over a long period of time. It is crucial to study a policy network as it changes during different administrations and congresses and to observe periods of quiet and of public controversy, if there are both.

To extend the analysis begun here, we should pay attention to the relationships between variation in the size of program expenditures and the existence of conflict; to the "nature of the issue"; to whether and what kinds of interest groups are participants in the policy process; to the incentives and/or disincentives for supportive behavior by bureaucratic and congressional actors; and to the way these incentives/disincentives are affected by changes in the larger political environment.

9

Community Health Centers and National Health Policy

Lessons for the Future

One of the lessons of the history of the neighborhood/community health center program is that change in the health care system in the United States cannot develop directly out of a program limited to the poor. Advocates of health centers within both OEO and DHEW believed that these projects would be supported by Medicare and Medicaid and that eventually the neighborhood health center model would be the basis of a restructured health care delivery system serving groups other than the poor. I have argued that it was precisely because the program was to be limited to the poor that the federal government could fund a program that attempted to provide social medicine and community-based care. The population to be served by this program was one that neither private practitioners nor hospitals wished to treat. However, such a population was also without the economic and political resources necessary to influence the continued allocation of funds to this kind of health care delivery model. The ability of most health centers to provide community health services was severely limited after the end of the War on Poverty, as federal policy required them to compete with other, favored providers for Medicare and Medicaid reimbursement.

Victor and Ruth Sidel (1984) come to a similar conclusion in their review of a number of the health system innovations initiated in the 1960s and early 1970s. They note that the women's health movement was one of the most successful attempts at health care reform because it included upper-middle-class women and health professionals with political resources. They suggest that future reform programs must be seen as beneficial to powerful as well as powerless groups in the society if they are to be fully implemented (1984:276–7). H. Jack Geiger makes a similar argument about the need for broad support for community health centers in the future (1984:31). Whether such political support can be mobilized is a difficult question. Ironically, actual health system restructuring is occurring in the 1980s, although not necessarily in the way that health care reformers in the 1960s hoped it would. The current situation may present the opportunity for CHCs to become an integral part of a restructured health care system.

As I discussed briefly in chapter 7, prospective hospital reimbursement, prepaid and managed health care, and the growth of profit-making health care corporations are transforming the delivery of care. The Reagan administration's success in reducing spending on social programs while unemployment has increased in some sectors of the American economy has resulted in more poverty and an expansion in the number of persons without health insurance. How to provide care to those not covered by public programs or private insurance has become a central question for business associations, hospital associations, and state and local governments (Richards, 1984; Iglehart, 1985). The future of CHCs will depend in part on how the debate on this question is structured. As has been shown repeatedly in this study, those with greater political resources are more able structure the terms of professional and public debate.

The major health policy issue in the United States in the 1980s has been the cost of care. In 1980, $247 billion, or $1,067 per capita, was spent for health services. This was 9.4 percent of the gross national product (GNP). In 1984, this had increased to 10.6 percent of the GNP; health care expenditures were $387.4 billion, or $1,580 per capita (DHEW, *Health U.S.*, 1981:2, 1985:2). The share of these costs paid by the government has increased mark-edly since the 1960s. In 1965, 22 percent of all health care expenditures were made by government (local, state, and federal); by 1980 public monies paid for 40 percent of all services (Weickert, 1981:81).

The development of a prospective system for hospital reimbursement under Medicare was an effort to reduce federal health care costs. Hospitals are paid at a rate calculated from the average cost of treating a specific category of illness, or diagnostic related group. Hospitals that operate for less than the prepaid rate keep the savings; those that spend more must absorb the additional cost. This system replaces one in which hospitals were paid on the basis of a daily rate calculated to cover costs and under which there were limited incentives to control costs.

One consequence of this change in reimbursement policy is that hospitals that treat the uninsured poor can no longer cover these costs from excess revenue generated by Medicare patients (Richards, 1984:106). At the same time, changes in Medicaid eligibility rules and reductions in the federal government's share of Medicaid funding that occurred between 1981 and 1985 have increased the numbers of uninsured patients (Iglehart, 1985:61).

This decrease in access to Medicaid and to other social programs for health and nutrition services, income maintenance, and housing since the Reagan administration took office appears to be related to a deterioration in the health status gains made since the 1960s. There has been an increase in anemia in pregnant woman and in the incidence of low-birth-weight babies. Both of these conditions are associated with the absence of prenatal care, which has also been on the rise since 1981. Data from several different cities indicate an increase in childhood diseases and conditions such as anemia, diarrhea and dehydration, "failure to thrive," measles, and lead poisoning. All of these are preventable illnesses. Since 1982, the infant mortality rate has decreased at a substantially slower rate than in the seventeen previous years. In contrast, during an economic recession in the mid-1970s, social program funding was not reduced and the rate of decrease in the infant mortality rate remained stable. (There has also been a reduction in the funding for the federal agencies that collect and analyze data on health status and this makes it even more difficult to assess the relationship between funding cuts and health) (Mundinger, 1985:45–46). The Reagan administration itself released a DHHS Task Force Report on the Health of Minorities in 1985. That report stated that the United States was not providing adequate health care to minority groups in general, and that the rates of mortality and morbidity among these groups has continued to be considerably higher than that of the population as a whole (APHA, *The Nation's Health*, December 1985:1, 6).

Along with the tremendous concern with the cost of care has come an awareness that a major factor in this increase is the orientation to high-technology, hospital-based inpatient care throughout the health services system. An assessment of the variables related to the increase in the cost of care between 1965 and 1980 found that much of the increase (58 percent) was due to increased prices for physician and hospital services rather than to population growth (9 percent) or to greater use of health services (33 percent). These price increases were in turn related to the greater use of complex tests and high technology treatment for a variety of conditions (Weickert, 1981:81–85). Studies have indicated that in many instances, these services are often provided when not really necessary or effective (Myers and Schroeder, 1981).

At the same time, there is evidence that relatively inexpensive treatments for simple conditions have had a large impact on reducing morality rates in the United States during the last twenty years. According to a 1983 report of the President's Commission for the Study of Ethical Problems in Medicine and Biomedical and Behavioral Research, deaths from infectious diseases such as influenza, tuberculosis, pneumonia, and other treatable conditions such as diabetes have declined since the expansion in the 1960s of publicly supported programs serving the medically underserved (President's Commission, 1983:53–55). Infant mortality rates dropped very rapidly between 1965 and 1974, after leveling off between 1950 and 1964. The death rates for children ages 1 to 4 also decreased, and the maternal mortality rate fell 50 percent during this period. During 1965–1974, infant mortality declined more rapidly for nonwhites than for whites (this was not true in the 1950–1964 period) and the decrease in the infant mortality rate was more substantial in states with higher poverty rates than in others (Davis and Schoen, 1978:32–34, 148). This suggests that the decline was greatest among low-income women (there is no national data on infant mortality and maternal income) and can be related to the expansion of income maintenance, nutrition, and health programs during the 1960s. Although declines in mortality and morbidity are related to improvements in general socioeconomic conditions as well as to the provision of care, this fact "does not diminish the evidence that improved health has paralleled the broadening of access to care" (President's Commission, 1983:55).

Prevention programs have also contributed to decreases in disease and death rates and have done so at a minute cost compared to what would have been spent on treatment. Hypertension programs, for instance, have reduced death rates from heart disease (Terris, 1983:253) and have decreased the incidence of serious kidney disease that would have been treated with dialysis or kidney transplants (President's Commission, 1983:70–71).

Community health centers have been a vehicle for providing the primary care and preventive services that are so clearly cost-effective in the long term. Numerous studies have documented improvements in health status in the areas served by these centers as compared to similar areas without centers. They have also documented the fact that these projects have reduced the hospitalization rates and length of hospital stays in their patient populations (see Geiger, 1984:28–29). Several recently published studies with large data bases have reaffirmed that health centers are cost-effective and, at the same time, improve health status.

Data from two large household surveys done prior to and then several years after the establishment of health centers in five different communities found that hospital admission rates for patients whose usual source of care was a community health center were about half the rate of those using a hospital outpatient department as their primary source of care. The hospitalization rate for health center patients was about one-quarter of the rate for the population usually treated by a private physician. Even when ethnicity, income, education, age, health, and insurance status are held constant, patients treated at health centers had lower rates of hospital admissions than patients whose usual source of care was a hospital outpatient department.

The authors of the household surveys study conclude that the use of health centers by even a portion of the population now using outpatient departments as their usual source of care would reduce government spending considerably. This is because inpatient hospitalization would be reduced and because the cost of primary care is lower in a health center than in a hospital outpatient department (Freeman et al., 1982:256–64). Another study in three communities that compared Medicaid patients using CHCs with Medicaid patients using other sources of care also found that health center patients had lower hospitalization rates and shorter hospital stays than did those not using CHCs as their primary source of care. Health center patients also used hospital emergency rooms less frequently than did others receiving Medicaid. Costs for health center patients in all three communities were lower than for the other Medicaid patients (Geiger, 1984:28).

Improvements in health status that have resulted from the establishment of CHCs are demonstrated in another large study, a multiple regression analysis using data from 678 of the largest counties in the United States during 1970–1978. This study found that the presence of several CHCs in a county had a statistically significant impact on both white and black infant mortality rates, but a larger impact on black rates. This study concluded that the expansion of the network of health centers would be important in the further reduction of infant mortality among blacks in the United States (Grossman and Goldman, 1985:21–23). The success of community health centers in providing high-quality and cost-effective care to low-income populations was recognized by the president's commission, mentioned above (1983:131–33). Further research needs to be done to isolate the factors that have made health centers more cost-effective than other modes of care. The role of physical accessibility to a community, of the employment of salaried physicians, of consumer participation in reducing barriers to access, and so forth, has not been studied separately in relation to either the cost of care or improvements in health status (see Geiger, 1984:30).

There has been some discussion of serious planning for a "cost-effective national health program." Such a program would include allocating resources to home health services rather than to nursing homes, major funding for prevention programs, and the delivery of primary care through group practices and community health centers (Terris, 1983:252–55). Participants at a 1982 conference sponsored by the Institute of Medicine of the National Academy of Sciences suggested that there were several factors that made the 1980s an auspicious period for developing systems of "community-oriented primary care." In addition to pressure at all levels of government to find means to deliver health services that would use limited resources most efficiently (Piore, 1982:129–32; Davis, 1982:174), there was an expanding supply of physicians that would increase the pool of potential primary care practitioners and also the recognition that many of the leading causes of morbidity and mortality were environmentally related and could be controlled by attending to the physical and social hazards that produce them (Davis, 1982:173). However, it is clear from this study that technocratic, "rational" values such long-term cost-efficiency are far less significant in determining how health care delivery will be organized than is ideology or the interests of politically powerful provider groups. The Reagan administration's philosophy of limited government and expansion of the "market" in health care is not compatible with a national health care program.

The issue of the uninsured poor has been central in current health policy discussions, but its focus has been on how existing providers (primarily hospitals) will get paid without increasing costs to the business community, not about how services can be made more accessible and cost-effective. Hospital associations view the "uncompensated costs" of caring for the uninsured poor as a high priority issue (Iglehart, 1985:59). Chambers of commerce and other coalitions of business groups, fearing that the costs of caring for the uninsured will be shifted to them via higher insurance premiums, have taken a leading role in persuading state governments to develop ways to finance care for the indigent from public monies (Richards, 1984:112). Proposed strategies (some of which have already been implemented at the state level) include: developing statewide "all payer systems" in which hospitals receive monies to pay for the "charity" and "bad debt" cases; a state trust fund financed by hospital assessments and state appropriations to pay for uncompensated care; a system of state insurance coverage for catastrophic illness for the uninsured poor; and federal grants to states to pay for such care (Iglehart, 1985; 63). According to a spokesperson for the American Public Health Association, "The whole issue has come up because hospitals are not getting paid. With the cutbacks that have occurred in Medicare and Medicaid the issue has turned from one of equity for the poor to equity for hospitals" (Richards, 1984:109).

As I discussed in chapter 7, planning for health services has shifted to the state level. As state governments are pressured by providers and business coalitions to underwrite care for the uninsured, they in turn are examining the options for alternative health care delivery plans. It is in this context that health centers are now competing with other providers to participate in prepaid contract arrangements with state governments. It was the recognition of the growing role of state governments in health policy that led to the 1981 restructuring of the NACHC and the development of a technical assistance program to state primary care associations under a grant from the Robert Wood Johnson Foundation. These activities were part of an effort to develop community health center policy networks at the state level. Such networks, however, operate within a context in which other providers, such as national health care companies, voluntary hospitals, and existing HMOs, will have far more political resources than do health centers.

The fact that decisions made by state officials about prepayment plans and Medicaid reimbursement are "political" decisions has brought us full circle, back to the discussion in chapter 2 of the history of ambulatory health care in the United States. This was a history of political mobilization and conflict, one in which the patterns of primary care delivery in the United States were shaped by political activity. So too, will be the nature of ambulatory health care in the 1990s—and beyond.

Notes
References
Index

Notes

Chapter 1. Perspectives on the Policymaking Process in Primary Care

1. See Michael P. Smith and Associates, 1974:3–8. A distinction can be made between "group theory" and "pluralism." The key argument of pluralists such as Robert Dahl was that "power is diffused and dispersed" and that "competition among various power centers is the essence of the political process" (Bill and Hardgrave, 1973:168; Hamilton, 1972:34–36). There is a general agreement that group theory is a form of "modern" or "analytical" pluralism (see Olson, 1965:118). Group theorists such as David Truman focused on the "group" as the basic analytic unit through which this competitive process takes place. Thus, while pluralists such as Dahl do not necessarily use a group approach, the fundamental assumptions of group theory were pluralist (see Bill and Hardgrave, 1973:140).

2. Much of this work is based on a typology of policy types developed by Theodore J. Lowi (1964). While there has been a debate about the broadness of the categories of Lowi's typology (see Wilson, 1973:328; Hayes, 1981:21), the distinction made between "distributive" and "redistributive" policies helps to explain the way that political conflicts are limited within the American policy process.

3. This gap in the literature may be explained by the fact that the study of all of these relationships simultaneously is time-consuming and that charting informal relationships between political actors requires the use of a qualitative methodology.

4. A modified "snowball" sampling strategy was used to select the interviewees. A preliminary set of interviews was conducted with key participants in the health center policy network in New York, and these participants suggested a list of important federal actors to interview. As these interviews proceeded, additional persons were suggested in the process of discussing events and issues related to the neighborhood/community health center program. In addition, at the end of each interview, participants were asked directly for the names of other individuals who were knowledgeable about the events or topics discussed. The author was also very generously given access to transcripts of interviews conducted

between 1974 and 1977 with neighborhood health center project directors and administrators and national program officials by Professors Jude Thomas May and Peter Kong-ming New (May and New transcripts).

5. A separate set of questionnaires was developed for each type of political actor (i.e., health center administrators, agency officials, congressional staff persons) for each time period being investigated. These questionnaires consisted of different "question sets" which focused on one research topic or theme. For example, one question set dealt with the history of regional and national health center associations; several sets dealt with the specific process of drafting authorizing legislation; another set was designed to elicit general opinions on the political future of the neighborhood/community health center program. The questions themselves were specific and focused, but open-ended, as most of them asked the informants to describe the behavior of political actors or the reasons why a particular course of action was undertaken. When new information was given, the interviewer asked additional questions that had not been prepared in advance. Question sets that were found to be inappropriate during the course of a specific interview were omitted. As the researcher proceeded with the interviews, questions were added in order to corroborate previous information given and to elicit further discussion on the issue or topic. Interviews lasted from one to four hours. All but two of the face-to-face interviews were tape-recorded with permission of the person being interviewed.

Chapter 2. The Mobilization of Bias and Primary Care Policy

1. Even so, "ideology" is complicated to measure, and they discuss the shift in the mobilization of bias "in favor of equality of opportunity" in qualified terms (see Bachrach and Baratz, 1970:94–100).

2. The first dispensaries in the United States were established in 1786, 1790, and 1796, in Philadelphia, New York, and Boston, respectively (Davis and Warner, 1918:4). In New York, in contrast to the other cities, almost all dispensaries, although privately run, received a state or city subsidy (Duffy, 1974:185; Rosenberg 1974:34).

3. Burrow reports that in some areas, citizens reacted to such fee-setting with protests and boycotts, but that in general "the profession succeeded in preventing popular outbursts far more often than it failed" (1977:109).

4. One Kentucky medical society prohibited its members from treating anyone on the "blacklist" unless emergency care was required and, in that case, only if the patient paid the doctor in cash (Burrow, 1977:110).

5. Paul Starr cautions that the number of health centers reported by writers in the 1920s and 1930s sometimes includes individual clinics such as those for tuberculosis, as well as the centers where a number of different services were offered (1982:194–95).

6. The Cincinnati Social Unit and its relationship to the neighborhood health center movement were brought to my attention by Dr. H. Jack Geiger.

7. The existence of a mobilization of bias, which precluded the introduction of proposals enlarging the federal role in the delivery of care, is demonstrated in Eric Redman's first-person account of the formulation and enactment of legislation establishing the National Health Service Corps (see Redman, 1973:37–38, 99).

Chapter 3. The Neighborhood Health Center Program

1. For more detailed analyses of the development of the OEO neighborhood health center program during the Johnson and early Nixon years, see the articles by May, Durham, and New, cited throughout (esp. 1980B), and Marcus, 1981.

2. While there are no data available on the exact number of health centers that employed family health workers, a major evaluation study of the neighborhood health center program conducted for the federal government in 1970–71 found that all twenty-one of the health centers surveyed had outreach programs, two-thirds of the health centers used teams to deliver care, and a majority of the programs studied offered health training programs to community residents (Lewis et al., 1976:192–96, 203).

3. Marcus identifies "mounting pressure regarding the costs of implementing the War on Poverty" as the reason for the changes but emphasizes that the eligibility criteria "diluted and compromised" the "initial community-based perspective of the program" (1981:43–45).

4. The first project directors were white physicians with medical school affiliations. In the 1970s, program directors were more likely to be nonwhite, nonphysician, health service administrators (Anderson et al., 1976:22–23).

5. When the sponsorship of the Mount Bayou Health Center was transferred from the Tufts University School of Medicine to a community corporation, the governor of Mississippi vetoed the transfer. The veto was overridden by the director of OEO (Interview, 31 March 1978).

6. The congressional debate also reflected the intrusion of the Vietnam War into social issues in terms of a tension between spending for the war versus domestic programs (CR, 26, 27, 29 September 1967).

7. The following discussion of DHEW funding of health centers is drawn primarily from David Blumenthal (1970).

8. An informal agreement was made between DHEW and OEO officials that when the number of OEO-funded projects had increased substantially and they were "well established," they would be transferred to DHEW (Interview, 12 October 1975:16, May and New transcripts).

Chapter 4. Program Survival and Institutionalization

1. The number of grant-in-aid programs (federal programs designed for a specific purpose which are locally administered within a set of federal guidelines) had increased dramatically during the 1960s. The total amount spent by the federal government for these programs was $2.2 billion in 1950, $7 billion in 1960, and $20.3 billion by 1969 (Judd, 1984:325).

2. Donald Rumsfeld, appointed by Nixon to head OEO, became convinced that the health programs supported by the agency were valuable. During 1969 and 1970 he acted as an advocate for the OEO health program with the White House. His support, however, was not necessarily for the neighborhood health center model. New grants were therefore made to other kinds of comprehensive health center programs (Interviews, 13 and 14 May 1975, May and New transcripts).

3. A revised version of Marcus's 1974 Ph.D. dissertation, which she wrote under the name of Isabel Walsh Pritchard, was published in 1981. In some instances, the dissertation (Pritchard, 1974) has been cited above.

4. Boston, like New York, had a relatively large number of health centers. In fact, the number of centers in Boston was larger than the number in New York. Many of these, however, were not funded by OEO and were smaller than the OEO centers. Boston, under Mayor Kevin White, had itself funded many small centers during the late 1960s (Interview A, 12 July 1979).

5. Michael T. Hayes conceptualizes congressional behavior in much the same way (1981:138–39).

6. Robert Hollister makes the same point in his study of the formative years of health center development in Denver and St. Louis (see 1971:256).

7. Bauman, who studied an overlapping health policy network concerned with HMO legislation, found the same phenomenon occurring (1976:137).

8. In contrast, several of the first DHEW grants under section 314(e) of the Public Health Service Act went to centers with boards composed of community residents.

9. It was more difficult for staff of the two appropriations committees to recall precisely the way in which the NHC program was perceived over time by committee members and staff than it was for the staff of the authorizing committees. This is because the appropriations committees deal with a very large number of health programs at one time and do so every year. Authorizing committees draft legislation far less frequently and spend more time on the details of each program.

Chapter 5. A Bureaucratic Strategy of Policy Change

1. See Hugh Heclo's 1977 discussion of the independence of career civil servants from the political appointees heading federal government agencies.

2. As a result of the creation of the Department of Education at the end of 1979, the Department of Health, Education, and Welfare (DHEW) became the Department of Health and Human Services (DHHS).

3. CHAP legislation passed the House during the Ninety-sixth Congress, but was never reported by the Senate Finance Committee (NACHC, *Legislative Status Report,* 7 January 1981:5).

4. The criterion for medical underservice "is that the area to be served by the project include at least one county which has at least three of the following designations: as a Medically Underserved Area, a Health Manpower Shortage Area, a High Infant Mortality Area, a High Migrant Impact Area or a High Impact Area" (NACHC, *Program Guidance Material,* 1978:8). For descriptions of the criteria of each of the above designations, see Samuels, 1978:166.

5. In 1978, approximately the same number of *older community* health centers were serving a population more than one-third greater than the population that they had served in 1975 (S. Rept. 95-860:10).

6. Studies have documented the effectiveness of health center programs in improving health status and reducing hospitalization rates (see chapter 9), but it has not been determined whether comprehensive health services, outreach services, or other aspects of the program singly or in combination are responsible for these outcomes (see Geiger, 1984:30 for the same point).

7. In the early 1980s the Reagan administration and Congress reduced funding for such primary care services (see chapter 7) and established a prospective reimbursement system to reduce Medicare payments for hospital services.

8. The central finding of a comparative study of health planning in the United States, England, France, and Québec is that provider behavior responds primarily to the structure of health financing (Rodwin, 1984).

Chapter 6. The Health Center Policy Network

1. In 1986, the sliding scale dues structure ranged from $150 to $4,000 per organizational member (NACHC, Membership Application, 1986).

2. This was also due to the fact that members knew that Chairman Paul Rogers "was reasonable" and that "he would always respond to their particular concerns" (Interview, 18 February 1980).

3. Many members of the association took the position that if their organization was to be an advocate for the needs of the medically indigent, then it would have to be concerned with changing the nature of hospital outpatient departments. This was because community health centers served only a small portion of the medically underserved and most low-income persons were dependent on hospital outpatient clinics and/or emergency rooms for medical care (Interview B, 24 July 1979).

Chapter 7. The Health Center Policy Network Under Siege

1. This discussion and a discussion of the Senate Labor and Human Resources Committee on pages 170–71 are based on the individual voting scores of members of the House and Senate during 1981 as developed by the *National Journal* and *The Baron Report* and reported in the *National Journal* of May 8, 1982. The scores were based on thirty-nine House and forty-one Senate votes selected from roll-call data collected by the Inter-University Consortium for Political and Social Research at Ann Arbor, Michigan. In comparing the scores of members of these two health sub-committees to the average scores of their party colleagues, only scores on economic and social issues are considered, although the *National Journal* and *The Baron Report* also assigned a score for foreign policy (see Cohen, 1982).

2. Those scores that are more liberal than the overall average are represented by positive numbers; those that are more conservative than average are represented by negative numbers. The average score of all Democratic members of the House was +75 on economic issues and +53 on social issues, while the average score of all Republican House members was −66 for social issues and −94 for economic issues.

3. The average score for the Democratic members of the Senate Committee on Labor and Human Resources was +161 on economic issues, in contrast to +79 for all Senate Democrats; and +111 on social issues, as compared to +39 for all Senate Democrats.

4. A 1980 report released by the House Appropriations Committee was also critical of the CHC and NHSC programs. Productivity and the cost of these programs were compared unfavorably with the private sector, and opposition was expressed to their expansion. Both BCHS and the national association responded to this critique and these responses were included in the report. Several informants stated that the impetus for this House committee report was also the projected expansion of the program by health policymakers within the Carter administration.

5. Initially Dr. Martin was appointed assistant HRSA administrator for clinical affairs while another long-time BCHS official became acting BHCDA director. This was done because Marjorie Mecklenberg, the conservative, "pro-family" administrator of the family planning program, objected to having Martin as her superior. The family planning program was later transferred out of BHCDA and Martin became BHCDA director (NACHC, *Washington Update,* 7 February 1983:4).

6. The medical care inflation rate was calculated from the Consumer Price Index for Medical Care, U.S. City Average, as reported in the Bureau of Labor Statistics CPI Detailed Report. The indexes for March of each year, the midpoint of that fiscal year, were used.

Chapter 8. Networks in Social Welfare Policy

1. Tierney's propositions (1985:5) are based on the work of Gais, Peterson, and Walker, 1984.

2. This term was suggested by the title of an article by A. Grant Jordon, "Iron Triangles, Woolly Corporatism and Elastic Nets: Images of the Policy Process" (1981). Jordon presents a very thoughtful examination of the applicability of four models of the policy process—iron triangles, issue networks, corporatism, and cabinet government—to the contemporary United States and United Kingdom, including insightful commentary on the clarity of the literature that discusses these concepts. Jordon uses the term "elastic nets" in the title (not in the text) of his article to refer to the more open issue network image, in contrast to the closed, rigid images of iron triangles and corporatism. We are using the term far more specifically, to represent one of three models in our typology.

3. During the early 1970s program administrators did consult with agriculture committees as they wrote regulations, but this appears to have been a "defensive" strategy rather than a cooperative relationship based on shared policy goals (see Berry, 1984:79–80).

4. Berry does say that the Community Nutrition Institute and the Food Research and Action Center "each received a good deal of federal funding" (1984:131), but he does not discuss the specific source of these funds nor how this fits with the "outsider" role these groups had for most of their existence.

5. The term "third party" is used to mean an interest group with substantial political resources that is supportive of a program that serves a group with very few such resources. This concept has been used in the analysis of protest politics (see Lipsky, 1968).

References

Written Sources

Abramowitz, Kenneth. *The Future of Health Care Delivery in America.* New York: Sanford C. Bernstein, 1985.
Abramson, Joseph H., and Sidney Kark. "Community Oriented Primary Care: Meaning and Scope." In *Community Oriented Primary Care: Conference Proceedings.* Institute of Medicine. Washington, D.C.: National Academy Press, 1982.
Accreditation Association for Ambulatory Health Care, Inc., Pamphlet, AAAHC, n.d.
"Amagrams." *JAMA* 229 (9 September 1974): 1414.
American Health Planning Association. *Crosscurrents: A Forum on Health Planning and Primary Care Programs.* Washington, D.C.: AHPA. Vol. 2, no 6 (November–December 1980); vol. 3, no. 2 (Summer 1981); "Update," September 1981.
American Hospital Association. *Reshaping Ambulatory Care Programs: Report and Recommendations of a Conference on Ambulatory Care.* Chicago: AHA, 1973.
American Public Health Association. *The Nation's Health.* Washington, D.C.: APHA, December 1985.
Anderson, Elizabeth J., Leda R. Judd, Jude Thomas May, and Peter K. New. *The Neighborhood Health Center Program, Its Growth and Problems: An Introduction.* Washington, D.C.: NANHC, 1976.
Anderson, James E. *Public Policy-Making,* 3d ed. New York: Holt, Rinehart and Winston, 1984.

Anderson, Odin W. *The Unequal Equilibrium: Private and Public Financing of Health Services in the U.S., 1875–1965.* New Haven, Conn.: College and University Press, 1968.

Arieff, Irwin B. "The New Bureaucracy: Growing Staff System on Hill Forcing Changes in Congress." *Congressional Quarterly* 37 (24 November 1979): 2631.

Arnold, R. Douglas. *Congress and the Bureaucracy, A Theory of Influence.* New Haven, Conn.: Yale University Press, 1979.

Association of New York Neighborhood Health Centers, Inc. "Memorandum Re: Notice of Proposed Rulemaking, Department of Health, Education, and Welfare, Health Services and Mental Health Administration. [42 CFR Part 50], *Federal Register,* May 21, 1973." 15 June 1973. (ANYNHC, 1973)

Bachrach, Peter, and Morton S. Baratz. *Power and Poverty, Theory and Practice.* New York: Oxford University Press, 1970.

Battistella, Roger M., and Thomas G. Rundall. *Health Care Policy in a Changing Environment.* Berkeley, Calif.: McCutchen, 1978.

Bauman, Patricia. "The Formulation and Evolution of the Health Maintenance Organization Policy, 1970–1973." *Social Science & Medicine* 10 (March–April 1976): 129–42.

Beer, Samuel H. "The Adoption of General Revenue Sharing: A Case Study in Public Sector Politics." *Public Policy* 24 (Spring 1976): 127–95.

Bellush, Jewel, and Stephen M. David, eds. *Race and Politics in New York City, Five Studies in Policy-Making.* New York: Praeger, 1977.

Berry, Jeffrey M. *Feeding Hungry People, Rulemaking in the Food Stamp Program.* New Brunswick, N.J.: Rutgers University Press, 1984.

Betten, Neil, and Michael Austin. "The Unwanted Helping Hand." *Environment* 19 (January–February 1977): 13–36.

Bill, James A., and Robert L. Hardgrave, Jr. *Comparative Politics, The Quest for Theory.* Columbus, Ohio: Charles E. Merrill, 1973.

Blumenthal, David. "Out-OEO-ing OEO': Institutional Innovation in the Public Health Service." Honors thesis, Department of Government, Harvard University, 1970.

Bornemeier, Walter C. "Shapers of the Future." *JAMA* 211 (21 December 1970): 2181–84.

Brandon, William. "Politics, Administration, and Conflict in Neighborhood Health Centers." *Journal of Health Politics, Policy and Law* 2 (Spring 1977): 79–99.

Brown, Lawrence D. "The Formulation of Federal Health Care Policy." *Bulletin of the New York Academy of Medicine* 54 (January 1978): 45–58.

"Budget Conferees Face Challenge on Reconciliation." *National Journal,* 13 September 1980, p. 1531.

"Budget: Congress Reaches Agreement on 'Reconciliation' Bill." *National Journal,* 29 November 1980, p. 1947.

Bureau of Community Health Services. See U.S. Department of Health, Education, and Welfare.

Burrow, James G. *Organized Medicine in the Progressive Era: The Move Toward Monopoly.* Baltimore, Md.: Johns Hopkins University Press, 1977.

Cairl, Richard E., and Allen W. Imershein. "National Health Insurance Policy in the United States: A Case of Non-Decision-Making." *International Journal of Health Services* 7 (1977): 167–77.

Califano, Joseph A., Jr. *Governing America.* New York: Simon and Schuster, 1981.

"Can Community Health Centers Cure Health Problems of the Poor?" *JAMA* 211 (23 March 1970): 1943–55.

Cater, Douglass. *Power in Washington.* New York: Vintage Books, 1965.

Center for Community Health Systems, Faculty of Medicine, Columbia University. *Community Hospitals and the Challenge of Primary Care.* New York: Columbia University Press, 1975 (CCHS, 1975).

Cigler, Allan J., and Burdett A. Loomis, eds. *Interest Group Politics.* Washington, D.C.: C.Q. Press, 1983.

Clark, Michael E. *Publicly Supported Preventive and Primary Care During the New York City Fiscal Crisis, 1974–1977.* New York: Health Policy Advisory Center, 1979.

Cohen, Richard E. "Rating Congress—A Guide to Separating the Liberals from the Conservatives." *National Journal,* 8 May 1982, pp. 800–10.

"Committee on Welfare Services." *JAMA* 198 (24 October 1966): 443–44.

Congressional Record. 90th Cong., 1st sess., 26, 27, 29 September; 3, 4 October; 15 November 1967; 95th Cong., 2d sess., 29 September 1978 (*CR*).

Connolly, William E., ed. *The Bias of Pluralism.* New York: Atherton, 1969.

Converse, Philip E., Jean D. Dotson, Wendy J. Hoag, and William

H. McGee III. *American Social Attitudes Data Sourcebook 1947–1978.* Cambridge, Mass.: Harvard University Press, 1980.

Davidson, Roger H. *The Politics of Comprehensive Manpower Legislation.* Baltimore, Md.: Johns Hopkins University Press, 1972.

_____. "Breaking Up Those 'Cozy' Triangles, an Impossible Dream?" In *Legislative Reform and Public Policy,* ed. Susan Welch and John G. Peters. New York: Praeger, 1977.

Davis, Karen. "Reagan Administration Health Policy." *Journal of Public Health Policy* 2 (December 1981): 312–32.

_____. "Discussion Paper." In *Community Oriented Primary Care: Conference Proceedings.* Institute of Medicine. Washington, D.C.: National Academy Press, 1982.

Davis, Karen, and Cathy Schoen. *Health and the War on Poverty.* Washington, D.C.: Brookings, 1978.

Davis, Michael M. *Clinics, Hospitals, and Health Centers.* New York: Harper, 1927.

_____. *America Organizes Medicine.* New York: Harper, 1941.

_____. *Medical Care for Tomorrow.* New York: Harper, 1955.

Davis, Michael M., and Andrew R. Warner. *Dispensaries, Their Management and Development.* New York: Macmillan, 1918.

Demkovich, Linda E. "It's A Whole New Ball Game, But Lobbyists Are Playing by Old Rules." *National Journal,* 10 October 1981, pp. 806–09.

De Haven-Smith, Lance, and Carl E. Van Horn. "Subgovernment Conflict in Public Policy." *Policy Studies Journal* 12 (June 1984): 627–42.

Donovan, John C. *The Politics of Poverty.* New York: Pegasus Books, 1967.

Downs, Anthony. *Inside Bureaucracy.* Boston: Little, Brown, 1967.

Drake, Bruce. "Report AMA Gave 1.6M to Kill Hospital Cost Bill," *New York Daily News,* 18 December 1979, p. 16.

Duffy, John. *A History of Public Health in New York City 1866–1966.* New York: Russell Sage, 1974.

Dye, Thomas R. *Understanding Public Policy.* 4th ed. Englewood Cliffs, N.J.: Prentice-Hall, 1981.

Feagin, Joe R. *Subordinating the Poor, Welfare and American Beliefs.* Englewood Cliffs, N.J.: Prentice-Hall, 1975.

Feingold, Eugene. "A Political Scientist's View of the Neighborhood Health Center as a New Social Institution." In *Neighborhood Health Centers,* ed. Hollister, Kramer, and Bellin.

Feldstein, Paul J. *Health Associations and the Demand for Legisla-*

tion: *The Political Economy of Health.* Cambridge, Mass.: Ballinger, 1977.

Foley, Henry A. *Community Mental Health Legislation, The Formative Process.* Lexington, Mass.: Lexington Books, 1975.

Freeman, Howard E., K. Jill Kiecolt, and Harris M. Allen II. "Community Health Centers: An Initiative of Enduring Utility." *Milbank Memorial Fund Quarterly/Health and Society* 60 (Spring 1982): 245–67.

Freeman, J. Leiper. *The Political Process: Executive Bureau-Legislative Committee Relations.* Rev. ed. New York: Random House, 1965.

Freymann, John Gordon. *The American Health Care System: Its Genesis and Trajectory.* Huntington, N.Y.: Robert E. Krieger, 1977.

Friedman, Lawrence M. "The Social and Political Context of the War on Poverty: An Overview." In *A Decade of Federal Antipoverty Programs, Achievements, Failures, and Lessons,* ed. Robert H. Haveman. New York: Academic Press, 1977.

Friedson, Eliot. *Profession of Medicine, A Study of the Sociology of Applied Knowledge.* New York: Dodd, Mead, 1972.

Fritschler, A. Lee. *Smoking and Politics: Policy Making and the Federal Bureaucracy.* 3d ed. Englewood Cliffs, N.J.: Prentice-Hall, 1983.

Gais, Thomas L., Mark A. Peterson, and Jack L. Walker. "Interest Groups, Iron Triangles and Representative Institutions in American National Government." *British Journal of Political Science* 14 (April 1984): 161–85.

Gallup, George H. *The Gallup Poll, Public Opinion, 1972–1977.* Vol. 2, 1976–77. Wilmington, Del.: Scholarly Resources, 1978.

Geiger, H. Jack. "A Health Center in Mississippi—A Case Study in Social Medicine." In *Medicine in A Changing Society,* ed. Lawrence Corey, Steven E. Saltman, and Michael F. Epstein. Saint Louis, Mo.: C. V. Mosby, 1972.

———. "Community Control or Community Conflict?" In *Neighborhood Health Centers,* ed. Hollister, Kramer, and Bellin.

———. "The Meaning of Community Oriented Primary Care in the American Context." In *Community Oriented Primary Care: Conference Proceedings.* Institute of Medicine. Washington, D.C., National Academy Press, 1982.

———. "Community Health Centers: Health Care as an Instrument of Social Change." In *Reforming Medicine: Lessons of the*

Last Quarter Century, ed. Victor W. Sidel and Ruth Sidel. New York: Pantheon Books, 1984.

Goldman, Fred, and Michael Grossman. "The Impact of Public Health Policy: The Case of Community Health Centers." *Eastern Economic Journal,* forthcoming.

Greenberg, George D. "Reorganization Reconsidered: The U.S. Public Health Service 1960–1973." *Public Policy* 23 (Fall 1975): 483–515.

Hamilton, Richard F. *Class and Politics in the United States.* New York: John Wiley, 1972.

Harader, William Harry. "The Committee on Veterans Affairs: A Study of the Legislative Process and Milieu as They Pertain to Veterans Legislation." Ph.D. diss., Johns Hopkins University, 1968.

Harris, Richard. *A Sacred Trust.* New York: New American Library, 1966.

Hartz, Louis. *The Liberal Tradition in America.* New York: Harcourt, Brace, 1955.

Hayes, Michael T. "The Semi-sovereign Pressure Groups: A Critique of Current Theory and an Alternative Typology. *Journal of Politics* 40 (1978): 134–61.

_____. *Lobbyists and Legislators, A Theory of Political Markets.* New Brunswick, N.J.: Rutgers University Press, 1981.

Heclo, Hugh. *A Government of Strangers, Executive Politics in Washington.* Washington, D.C.: Brookings, 1977.

_____. "Issue Networks and the Executive Establishment." In *The New American Political System,* ed. Anthony King. Washington, D.C.: American Enterprise Institute, 1978.

Heidenheimer, Arnold J., Hugh Heclo, and Carolyn Teich Adams. *Comparative Public Policy, The Politics of Social Choice in Europe and America.* New York: St. Martin's, 1975.

Hiscock, Ira V. "The Development of Neighborhood Health Services in the United States." *Milbank Memorial Fund Quarterly* 13 (January 1935): 30–51.

Hollingsworth, Ellen Jane. "Ten Years of Legal Services for the Poor." In *A Decade of Federal Antipoverty Programs, Achievements, Failures, and Lessons,* ed. Robert H. Haveman. New York: Academic Press, 1977.

Hollister, Robert M. "From Consumer Participation to Community Control of Neighborhood Health Centers." Ph.D. diss., Massachusetts Institute of Technology, 1971.

Hollister, Robert M., Bernard M. Kramer, and Seymour S. Bellin, eds. *Neighborhood Health Centers.* Lexington, Mass.: Lexington Books, 1974.

Hollister, Robert M., Bernard M. Kramer, and Seymour S. Bellin. "Neighborhood Health Centers as a Social Movement." In *Neighborhood Health Centers,* ed. Hollister, Kramer, and Bellin.

Hudson, C. L. "Inaugural Address: Finding Our Way on a Path to the Future." *JAMA* 197 (11 July 1966): 97–99.

Hudson, James I., and Marcel D. Infeld. "Ambulatory Care Reorganization in Teaching Hospitals." *Journal of Ambulatory Care Management* 3 (February 1980): 31–50.

Iglehart, John K. "Health Report/Executive Legislative Conflict Looms over Continuation of Health Care Subsidies." *National Journal* 5 (May 1973): 645–52.

————. "Health Report/Congress Expands Capacity to Contest Executive Policy." *National Journal,* 17 May 1975, pp. 730–39 (1975A).

————. "Health Report/Ford Eyes Consolidation of Federal Grant Programs." *National Journal,* 27 December 1975, pp. 1741–42 (1975B).

————. "The Carter Administration's Health Budget: Charting New Priorities with Limited Dollars." *Milbank Memorial Fund Quarterly/Health And Society* 56 (Winter 1978): 51–77.

————. "Health Policy Report: Medical Care of the Poor—A Growing Problem." *New England Journal of Medicine* 313 (July 1985): 59–63.

Jacobs, Barry. "Role Models: Innovation in Health Care." *New York Affairs* 7 (1981): 79–97.

Jonas, Steven. *Health Care Delivery in the United States.* New York: Springer, 1977 (1977A).

————. "Organized Ambulatory Services and the Enforcement of Health Care Quality Standards in New York State." In *The Impact of National Health Insurance on New York,* ed. Marvin Lieberman. New York: Prodist, 1977 (1977B).

————. *Health Care Delivery in the United States,* 3d ed. New York: Springer, 1986.

Jones, Charles O. *An Introduction to the Study of Public Policy.* 3d ed. Monterey, Calif.: Brooks-Cole, 1983.

Jordan, A. Grant. "Iron Triangles, Woolly Corporatism, and Elastic Nets: Images of the Policy Process." *Journal of Public Policy* 1 (February 1981): 95–123.

Judd, Dennis R. *The Politics of American Cities, Private Power and Public Policy,* 2d ed. Boston: Little, Brown, 1984.

Julius Rosenwald Fund. "Eight Years Work in Medical Economics 1929–1936." Chicago: Julius Rosenwald Fund, 1937.

Kalmans, Patricia A. *Medicaid Reimbursement of Community Health Centers.* Washington, D.C.: Georgetown University Health Policy Center, 1977.

Kariel, Henry S. *The Decline of American Pluralism.* Stanford, Calif.: Stanford University Press, 1961.

Katz, Michael B. *Poverty and Policy in American History.* New York: Academic Press, 1983.

Kirkham, Frederick, T., Jr. "Opening Statement at the 1976 Annual Conference of the New York Academy of Medicine, Issues in Primary Care." *Bulletin of the New York Academy of Medicine* 53 (January–February 1977): 7–9.

Kirschten, Dick. "The 'Revolution' at the White House: Have the People Caught up with the Man?" *National Journal,* 29 August 1981, pp. 1532–39.

Klaw, Spencer. *The Great American Medicine Show.* Harmondsworth: Penguin Books, 1976.

Knowles, John H. "The Medical Center and the Community Health Center." In *Social Policy for Health Care.* Papers reprinted from the *Bulletin of the New York Academy of Medicine.* New York: New York Academy of Medicine, 1969.

Kotz, Nick. "Discussions." In *A Decade of Federal Antipoverty Programs, Achievements, Failures, and Lessons,* ed. Robert H. Haveman. New York: Academic Press, 1977.

Lander, Louise. "HSA's: If At First You Don't Succeed. . . . " *Health Pac Bulletin* 70 (May–June 1976): 1–7, 10–15.

Lavery, Thomas J. "Consumer Participation at a Neighborhood Health Center." Ph.D. diss., University of Iowa, 1978.

Levitan, Sar. "Healing the Poor in Their Backyard." In *Neighborhood Health Centers,* ed. Hollister, Kramer, and Bellin. 1974.

Lewis, Charles E., Rashi Fein, and David Mechanic. *A Right to Health: The Problem of Access to Primary Medical Care.* New York: John Wiley, 1976.

Lijphart, Arend. "Comparative Politics and the Comparative Method." *American Political Science Review* 65 (September 1971): 682–93.

Lipsky, Michael. "Protest as a Political Resource." *American Political Science Review* 62 (December 1968): 1144–58.

Lipsky, Michael, and Morris Lounds. "Citizen Participation and Health Care: Problems of Government Induced Participation."

Journal of Health Politics, Policy and Law 1 (Spring 1976): 85–111.

Long, Norton E. "Bureaucracy and Constitutionalism." *American Political Science Review* 46 (September 1952): 808–18.

Loomis, Burdett A., and Allan J. Cigler. "Introduction: The Changing Nature of Interest Group Politics." In *Interest Group Politics,* ed. Allan J. Cigler and Burdett A. Loomis. Washington, D.C.: C.Q. Press, 1983.

Lowi, Theodore J. "American Business, Public Policy, Case Studies and Political Theory." *World Politics* 15 (July 1964): 677–715.

––––––. *The End of Liberalism.* New York: W.W. Norton, 1969.

McConnell, Grant. *Private Power and American Democracy.* New York: Vintage, 1966.

McDermott, Walsh. "General Medical Care, Identification and Analysis of Alternative Approaches." *Johns Hopkins Medical Journal* 135 (November 1974): 292–321.

McDonagh, Edward C. "Social Phases of the Group Health Association Movement in the United States." Ph.D. diss., University of Southern California, 1942.

Maloney, William F. "The Tufts Comprehensive Community Action Program." *JAMA* 202 (30 October 1967): 411–14.

Marcus, Isabel. *Dollars for Reform: The OEO Neighborhood Health Centers.* Lexington, Mass.: Lexington Books, 1981.

Markowitz, Gerald E., and David Karl Rosner. "Doctors in Crisis: A Study of the Use of Medical Education Reform to Establish Modern Professional Elitism in Medicine." *American Quarterly* 25 (March 1973): 83–107.

Marmor, Theodore R. *The Politics of Medicare.* Chicago: Aldine, 1973.

Martin, Edward D. "The Federal Initiative in Rural Health." *Public Health Reports* 90 (July–August 1975): 291–97.

May, Jude Thomas, Katherine Knoop Parry, Mary L. Durham, and Peter Kong-Ming New. "Institutional Structure and Process in Health Services Innovation: The Reform Strategy of the Neighborhood Health Center Program." In *Assessing the Contributions of the Social Sciences to Health,* ed. M. Harvey Brenner, Anne Mooney, and Thomas Nagy. American Association for the Advancement of Science Selected Symposium. Boulder, Colo.: Westview Press, 1980 (1980A).

May, Jude Thomas, Mary L. Durham, and Peter Kong-ming New. "The Process of Problem Definition: A Model from the Neighborhood Health Center Program." Presented at the meeting of the Society for the Study of Social Problems, Boston, August 1979.

May, Jude Thomas, Mary L. Durham, and Peter Kong-ming New. "Structural Conflicts in the Neighborhood Health Center Program: The National and Local Perspectives." *Journal of Health Politics, Policy and Law* 4 (Winter 1980): 581–604 (1980B).

May, Jude Thomas, Mary L. Durham, and Peter Kong-ming New. "Professional Control and Innovation: The Neighborhood Health Center Experience." In vol. 1 of *Research in the Sociology of Health Care,* ed. Julius A. Roth. Greenwich, Conn.: JAI Press, 1980 (1980C).

May, Jude Thomas, and Peter Kong-ming New. Transcripts from Oral History Project, interviews conducted by Drs. May and New. Washington, D.C.: NACHC, 1974–1977.

Merten, Walter, and Sylvia Nothman. "Neighborhood Health Center Experience, Implications for Project Grants." *American Journal of Public Health* 65 (March 1975): 248–52.

Miles, Rufus E., Jr. *The Department of Health, Education and Welfare.* New York: Praeger Publishers, 1974.

Mullan, Fitzhugh, S.M. "The National Health Service Corps." *Caring for the People, the National Health Service Corps in Action. Public Health Reports,* supplement, July–August 1979, pp. 2–6.

_____. "The National Health Service Corps and Health Personnel Innovations: Beyond Poorhouse Medicine." In *Reforming Medicine: Lessons of the Last Quarter Century,* ed. Victor W. Sidel and Ruth Sidel. New York: Pantheon Books, 1984.

Mundinger, Mary O'Neil. "Sounding Board: Health Service Funding Cuts and the Declining Health of the Poor." *New England Journal of Medicine* 313 (4 July 1985): 44–47.

Myers, Lois B. and Steven A. Schroeder. "Physician Use of Services for the Hospitalized Patient: A Review with Implications for Cost Containment." *Milbank Memorial Fund Quarterly/Health and Society* 59 (Summer 1981): 481–507.

Nachmias, David, and David H. Rosenbloom. *Bureaucratic Government USA.* New York: St. Martin's, 1980.

Nathan, Richard P. *The Plot that Failed: Nixon and the Administrative Presidency.* New York: John Wiley, 1975.

_____. "The Reagan Presidency in Domestic Affairs." In *The Reagan Presidency, An Early Assessment,* ed. Fred I. Greenstein. Baltimore, Md.: Johns Hopkins University Press, 1983.

National Association of Community Health Centers, Inc. (NACHC).

Fifth Annual Policy and Issues Forum Guidebook. 17–21 February 1980. (*Guidebook,* 1980)

————. "Guidance for the Implementation of the Restructuring of NACHC," [1981]. ("Restructuring")

————. *Health Centers: At the Crossroads. Guidebook for the 1985 Health Policy Seminars.* (*Guidebook,* 1985)

————. *Legislative Status Report.* Washington, D.C., 4 September 1975–2 October 1981.

————. *Medicaid Study,* 1981.

————. Membership application, 1986.

————. Memos, 29 June and 28 July 1981.

————. *News,* January–February 1980.

————. "Organizational Membership Benefits," 1986.

————. Pamphlet, 1980.

————. Program, *Community Health Institute 16th Annual Convention,* 7–11 September 1985.

————. "Update—Congressional Action," 12 June 1981.

————. *Washington Update,* 1982–1986.

————. *Weathering the Storm: Techniques for Overcoming Adversity. Guidebook for the 1982 Health Policy Seminars.* (*Guidebook,* 1982)

Nelson, Barbara J. *Making an Issue of Child Abuse.* Chicago. University of Chicago Press, 1984.

New York State Office of Health Systems Management. *Evaluation of the Ghetto Medicine Program, Executive Summary.* Albany, N.Y., March 1979 (NYS–HSM, 1979A).

————. *Preliminary Report to the Legislature on Ambulatory Care.* Albany, N.Y., September 1979 (NYS–HSM, 1979B).

————. *Final Report to the Legislature on Ambulatory Care.* Albany, N.Y.: OHSM, 15 January 1980 (NYS–HSM, 1980).

New York Times, 19 February 1971, 21 June 1973, 29 December 1980, 3 April 1981, 19 May 1981, 29 May 1981, 27 October 1982, 8 June 1984.

Numbers, Ronald L. *Almost Persuaded, American Physicians and Compulsory Health Insurance, 1912–1920.* Baltimore, Md.: Johns Hopkins University Press, 1978.

Olson, Mancur. *The Logic of Collective Action, Public Goods and the Theory of Groups.* Cambridge, Mass.: Harvard University Press, 1965.

Parenti, Michael. "Power and Pluralism: A View from the Bottom." *Journal of Politics* 32 (August 1970): 501–30.

Parker, Alberta W. "The Dimensions of Primary Care: Blueprints for Change." In *Primary Care: Where Medicine Fails,* ed. Spyros Andreopoulos. New York: John Wiley, 1974.

Parker, R. Andrew. "The Case of Ghetto Medicine." In *The Politics of Health Care, Nine Case Studies of Innovative Planning in New York City,* ed. Herbert Harvey Hyman. New York: Praeger, 1973.

Peirce, Neal R., and Carol Steinbach. "Some Friends in High Places May Save Legal Aid for Poor from Extinction." *National Journal,* 6 June 1981, pp. 1025–26.

Peters, Jean. "Reconciliation 1982: What Happened?" *PS* 14 (Fall 1981): 732–36.

Peterson, Mark A., and Jack L. Walker. "The Impact of the First Reagan Administration upon the National Interest Group System." Presented at the annual meeting of the American Political Science Association, New Orleans, 31 August 1985.

Piore, Nora. "Discussion Paper." In *Community Oriented Primary Care, Conference Proceedings,* Institute of Medicine. Washington, D.C.: National Academy Press, 1982.

Pious, Richard. "Congress, the Organized Bar, and the Legal Services Program." *Wisconsin Law Review,* 1972: 418–46.

Piven, Frances Fox, and Richard A. Cloward. *Poor People's Movements, Why They Succeed, How they Fail.* New York: Pantheon, 1979.

Piven, Frances Fox, and Richard A. Cloward. *Regulating the Poor: The Functions of Public Welfare.* New York: Vintage, 1971.

Polsby, Nelson W. *Political Innovation in America, The Politics of Policy Initiation.* New Haven, Conn.: Yale University Press, 1984.

Pratt, Henry J. *The Gray Lobby.* Chicago, Ill.: University of Chicago Press, 1976.

President's Commission for the Study of Ethical Problems in Medicine and Biomedical and Behavorial Research. *Securing Access to Health Care, A Report on the Ethical Implications of Differences in the Availability of Health Services.* Vol. 1. Washington, D.C.: March, 1983.

Price, David E. "Policy-Making in Congressional Committees: The Impact of 'Environmental' Factors." *American Political Science Review* 72 (June 1978): 548–74.

Price, Don K. "Planning and Administrative Perspectives on Adequate Minimum Personal Health Services." *Milbank Memorial Fund Quarterly/Health and Society* 56 (Winter 1978): 22–50.

Pritchard, Isabel Walsh. "Health Care and Reform: The Dilemmas of a Demonstration Program." Ph.D. diss., University of California, Berkeley, 1974.

Pumphrey, Ralph E. "Michael M. Davis and the Development of the Health Care Movement, 1900–1928." *Societas* 2 (Winter 1972): 27–41.

———. "Michael Davis and the Transformation of the Boston Dispensary, 1910–1920." *Bulletin of the History of Medicine* 49 (Winter 1975): 451–65.

Rayack, Elton. *Professional Power and American Medicine.* Cleveland, Ohio: World Publishing, 1967.

Redman, Eric. *The Dance of Legislation.* New York: Simon and Schuster, 1973.

Reichley, A. James. *Conservatives in an Age of Change: The Nixon and Ford Administrations.* Washington, D.C.: Brookings, 1981.

Rhee, Y. B. "HSA Capacity Building Strategy." Bureau of Community Health Services, U.S. Public Health Service, Rockville, Maryland, 15 October 1976. Unpublished.

Richards, Glenn. "Special Interests Push Indigent Care Solutions." *Hospitals,* 16 October 1984, pp. 106, 109, 112–13.

Richmond, Julius B. *Currents in American Medicine.* Cambridge, Mass.: Harvard University Press, 1969.

Ripley, Randall B., and Grace A. Franklin. *Congress, the Bureaucracy and Public Policy,* 3d, 4th eds. Chicago: Dorsey, 1984, 1987.

Ripley, Randall B., and Grace A. Franklin. *Policy Implementation and Bureaucracy,* 2d ed. Chicago: Dorsey, 1986.

Rodwin, Victor G. *The Health Planning Predicament, France, Québec, England and the United States.* Berkeley, Calif.: University of California Press, 1984.

Roemer, Ruth, Charles Kramer, and Jeanne E. Frink. *Planning Urban Health Services, From Jungle to System.* New York: Springer, 1975.

Rogers, David E. "Medical Academe and the Problems of Health Care Provision." *Archives of Internal Medicine* 135 (October 1975): 1364–69.

Rosen, George. "The Idea of Social Medicine in America." *Canadian Medical Association Journal* 61 (September 1949): 316–23.

———. "Michael M. Davis (November 19, 1879–August 19, 1971): Pioneer in Medical Care." *American Journal of Public Health* 62 (March 1972): 321–23.

———. "The Efficiency Criterion in Medical Care, 1900–1920: An

Early Approach to the Evaluation of Health Service." *Bulletin of the History of Medicine* 50 (Spring 1976): 28–44.

Rosenbaum, Sara. "Implementation of the Rural Health Clinic Services Act of 1977: Keepin' Em Down on the Farm." *Health Law Project Library Bulletin* 4 (May 1979): 142–52.

Rosenberg, Charles E. "Social Class and Medical Care in Nineteenth Century America: The Rise and Fall of the Dispensary." *Journal of the History of Medicine and Allied Sciences* 29 (January 1974): 32–54.

Rosenfeld, Leonard S. *Ambulatory Care: Planning and Organization.* Rockville, Md.: National Center for Health Services Research and Development, U.S. Department of Health Education and Welfare, 1971.

Rourke, Francis E. *Bureaucracy, Politics and Public Policy.* 2d ed. Boston: Little, Brown & Company, 1976.

Rouse, M. O. "Inaugural Address: To Whom Much Has Been Given." *JAMA* 201 (17 July 1967): 169–71.

Salisbury, Robert H. "Interest Representation: The Dominance of Institutions." *American Political Science Review* 78 (March 1984): 64–76.

Samuels, Michael E. "Federal Strategy for Rural Health: A Systems Approach." *Annals of the New York Academy of Sciences* 310 (21 June 1978): 163–68.

Schattschneider, E. E. *The Semisovereign People, A Realist's View of Democracy in America.* 1960. Rpt. Hinsdale, Ill.: Dryden Press, 1975.

Schlozman, Kay L., and John T. Tierney. "More of the Same: Washington Pressure Group Activity in a Decade of Change." Presented at the 1982 annual meeting of the American Political Science Association, Denver, Colorado.

Schoen, Cathy. Presentation to a meeting of the Health Planners Network. New York, 15 April 1978.

Schorr, Lisbeth Bamberger, and Joseph T. English. "Background, Context and Significant Issues in Neighborhood Health Centers." In *Neighborhood Health Centers,* ed. Hollister, Kramer, and Bellin.

Seidman, Harold. *Politics, Position, and Power: The Dynamics of Federal Organization,* 2d ed. New York: Oxford University Press, 1975.

Shenkin, Budd N. *Health Care for Migrant Workers: Policies and Politics.* Cambridge, Mass.: Ballinger, 1974.

Sidel, Victor W., and Ruth Sidel. *A Healthy State.* New York: Pantheon, 1977.

———. *Reforming Medicine: Lessons of the Last Quarter Century.* New York: Pantheon, 1984.

Smith, Michael P., and Associates. *Politics in America: Studies in Policy Analysis.* New York: Random House, 1974.

Somers, Anne R. *Health Care in Transition: Directions for the Future.* Chicago, Ill.: Hospital Research and Educational Trust, 1971.

Stanfield, Rochelle L. "Social Lobbies—Battered but Stronger After Round Two with Reagan." *National Journal,* 2 October 1982, pp. 1673–76.

Starr, Paul. *The Transformation of American Medicine.* New York: Basic Books, 1982.

Stern, Bernhard J. *Medical Services by Government: Local, State and Federal.* New York: Commonwealth Fund, 1946.

Stevens, Rosemary. *American Medicine and the Public Interest.* New Haven, Conn.: Yale University Press, 1971.

Stoeckle, John D., and Lucy M. Candib. "The Neighborhood Health Center—Reform Ideas of Yesterday and Today." In *Neighborhood Health Centers,* ed. Hollister, Kramer, and Bellin.

Stone, Clarence N. "Systemic Power in Community Decision Making: A Restatement of Stratification Theory." *American Political Science Review* 74 (December 1980): 978–90.

Stumpf, Harry P. *Community Politics and Legal Services: The Other Side of the Law.* Beverly Hills, Calif.: Sage, 1975.

Sundquist, James L. *Politics and Policy, The Eisenhower, Kennedy, and Johnson Years.* Washington, D.C.: Brookings, 1968.

Taylor, Lloyd C., Jr. *The Medical Profession and Social Reform, 1885–1945.* New York: St. Martin's, 1974.

Terris, Milton. "Herman Biggs' Contribution to the Modern Concept of the Health Center." *Bulletin of the History of Medicine* 20 (October 1946): 387–412.

———. "Editorial, A Cost-Effective National Health Program." *Journal of Public Health Policy* 4 (September 1983): 252–58.

Tierney, John T. "Subgovernments and Issue Networks." Presented at the 1985 annual meeting of the American Political Science Association, New Orleans, 29 August–1 September 1985.

Thompson, Frank J. *Health Policy and the Bureaucracy, Politics and Implementation.* Cambridge, Mass.: MIT Press, 1981.

Truman, David B. *The Governmental Process, Political Interests and Public Opinion.* New York: Knopf, 1951.

U.S. *Code, Congressional and Administrative News.* 95th Cong., 2d sess., 1978. Vol. 7. St. Paul, Minn.: West Publishing, 1979.

U.S. Congress. House. Committee on Education and Labor. *Economic Opportunity Amendments of 1967.* 90th Cong., 1st sess., 1967. H. Rept. 90-866.

_____. Committee on Energy and Commerce. *The Health Services Amendments Act of 1985.* 99th Cong., 1st sess., 1985. H. Rept. 99-157.

_____. Committee on Interstate and Foreign Commerce. *Health Centers Amendments of 1978.* 95th Cong., 2d sess., 1978. H. Rept. 95-1186.

_____. Committee on Interstate and Foreign Commerce. *Health Revenue Sharing and Health Services Act of 1975.* 94th Cong., 1st sess., 1975. H. Rept. 94-192.

_____. Committee on Interstate and Foreign Commerce. *The Health Services Amendments of 1978. Hearings Before the Subcommittee on Health and the Environment on H.R. 10533.* 95th Cong., 2d sess., 1978 (House Hearings 1978A).

_____. Committee on Interstate and Foreign Commerce. *Hearings Before the Subcommittee on Health and the Environment on Development of Primary Health Care Services to Meet the Health Needs of the Medically Underserved Areas of Our Country.* 95th Cong., 2d sess., 1978 (House Hearings 1978B).

_____. Committee on Interstate and Foreign Commerce. *Hearings Before the Subcommittee on Health and the Environment on H.R. 1954 and H.R. 2955.* 94th Cong., 1st sess., 1975.

_____. Committee on Interstate and Foreign Commerce. *Hearings Before the Subcommittee on Health and the Environment on H.R. 11511.* 93rd Cong., 2d sess., 1974.

_____. Subcommittee on Health and the Environment of the Committee on Interstate and Foreign Commerce. *A Discursive Dictionary of Health Care.* Washington, D.C.: GPO, 1976.

U.S. Congress. Senate. *A Bill to Amend the Public Health Act.* 95th Cong., 2d sess., 1979. S. 2879.

_____. Committee on Appropriations. *Departments of Labor and Health, Education, and Welfare, and Related Agencies Appropriation Bill, 1975.* 93rd Cong., 2d sess., 1974. S. Rept. 93-1146.

_____. Committee on Human Resources. *Health Services Extension Act of 1978: Hearings Before the Subcommittee on Health and Scientific Research on S. 2474.* 95th Cong., 2d sess., 1978 (Senate Hearings, 1978).

_____. Committee on Human Resources. *Health Services Exten-*

sion and Primary Health Care Act of 1978. 95th Cong., 2d sess., 1978. S. Rept. 95-860.

————. Committee on Labor and Human Resources. *The Primary Care Amendments of 1985.* 99th Cong., 1st sess., 1985. S. Rept. 99-104.

————. Committee on Labor and Public Welfare. *Special Health Revenue Sharing Act of 1975.* 94th Cong., 1st sess., 1975. S. Rept. 94-29.

U.S. Department of Health, Education, and Welfare. Bureau of Community Health Services. *Bureau of Community Health Services Programs.* DHDW Publ. No. (HSA) 78-5002, 1978. (*BCHS Programs*)

————. Bureau of Community Health Services. *Public Health Service Health Care Initiatives: Program Guidance Material for the Rural Health Initiative, Urban Health Initiative, National Health Service Corps.* Rockville, Md.: GPO, April 1978 (BCHS, *Program Guidance Material*).

————. Bureau of Health Care Delivery and Assistance. Memorandum, 1985.

————. National Center for Health Statistics. *Health—United States 1981; Health—United States 1985.* Hyattsville, Md.: GPO, 1981, 1985.

U.S. Government Accounting Office. "Implementation of a Policy of Self-Support by Neighborhood Health Centers." Report to the Subcommittee on Health, Committee on Labor and Public Welfare, U.S. Senate, 2 May 1973.

Walker, Jack L. "The Origins and Maintenance of Interest Groups in America." *American Political Science Review* 77 (June 1983): 390–406.

Weickert, Barbara G. In *Health—United States, 1981.*

Wilensky, H. L. *Organizational Intelligence.* New York: Basic Books, 1967.

Wilinsky, C. F. "The Health Center." *American Journal of Public Health* 17 (July 1927): 677–82.

Wilsford, David. "Exit and Voice: Strategies for Change in Bureaucratic-Legislative Policymaking." *Policy Studies Journal* 12 (March 1984): 431–44.

Wilson, James Q. *Political Organizations.* New York: Basic Books, 1973.

Winston, David, A. "The Department of Health and Human Services." In *Mandate for Leadership, Policy Management in* a *Conservative Administration,* ed. Charles L. Heatherly. Washington, D.C.: Heritage Foundation, 1981.

Wise, Harold B., E. Fuller Torrey, Adrienne McDade, Gloria Perry, and Harriet Bograd. "The Family Health Worker." In *Neighborhood Health Centers,* ed. Hollister, Kramer, and Bellin.

Woll, Peter. *American Bureaucracy,* 2d ed. New York: W.W. Norton, Company, Inc., 1977.

Woodward, Kenneth. "Impacts of the New Federal Health Policy on the Future of the Community Health Centers and Primary Care Programs." Presented at the Symposium on Changing Roles in Serving the Underserved: Public and Private Responsibilities and Interests, American Health Planning Association and National Association of Community Health Centers, Leesburg, Va., October 11–13, 1981.

Zwick, Daniel I. "Some Accomplishments and Findings of Neighborhood Health Centers." In *Neighborhood Health Centers,* ed. Hollister, Kramer, and Bellin.

Interviews

A few of the individuals interviewed requested that their names not be used; I therefore decided to use general titles or the former titles that were relevant to this study to identify all interviewees. All of those interviewed agreed to this use of titles. Further identifying information is available from the author for those interviewed who did not request anonymity. Since interviews are cited in the text by date, multiple interviews conducted with one person are listed separately in chronological order.

29 September 1977, 13 October 1977	Assistant Director, Association of New York Neighborhood Health Centers, Inc., New York, N.Y.
13 October 1977	Executive Director, Association of New York Neighborhood Health Centers, Inc., New York, N.Y. (tenure 1975–1979).
30 March 1978	Director, Department of Policy Analysis, National Association of Community Health Centers, Washington, D.C.
31 March 1978	Public health service official #1, Washington, D.C.

6 April 1978	Former director of two neighborhood health centers, New York, N.Y.
26 June 1979	Former Chief Counsel, Subcommittee on Health, House Committee on Interstate and Foreign Commerce, telephone interview.
2 July 1979	Former Executive Director, New York Association of Neighborhood Health Centers, Inc., New York, N.Y. (tenure from 1971–1974).
3 July 1979	Executive Director, Association of New York Neighborhood Health Centers, Inc., New York, N.Y. (tenure began in 1979).
5 July 1979	Former Associate Project Director, health center in New York, N.Y.
10 July 1979	A: Professional staff member #1, Senate Committee on Labor and Human Resources, Washington, D.C.
10 July 1979	B: Professional staff member #2, Senate Committee on Labor and Human Resources, Washington, D.C.
10 July 1979	C: Former professional staff member, House Appropriations Committee, Washington, D.C.
10 July 1979	D: Director, Department of Policy Analysis, NACHC, Washington, D.C.
11 July 1979	Former professional staff member, Senate Committee on Labor and Public Welfare, Silver Spring, Md.
12 July 1979	A: Former official, NACHC, Washington, D.C.
12 July 1979	B: Former professional staff member, Senate Appropriations Committee, Washington, D.C.
13 July 1979	A: Public health service official #2, Washington, D.C.
13 July 1979	B: Bureau of Community Health Services official #1, Rockville, Md.
16 July 1979	Project Director, health center in Brooklyn, N.Y.
17 July 1979, 10 August 1979	Associate Director for Health Services, health center in New York, N.Y.

24 July 1979	A: Former professional staff member #1, House Committee on Interstate and Foreign Commerce, Washington, D.C.
24 July 1979	B: Director, Department of Policy Analysis, NACHC. Washington, D.C.
25 July 1979	A: BCHS official #2, Washington, D.C.
25 July 1979	B: BCHS official #3, Rockville, Maryland.
25 July 1979	C: Regional legislative representative, American Hospital Association, Washington, D.C.
27 November 1979	Former professional staff member #2, House Committee on Interstate and Foreign Commerce, telephone interview.
18 February 1980	Counsel, House Subcommittee on Health and the Environment, Committee on Interstate and Foreign Commerce, Washington, D.C.
21 March 1980	Counsel, House Subcommittee on Health and the Environment, Committee on Interstate and Foreign Commerce, Washington, D.C., telephone interview.
2 February 1982	Former professional staff member #3, House Committee on Interstate and Foreign Commerce, telephone interview.
5 February 1982	A: Professional staff member, Senate Committee on Human Resources, Washington, D.C.
5 February 1982	B: Professional staff member, Senate Appropriations Committee, Washington, D.C.
22 June 1982	Former professional staff member #2, House Committee on Interstate and Foreign Commerce, telephone interview.
14 July 1982	Staff person, American Medical Association, Washington, D.C., telephone interview.
4 August 1982	Regional BCHS official #1, New York, N.Y.
6 August 1982	Regional BCHS official #2, New York, N.Y.
16 August 1982	Executive Director, NACHC, Washington, D.C.
17 August 1982	A: Executive Director, NACHC, Washington, D.C.
17 August 1982	B: BCHS official #4, Rockville, Md.
18 August 1982	Official, Office for Planning and Evaluation, Office of the Secretary of DHHS, Washington, D.C.

5 March 1984   A: Former Assistant Minority Counsel to the House Energy and Commerce Committee, Washington, D.C.

5 March 1984   B: Former Legislative Assistant for Health and Human Services, U.S. Senate, Washington, D.C.

6 March 1984   BCHS/BHCDA official #5, Washington, D.C.

7 March 1984   A: Counsel, House Subcommittee on Health and the Environment, Energy and Commerce Committee, Washington, D.C.

7 March 1984   B: Health Director, Senate Committee on Labor and Human Resources, Washington, D.C.

Communications, NACHC: 7, 8, and 22 November 1983; 11 July, 26 August, 5 September 1986. These were telephone conversations in which NACHC staff persons supplied the author with specific data.

Index

ABA. *See* American Bar Association

Accreditation Association for Ambulatory Health Care (AAAHC), 139

Advisory boards, for primary care centers, 156

Aid to Families with Dependent Children (AFDC), 127, 196

Alternatives to Abortion, 120

American Association for Labor Legislation, 30

American Association of Medical Colleges, 180

American Association of Retired Persons (AARP), 138

American Bar Association (ABA), 219–20, 221, 223

American College Health Association, 139

American Dental Association (ADA), 204

American Farm Bureau Federation, 85

American Federation of State, County and Municipal Employees (AFSCME), 154

American Group Practice Association, 139

American Hospital Association (AHA), 16, 43, 61, 84, 87, 93, 155, 158, 163, 204

American Indian Health Care Association, 137

American Medical Association (AMA), 16, 86, 92–93, 180, 204; access to Reagan administration of, 182–83, 186; Committee on Welfare Services of, 63, 80–81; during Progressive Era, 25; and government contracts for technical assistance, 84–85; opposition of to community mental health centers, 217; opposition of to government administered health insurance, 47–48; opposition of to group practice, 27–28, 31, 43, 44, 56; opposition of to Javits amendment, 159–60, 162; opposition of to neighborhood health center programs, 61–66, 80, 106, 202–03; opposition of to prepaid health insurance, 31, 32; and support for funding categorical grants, 70

American Public Health Association (APHA), 87, 232

American Statistical Association, 32–33

Association of American Medical Colleges, 87

Association of New York Neighborhood Health Centers (ANYNHC), 85

267

Health Care Financing Administration
(HCFA), Department of Health and
Human Services (DHHS), 131, 191,
198
Health care: federal role in, 46–49;
and ideology, 29–32; and reformers,
68, 69, 72, 73, 81, 226. *See also*
Health system reform
Health Center Amendments of 1978
(H.R. 12460), 142, 157
Health Center Amendments to the
Office of Economic Opportunity
Act of 1966 and 1967, 201
Health centers policy network, 108,
125, 176, 200–07, 237n4; compared
with food stamp policy network,
207–16; challenge and response,
164–99; as elastic net, 207, 208, 215;
functioning of, 140; and institutionalization of health centers
program, 77–107, 205; and resource
allocation and conflict, 133–63;
and urban/rural equity, 143–45.
See also Policy networks
Health education, 18, 33, 34, 100,
101, 125, 126, 129, 130, 147
Health financing. *See* Financing
policy
Health insurance, 226; compulsory,
30; by employers, 78; European, 30;
national (U.S.), 9, 47–48, 60, 78, 91,
94, 95, 99, 117, 173–74, 214; state-
administered, 30; voluntary, 43
Health maintenance clinic, as new
concept, 42
Health maintenance organizations
(HMOs), 4, 18, 78, 79, 98, 146, 191,
196–97, 232, 240n7
Health Planning and Resources
Development Act, 95
Health Resources Administration,
Public Health Service (PHS), 185
Health Resources and Services
Administration (HRSA), Public
Health Service (PHS), 185
Health Services Administration,
Public Health Service (PHS), 174,
185
Health Services Amendments of 1978
(H.R. 12370), 142
Health Services Block Grant, 167

Health Services Extension Act of 1977
(P.L. 95–83), 140
Health Services and Mental Health
Administration (HSMHA), Public
Health Service (PHS), 72, 82, 83,
97
Health system reform, 39–48;
neighborhood health centers as,
53–56, 92, 212; and ideology, 29–32;
and policy entrepreneurs, 56–59.
See also Health care reformers
Health [for] Underserved Rural
Areas Program (HURA), 115, 116,
143–45, 154
Heclo, Hugh, 11–13, 14, 15, 73, 106,
206, 207, 240n1
Heritage Foundation, 174, 180, 181;
Report of, 189
Hill-Burton Act (Hospital Survey and
Construction Act of 1946), 47, 92,
147
HIRE program, 14
Hollings, Ernest, 177, 178
Hollister, Robert, 240n6
Holloman, John, 80–81
Hospital-affiliated group practices,
31
Hospital affiliated primary care
centers, 149–63
Hospital-centered health system, 23
Hospital outpatient departments, 24,
30, 37, 42, 45, 46, 57, 78, 79, 122,
139, 145, 149–63, 229–30, 241n3
Hospital Survey and Construction Act
of 1946 (Hill-Burton Act), 47
House Appropriations Committee,
104–05, 110, 118, 161, 177, 242n4;
Subcommittee on Health,
Education and Labor, 104
House Budget Committee, 171
House Committee on Interstate and
Foreign Commerce, 157, 158; Sub-
committee on Public Health and
the Environment, 86–88, 89, 91,
93, 142, 168, 201
House Energy and Commerce Com-
mittee, 169, 170–71, 173; Health
Subcommittee of, 99–100, 103,
148, 158, 159, 160, 167–71, 208
House of Representatives, during early
Reagan administration, 167–71

National Conservative Political
  Action Committee, 221
National Council of Churches, 221
National Council of Community
  Hospitals, 154
National health insurance. *See* Health
  insurance, national
National Health Service Corps
  (NHSC); administration of, 180,
  185; and Bureau of Community
  Health Services (BCHS), 109;
  coordination with community
  health center program of, 113, 123,
  195; establishment of, 4, 115, 215,
  216, 239n7; funding for, 121, 173;
  and government grants for techni-
  cal assistance, 85; policy network
  of, 223; support for in Congress,
  222
National Institute of Mental Health
  (NIMH), 216–17, 222
National Journal, 242n1
National Medical Association, 80–81
National Rural Primary Care
  Association, 137
Neighborhood Health Center
  Program; creation of, 51–53; early
  politics of, 60; goals of, 58–59; and
  hospitals and medical schools,
  64–66; and presentation of health
  center issue in Congress, 66–68
Neighborhood Service Program, 71
Nelson, Gaylord, 166
New, Peter Kong-ming, 238n4, 239n1
New Deal, 32, 36
New Federalism, 78
New York Academy of Medicine, 35,
  46
New York Association for Improving
  the Conditions of the Poor, 33
New York Association of Neighbor-
  hood Health Centers, 83–84, 102,
  134, 135
New York City Ambulatory Care
  Program, 149
New York City Department of Health,
  35, 150
New York City Health and Hospitals
  Corporation, 154

New York State Health Department,
  149
New York University, 71
Nixon, Richard M., 77, 89, 109, 111,
  164, 165, 240n2
Nixon administration; and community health centers, 96–99; and food
  stamp program, 209; issue salience
  during, 104; and legal services
  program, 221; legislative action
  during, 88–89, 99–103; and
  National Health Service Corps,
  219; and neighborhood health center policy network, 16, 82, 83, 181,
  186, 201, 202, 206; Office for Planning and Evaluation during, 120;
  and opposition to neighborhood
  health center program, 77–81, 87,
  88, 103, 105, 118, 119, 205, 239n1;
  relationship with Congress of, 91,
  96–99, 100, 107, 193
Nondecision-making, 20–22, 31, 32,
  48, 49
North East Neighborhood Association
  (NENA), 72

Obey, David, 177
Office of the Assistant Secretary for
  Health, Department of Health and
  Human Services (DHHS), 181
Office of the Assistant Secretary for
  Planning and Evaluation,
  Department of Health and Human
  Services (DHHS), 120, 174, 180,
  193–94
Office of the Deputy Assistant
  Secretary for Health Planning and
  Evaluation, Department of Health
  and Human Services (DHHS), 183
Office of Economic Opportunity
  (OEO): agreement of with Depart-
  ment of Health, Education and
  Welfare, 239n8; Community
  Action Agency of, 217; and crea-
  tion of neighborhood health
  centers program, 3, 5, 16, 51–73,
  119, 202, 205, 208, 210, 212, 225,
  239n1, 239n5, 240n2; health
  centers not funded by, 240n4;
  legal services program of, 220;
  Office of Comprehensive Health

Pitt Series in Policy and Institutional Studies
Bert A. Rockman, Editor

The Acid Rain Controversy
James L. Regens and Robert W. Rycroft

Agency Merger and Bureaucratic Redesign
Karen M. Hult

The Aging: A Guide to Public Policy
Bennett M. Rich and Martha Baum

Clean Air: The Policies and Politics of Pollution Control
Charles O. Jones

Comparative Social Systems: Essays on Politics and Economics
Carmelo Mesa-Lago and Carl Beck, Editors

Congress and Economic Policymaking
Darrell M. West

Congress Oversees the Bureaucracy: Studies in Legislative Supervision
Morris S. Ogul

Foreign Policy Motivation: A General Theory and a Case Study
Richard W. Cottam

Homeward Bound: Explaining Changes in Congressional Behavior
Glenn Parker

Imagery and Ideology in U.S. Policy Toward Libya, 1969–1982
Mahmoud G. ElWarfally

The Impact of Policy Analysis
James M. Rogers

Iran and the United States: A Cold War Case Study
Richard W. Cottam

Japanese Prefectures and Policymaking
Steven R. Reed

Managing the Presidency: Carter, Reagan, and the Search for Executive Harmony
Colin Campbell, S.J.

Organizing Governance, Governing Organizations
Colin Campbell, S.J., and B. Guy Peters, Editors

Perceptions and Behavior in Soviet Foreign Policy
Richard K. Herrmann

Pesticides and Politics: The Life Cycle of a Public Issue
Christopher J. Bosso

Contemporary Community Health Series

Made in the USA
Monee, IL
08 February 2020